THE
THUMPIN'

THE THUMPIN'

How Rahm Emanuel and the
Democrats Learned to Be
Ruthless and Ended the
Republican Revolution

Naftali Bendavid

DOUBLEDAY
New York London Toronto Sydney Auckland

PUBLISHED BY DOUBLEDAY

Copyright © 2007 by Naftali Bendavid

All Rights Reserved

Published in the United States by Doubleday, an imprint of The Doubleday Broadway
Publishing Group, a division of Random House, Inc., New York.
www.doubleday.com

DOUBLEDAY and the portrayal of an anchor with a dolphin are registered trademarks of
Random House, Inc.

Book design by Chris Welch

Cataloging-in-Publication Data is on file with the Library of Congress.

ISBN: 978-0-385-52328-8

PRINTED IN THE UNITED STATES OF AMERICA

1 3 5 7 9 10 8 6 4 2

First Edition

For Dara

CONTENTS

THE
THUMPIN'

INTRODUCTION

Rahm Emanuel was racing down the highway from Albany to Utica on the forty-seventh trip of his two-year campaign to win back the House. He'd just come from a fund-raiser for a struggling candidate named Kirsten Gillibrand, and his next stop was a tiny senior center in Utica where he would schmooze with senior citizens on behalf of another candidate. Evening would find him in Syracuse, urging two dozen Democrats to give money to still a third congressional hopeful. It was October 26, 2006, and the pressure was becoming hard to tolerate. With Election Day twelve days away, Emanuel and the Democrats soon would either cap an unprecedented campaign by retaking the House, ensuring Emanuel's political future, or they would blow it yet again, and he would become another in a long line of Democratic failures. Polls showing a likely Democratic victory only increased the pressure; anything less would now be seen as a disaster. President Bush and other top Republicans were confidently assuring the Democrats their hopes of victory were ill-founded. Emanuel, like other Democrats, faced a perpetual fear that the Republicans would find a way to snatch away the victory, as they had done to devastating effect in each of the previous three elections.

Every decision Emanuel made in these final days was immediately second-guessed and criticized: where to spend money, what message to push, which Republicans to attack. Fear of fatal error was constant. The drive from Albany to Utica on this cloudy afternoon took about ninety minutes, and Emanuel spent virtually every one of those minutes on his cell phone with candidates, strategists, reporters, contributors. At one point he put his hand over the receiver and asked the driver to stop so he could use the rest room. As the driver pulled into a rest stop, Emanuel continued talking on the phone, never taking a break, as he entered the bathroom and relieved himself at a urinal.

The last thing Emanuel needed at this point was a lecture from someone sitting in Washington. But he found himself on a conference call with two of his top consultants, James Carville and Stan Greenberg. They were old friends as well as two of the best-known strategists in Democratic politics. Emanuel had known Carville, with his famous bald head and Cajun bark, since they'd worked together on Bill Clinton's 1992 presidential campaign. They talked so often, their wives joked that they should install an 800 number. By this point in the campaign they were frequently fighting; Carville would tell Emanuel that the Democrats would fail—"It doesn't look so good out there," he'd say—just to get a rise out of him. "He's driving me crazy. I'm probably driving him crazy," Carville said around this time. "We're probably bad for each other. We talk seven times a day. We're like an old married couple." As for Greenberg, a pollster, Emanuel made his home in Greenberg's basement when he was in Washington.

But on the ride to Utica, any tone of camaraderie evaporated. Carville and Greenberg told Emanuel his candidates needed to wrap up their campaigns with ads promising to "move beyond partisanship" and "work to change Washington." Emanuel was reluctant to impose this sort of cookie-cutter message, but Carville and Greenberg kept pressing. Finally, Emanuel's entire body tensed and he exploded at Carville, "James—*No, James, you listen.* Can you listen for one fucking minute? I'm working these campaigns all the time. The campaigns all have different textures." Undaunted, Carville kept interrupting. "Okay, what am I too *stupid* to understand?" Emanuel said, gripping the little silver phone with all his might.

Emanuel reminded Carville that he did not have the power to order candidates to air specific commercials. "I know it comes as a rude shock, but every one of these media consultants doesn't like having it shoved down their throats," Emanuel said. "It takes a lot of time. I'm working it race by race." All the tension of the campaign's final stretch, with any number of critics telling Emanuel he had to take their advice or the Democrats would blow their best chance in a generation, boiled over. Emanuel's voice was shrill, breaking with the stress. Carville and Greenberg urged him to exercise his leadership and force the campaigns to bend to his will. This was too much. "I am exercising it, with every fucking fiber in my body," Emanuel shouted. "If you don't see what you like, I highly recommend you pick up the fucking phone and do it yourself." His friends told him to relax. "*I am fucking relaxed,* but I'm telling you I'm trying to get it done," Emanuel said.

The midterm elections of 2006 came at a pivotal time in American politics. With the reelection of a Republican president, Senate, and House in 2004, Republicans were looking forward to a generation of GOP dominance, hoping to rival Franklin D. Roosevelt's accomplishment for the Democrats seventy years earlier. With the South firmly in their control and evangelical conservatives marching like soldiers to the polling place, Republicans faced no foreseeable prospect of losing power. Yet undercurrents of anxiety ran through the electorate. George Bush's presidency had been driven by the September 11 terrorist attacks and the Iraq war that followed, and Bush had been reelected by a nation concerned about its security. But the war was not going well, and the pillars of middle-class economic security, such as health care and retirement benefits, seemed shakier than ever. The Congress installed by the 2006 election would face those challenges. More immediately, it would control the final two years of a president who'd enjoyed great political success and governed almost exclusively with a Congress of his own party. This election would largely determine Bush's legacy, and it would set the stage for the presidential election of 2008, when for the first time in decades neither a sitting president nor vice president would be seeking the nomination.

All that seemed remote in December 2004, when House Democratic leader Nancy Pelosi, tired of being in the minority and driven to become the first woman Speaker of the House, asked Emanuel to take on the thankless job of running the Democratic campaign. Every two years, party leaders chose lawmakers to spearhead their House and Senate campaigns—recruiting candidates, raising money, crafting strategy. Often this job went to a distinguished senior statesman. Emanuel, on the other hand, was new to Congress, having just been elected to his second term. But he was known as a political assassin, willing to launch relentless, nasty attacks on his opponents, and Pelosi believed that was what the Democrats needed when she appointed Emanuel chairman of the Democratic Congressional Campaign Committee, or DCCC. Not that there was any committee in the normal sense; it was just Emanuel, his DCCC staff of about a hundred, and whatever lawmakers he chose to involve in the campaign.

No one expected the Democrats actually to win control of the House. The obstacles to knocking off sitting congressmen were simply too great. At best, if the Democrats were lucky, they might retake a handful of the fifteen seats they needed for the majority, and perhaps set the stage for finishing the job in 2008.

Into that difficult landscape stepped Emanuel. In a world where congressmen referred to each other as "my distinguished colleague" or "my good friend from Illinois," Emanuel often was unable to get through a single sentence without several obscenities. He was forty-five when the campaign began. He had risen through Chicago politics before joining Bill Clinton's presidential campaign and becoming one of his closest advisors. Emanuel's politics were carefully centrist, but his style was extremist. Impatient at delay and resistance, he sought to force action through sheer willpower. He browbeat or harangued associates and subordinates when he wanted something done. When he joined Clinton's team as a fund-raiser, he yelled at donors he felt were not giving enough. He mailed a dead fish to a pollster with whom he'd had a dispute. Part of his right middle finger had been severed when he was a teenager, adding to his aura of toughness—especially when he extended that middle finger, which he did with some regularity. At the White House, his abrasive style had so alienated his colleagues that he was demoted; even so, Emanuel battled relentlessly and pushed through two of Clinton's signature initiatives, the North American Free Trade Agreement (NAFTA) and a crime bill.

Five foot eight and 150 pounds, Emanuel was always moving, jiggling his foot or collapsing theatrically to the floor to make a point. He rarely finished one sentence before starting the next. His presence was such that he was called "Rahm"—not "Congressman" or "Emanuel"—by ally and enemy alike. A number of his colleagues genuinely disliked him, but others were attracted by his intensity, force, and charisma.

Whatever the merits of his temperament, Emanuel had piled one success on another. By age thirty-seven, he was working adjacent to the Oval Office. After leaving the Clinton administration in 1998, he had made millions as an investment banker. When he ran for Congress in 2002, he won a bruising campaign. He combined the savvy of an operative with the stature of a congressman. Democrats hoped the very abrasiveness that bothered so many of them would also equip him to take on the Republican electoral machine. Republicans had become so much better than Democrats at raising money, enforcing discipline, and turning out voters that Democrats had become spooked. Much of the battle was psychological; many Democrats no longer believed they could win. For the Democrats to retake the House, University of Virginia political scientist Larry Sabato said during the campaign, "You need someone whose favorite word is not *a* or *the,* but *fuck*. And that is Rahm."

The 2006 campaign so far had been an exercise in pure politics, in all its ugliness and grandeur. A presidential campaign revolves around two people, their strengths and their weaknesses. The campaign for the House, in contrast, required familiarity with dozens of individual campaigns—the candidates, the interest groups, the voting blocs. It was a game of three-dimensional chess, in that what happened in one district affected many others; a single message—"We favor withdrawing from Iraq"—might play well in one area but court catastrophe in another. "It's the hardest job in politics, bar none," Carville said. "You have all these candidates and everyone needs something. I'd run five presidential campaigns before I'd do one DCCC." Emanuel focused on about fifty key races, meaning he had to keep up with the moods, tactics, and problems of fifty different candidates. "It is incredibly fucking grueling," Emanuel said early in the race. "I'll tell you this: It is so fucking stressful. If anybody does anything on either side, it's your problem. It's one thing if I'm managing my life, my set of problems. It's one thing if I have to think about part of Bill Clinton's developments. But this—everything that happens is my problem. [Congressman] Bill Jefferson in Louisiana has an FBI investigation, that's my problem. Some [candidate] loses a loved one—how that will affect him psychologically? . . . Anything that happens anywhere, personal or professional, is my problem."

A big part of what had happened by October 2006 was that a Republican majority too long in power began to succumb to its own overreaching. Emanuel did not make that happen. He did not affect the course of the Iraq war and had nothing to do with President Bush's response to Hurricane Katrina. His job had been to position the Democrats to take advantage of a political tidal wave if it came. He had thrown himself into that task with a ferocity that had not been seen before, going full force from day one. He had scrutinized the smallest details, even crafting radio ads for individual candidates. At no point had the Democratic campaign been a confident march to victory. The recent defeats of Democratic presidential candidates Al Gore and John Kerry, each of whom had the momentum at key points in their campaigns, together with a string of congressional losses, had instilled in Democrats a deep insecurity about their ability to win. The more their fortunes improved in the 2006 campaign, the more they feared they would blow it. Many Democrats in their hearts wondered if the Republicans were right when they claimed to be more in touch with mainstream voters when it came to terrorism, taxes, guns, and basic values. Even Emanuel, who had seen it as part of his job to instill confidence in his fellow Democrats, had been constantly seized by doubt. The campaign had a dizzying quality for Democrats, a feeling of giddiness every time the Republicans stumbled, followed by nauseatingly familiar misgivings.

As he sped down that highway in upstate New York with less than two weeks before it all ended, Emanuel was sharply aware that the only thing that mattered—for the Democrats, the country, his own career—was how many seats the Democrats would win on November 7, 2006. Bill Paxon, a former New York congressman who had Emanuel's job for the Republicans when they took the House in 1994, had found the task was so stressful he had instituted a four-year limit. "It's exhausting, but very fulfilling, and unlike a lot of things in government where there is compromise, there is only one result: You either win or you lose, and you are judged on that," Paxon said. "You can look at fund-raising, candidate recruitment, and other things, but they are meaningless. The only thing that matters is if you win or lose."

This is the story of what Emanuel and the Democrats did to win.

1

AN IMMOVABLE OBJECT

F ive hundred conservatives applauded excitedly as Karl Rove rose to speak in an elegant ballroom at the Sheraton New York Hotel and Towers on the evening of June 22, 2005. This was a heady time for the activists who had gathered to honor Rove and give him an award that had previously been bestowed on such stars as Ronald Reagan and Jack Kemp. President Bush had been reelected five months earlier by a margin of 3.5 million votes, despite fierce campaigning by grassroots Democrats and millions of dollars poured into the race by liberal donors. Republicans and conservatives viewed Bush's victory over John Kerry as nothing less than an emphatic affirmation of Americans' support for their principles. Bush himself said at a press conference two days after the election, "I've got the will of the people at my back." The Republican victory in fact owed a good deal to superior political tactics, and Bush and his party were still benefiting from the emotions surrounding the September 11 terrorist attacks, but those factors were downplayed in the post-election euphoria. "I earned capital on the campaign—political capital," Bush said. "And now I intend to spend it."

It wasn't just Bush's victory that lent credence to the notion that America was becoming more Republican in a fundamental way. In the Senate,

Republicans swept six open seats in the South and increased their majority to 55–45. For some conservatives, the sweetest part of that outcome was the defeat of Senate Democratic leader Tom Daschle of South Dakota, a frequent Bush critic. Republicans had fared well in the House also, increasing their majority by three, to 232–203. Never had the party's future seemed more assured. That was the landscape as members of the Conservative Party of New York gathered to hear Rove's speech at the Sheraton. Founded in 1962 in the belief that even the Republican Party was too liberal, the Conservative Party had become an important political force in the state. The audience could not have been more friendly to Rove, widely praised as the architect of Republican victories in 2000, 2002, and 2004. "It was fantastic," Shaun Marie Levine, the Conservative Party's executive director, said of the celebratory atmosphere that night. "When a gentleman gets up and says what you believe, it's refreshing and wonderful to know he is right up there with the leader of the free world. . . . People went wild."

The pudgy, bespectacled, buzz-cut Rove was to make news that night with the sort of cutting comment that had become his trademark. "Conservatives saw the savagery of 9/11 and the attacks and prepared for war," Rove said. "Liberals saw the savagery of the 9/11 attacks and wanted to prepare indictments and offer therapy and understanding for our attackers." In the following days, Democrats angrily demanded that Rove retract his statement that liberals wanted to offer terrorists "therapy." It was a reflection of the political moment that Rove shrugged off their demands without consequence, while the White House stood by his comments.

But by far the greater significance of Rove's speech was the vision he outlined of an imminent era of conservative Republican dominance. Rove was a student of history; his White House office featured two pictures of Abraham Lincoln, a Lincoln campaign banner, letters from James Madison, and a Theodore Roosevelt campaign ribbon. The first book Rove had ever read, in second grade, was *Great Moments in History,* and he kept a framed copy of its first page. The strategist was fascinated by the presidency of William McKinley, who had ushered in a Republican era at the beginning of the twentieth century. Rove's grand theory, as he offered it in his speech, was this: American liberalism had peaked forty years earlier with the landslide election of Lyndon Johnson in 1964. Back then, it was liberals who had energy, idealism, and momentum. With the just-concluded 2004 election, the pendulum had swung forcefully in the other direction, and it was now the conservatives' turn to dominate the American scene. "Today conservatism is the guiding philosophy in the White House, the Senate, the House, and in governorships and state legislatures throughout America," Rove said. "Liberalism is edging toward irrelevance." He added, "The conservative movement has gone from a small, principled opposition to a broad, inclusive movement that is self-assured, optimistic, forward-leaning, and dominant. . . . This president and today's conservative movement are shaping history, not trying to stop it."

That was certainly how it felt to the conservatives in the room—that they were shaping history. "It was natural for Republicans and conservatives to have felt pretty full of themselves after that election," said Howard Lim, secretary of the Conservative Party, who was there. "It bucked so many trends in terms of reelecting a president and having a ripple effect on his party in Congress." Party chairman Michael Long, for his part, well remembered the darkness of the 1964 election that Rove had cited. Fresh out of the Marine Corps, an idealistic Long had volunteered for Barry Goldwater's presidential campaign, only to see his hero lose forty-four of fifty states and get crushed by Johnson. "Election Night was tough to take at that time for a young, aggressive conservative like myself," Long said. "I clearly thought the lights were going out forever. You feel you're never going to be able to overcome that." But listening to Rove, he felt the opposite. "It struck a chord from a conservative point of view in the audience—not just Republican dominance, but conservative Republican dominance," Long said.

Rove's speech that night crystallized the triumphalist mood, but he was far from the only Republican to assert that Bush's reelection had sealed the Democrats' fate as a minority party for decades. That became a fashionable view among conservative intellectuals, and even many Democrats fatalistically accepted the idea. Fred Barnes, executive editor of the conservative *Weekly Standard,* cited the "breadth and depth" of the Republicans' strength in the *Wall Street Journal* on January 1, 2005. "They have all but completed the sweeping political realignment they could only dream about a generation ago," Barnes wrote. "In the dark days after the 1964 rout, those dreams seemed quixotic, farfetched, even crazed. Now they've been realized." Barnes emphasized Bush's growing support among blacks, Hispanics, Jews, Catholics, and women—all traditionally Democratic groups. "There's reason to believe Republican dominance, absent a catastrophe such as a depression, will last," Barnes wrote. The *National Review,* in an editorial in its edition of November 29, 2004, titled "Victory," predicted that "a conservative era in American governance could be starting now."

This portrait of the Democratic Party as the victim of large historical trends rather than more transient factors made its plight seem all the more hopeless. Few were more definitive about this than Grover Norquist, the hard-hitting activist who served as the nerve center of the conservative movement. Bearded and bespectacled, Norquist ran a meeting of conservative leaders in Washington every Wednesday morning to discuss issues and strategy over bagels. The power of this "Wednesday group" was such that virtually any Republican thinking of running for national office dropped by to try to win its favor. The Bush White House was careful always to send a representative. Among Norquist's missions was to try to get Ronald Reagan's name on as many buildings as possible, to balance the impression made by all those Franklin D. Roosevelt schools and highways. In his official job, as president of Americans for Tax Reform, Norquist had persuaded hundreds of politicians to sign a "Taxpayer Protection Pledge" vowing opposition to any tax increase. A combative true believer, Norquist was given to outrageous statements that a more circumspect figure would avoid. "I don't want to abolish government—I simply want to reduce it to the size where I can drag it into the bathroom and drown it in the bathtub," he said once. He told National Public Radio that those who opposed cutting the estate tax were adhering to "the morality of the Holocaust." After the 2004 election, Norquist took his usual nuanced approach. He flatly told PBS *Frontline* that "Republicans have the House until at least 2012, but probably another decade. They have the Senate indefinitely." If the Iraq war went badly, it could slow the GOP ascent, he acknowledged, but that was unlikely. "I think it would be difficult to see what would turn it around," Norquist said. "Obviously some great depression or something could do it." The assessment was not limited to conservatives. The independent political analyst Charlie Cook wrote in his newsletter, the *Cook Political Report*, on January 22, 2005, "[Democrats] run the risk of becoming perpetual losers, with a self-defeating mentality to match."

It was against that backdrop that Nancy Pelosi, who'd been in Congress for seventeen years and leader of the House Democrats for two, called Rahm Emanuel, the volatile second-term congressman from Chicago, and asked him to run the Democratic House campaign. Pelosi came from a political family, and her father and brother had both been mayors of Baltimore. After moving to San Francisco, marrying a businessman, having five children, and throwing herself into California politics, Pelosi had won a congressional seat representing San Francisco in 1987. Derided by Republicans as a "San Francisco liberal," which she was, Pelosi also was sometimes mocked for a wide-eyed, saccharine television persona. Pelosi tried to soften her image, referring to herself often as an "Italian grandmother," but she had a hard edge. She ran the House Democrats with a combination of charm and toughness, known for providing colleagues with chocolates and also for rules that punished them if they failed to follow the party line. In her climb to the party leadership, Pelosi had raised enormous sums of money, donating it to colleagues to build a bank of favors, and she had no problem challenging powerful Democrats or holding grudges against her rivals. She had waged a tough fight against Maryland congressman Steny Hoyer for the number two spot in the Democratic hierarchy before becoming party leader. In that race, she had marshaled the support of the California delegation, Democratic women, and the party's liberals to win the race almost before it started. She wanted to lead the party in part because she felt current Democratic leaders were doing too little to regain the majority. "She looked around and thought these people either were not interested or did not know how to win," said Democratic congressman George Miller of California, one of Pelosi's closest allies in the House. "We were not winning. We weren't moving anywhere. She decided there had to be a different dynamic. She just said, 'This is untenable. I did not come to sit in the minority, to be stagnant.'" Pelosi badly wanted to make history by becoming the first female Speaker of the House. That, of course, would happen only if the Democrats regained the majority.

Pelosi faced significant pressure to choose someone other than Emanuel to bring this about. Members of Congress valued seniority, and Emanuel, first elected just two years earlier, was a newcomer. One candidate was California congressman Mike Thompson, a personal friend of Pelosi. Leaders of the labor movement, close allies of Pelosi, were opposed to Emanuel because of his role in pushing through the NAFTA treaty, which they despised.

Pelosi chose Emanuel anyway. The two had known each other a long time. Emanuel had been a young staffer at the DCCC in 1987 when Pelosi won her first congressional race, and he was at the Clinton White House when she was a rising Democratic star. The Democratic leader was familiar with Emanuel's background and temperament. The average House member came to Congress after becoming a respected community leader— a prominent attorney, perhaps, or a state senator. Emanuel, in contrast, had spent twenty years getting his hands dirty in politics—raising money, studying polls, crafting attacks, planning strategy. He had done this at a relatively low level—in high school he had walked the streets for former Chicago congressman Abner Mikva—and at the highest, as President Bill Clinton's senior advisor. Pelosi, a former party operative herself, was keenly aware of Emanuel's ability to raise money. Most important, Emanuel was known to be tireless, aggressive, and pushy. Given the job's grueling nature, it was crucial to find someone who would never let up, and nobody could compete with Emanuel on that score. "There were many people who wanted to be considered for it," Pelosi said. "It was a decision I had to make. Some questioned it because he was brand-new. To me it wasn't a minus he was new, it was a plus." Miller added, "She is about matching what had to be done with who could get it done. Everything else was interesting, but not terribly important."

Pelosi called Emanuel in December 2004, a month after the election, reaching him at his family vacation home in Michigan. After saying he would accept the job, Emanuel warned Pelosi there was no way the Democrats could win the House in 2006. At best, he said, they would capture a few seats and perhaps finish the job in the 2008 election cycle. "Nancy, the truth is, rather than keep telling people we're going to take back the House, we have to start realizing this is a two-cycle process," Emanuel said. He reminded Pelosi that the Republicans had captured nine Democratic House seats in 1992, setting the stage for their fifty-four-seat blowout two years later. Similarly, he thought, a handful of Democratic wins in 2006 could pave the way for retaking the House in 2008. Undaunted by this pessimistic forecast, Pelosi on January 9 officially named Emanuel to head the Democratic Congressional Campaign Committee, putting her future in his hands.

It was less clear why Emanuel would want the job, given the Democrats' bleak political outlook. One explanation he gave was that it would be even harder for him to do it in future years, when his three young children—Zachariah, Ilana, and Leah—were older. "Given my background in politics, having worked at the DCCC and the White House and campaigns, I was never going to get through my life in the House and not do this," Emanuel said. "So I made a determination that I wanted to get it done while the kids are nine, seven, and six, rather than have this job when they're twelve, eleven, and ten. There's a difference. There is a higher-than-normal suicide rate among members' kids, when you look at it on a per capita basis. And nothing is that important. I'm going to be around for them."

Be that as it may, Emanuel also saw, with his shrewd political eye, that this was an opportunity for him to gain power quickly in a Congress where power usually accrues with maddening slowness. A president's party often loses House seats in the sixth year of his term, Emanuel knew. If he exceeded expectations and won more seats for the Democrats than predicted—perhaps nine or ten—his appreciative Democratic colleagues might elevate him to an influential position. At forty-five, Emanuel was restless. He had already served as a president's top counselor and could see being House Speaker one day. "If I make gains—and I'm not talking about one or two seats, I mean, make gains—I'll be seen as part of it," Emanuel said. "Your ability in the House just grows if you're part of people getting closer to being able to accomplish their objectives."

After talking it over with his wife, Emanuel took the job. With his driven personality, there was in fact never much chance he would do anything else. And once he jumped in, Emanuel moved fast. Previous DCCC heads had taken too long to get started, he believed, and he did not want to make that mistake. He also had no interest in being titular head of a campaign that was actually controlled by the staff.

Emanuel began by pulling together a team of fellow members of Congress. Virtually all of the lawmakers he chose had come to Congress recently—and as the result of a particularly impressive or bloody election. They had shown themselves willing to take on Democrats as well as Republicans, they relished political battle, and they'd won against the odds. Emanuel shied away from respected older members who had not faced a tough rival in years. "He wants that lean and hungry look," political scientist Larry Sabato said. "If you've been in Washington for a while and you're in a safe district, you're in early retirement. Rahm will never be in early retirement. He'll probably never be in late retirement; he'll die with his boots on, making a deal." The same could be said for the others on his team. Emanuel wanted allies who were not afraid to draw blood, who had no problem launching a harsh attack against a Republican and smiling at him in the Capitol the next day.

Congressman Chris Van Hollen of Maryland, forty-seven, had, like Emanuel, come to Congress just two years earlier. He was tall, with short blond hair and an affable look. To get elected, Van Hollen had first had to win a Democratic primary against Mark Shriver, a well-financed member of the Kennedy family. Van Hollen, then a state senator, had a history of ferocious campaigning, and he attacked Shriver as an empty suit who was running on the Kennedy name. At one debate with Shriver, Van Hollen supporters groaned in unison whenever Shriver spoke, in what appeared to be an orchestrated tactic. After squeaking past Shriver, Van Hollen defeated Congresswoman Connie Morella, a likeable Republican whom Democrats had been trying to knock off for sixteen years. Van Hollen relentlessly emphasized Morella's party affiliation in the heavily Democratic district. In the end, Morella was one of only two GOP incumbents to lose that year. Shortly after being named DCCC chairman, Emanuel called Van Hollen and asked him to help out.

Emanuel also turned to Congresswoman Debbie Wasserman Schultz. A small, slim woman with pronounced features and frizzy hair, Wasserman Schultz, thirty-nine, came off as a nice Jewish girl from New York, which essentially she was, having moved from Long Island to Florida. Her attachment to Judaism created an immediate bond with Emanuel. When she ran in 2004, Wasserman Schultz raised enough money to scare off any Democratic opponents, ensuring her election in the heavily Democratic district. Once in Congress, Wasserman Schultz became a leader of the "30-Something Working Group," a gang of young Democrats who took to the House floor to ridicule Republicans. On one occasion, Wasserman Schultz brought a bobble-head elephant doll to the floor to make the point that House Republicans only knew how to nod yes to Bush, not how to shake their heads no.

These young House members, and others in Emanuel's inner circle, were not put off by Emanuel's pushy manner, as were some of his older colleagues. As a Jewish woman from New York, Wasserman Schultz said, she was used to abrasive types. "There is no question that I've encountered my share of strong personalities as a member of the Jewish community in New York and now in south Florida," Wasserman Schultz said. Then she laughed self-consciously, apparently worried she'd said something impolitic. "I represent a lot of strong personalities, and I mean that affectionately," she rephrased. "So it's not unusual for me to interact with people like Rahm."

As the House members began meeting on Thursdays in early 2005, they faced long odds. The Democrats needed just 15 of the Republicans' 232 seats to retake the House, but fewer than 10 seemed remotely vulnerable. The rest were in heavily Republican areas or were occupied by long-time incumbents. And incumbents almost never lost. They had name recognition, the ability to raise money, and the opportunity to do favors for their constituents. In 2004, of the 400 incumbents seeking reelection, 393 had prevailed, with a startling average victory margin of 40 percent.

Adding to their advantage, Republicans always raised more money than Democrats. Then there was the power of the White House. President Bush and Vice President Dick Cheney could campaign with candidates and help them raise money, and Bush could aid Republicans simply by shifting the public dialogue to terrain more favorable to the GOP, such as the fight against terrorism.

But none of those factors was as important as the country's electoral map, which inherently favored Republicans. Democratic voters were packed into urban areas, while Republicans were distributed much more efficiently in large rural stretches. This Republican tilt was not limited to the House. President Bush had captured the White House even though Democrat Al Gore had received significantly more votes. In the Senate, liberal, populous New York had two senators, just like conservative, sparsely populated Wyoming. In fact, Democrats had received 51 percent of all votes cast for the Senate from 2000 through 2004, yet Republicans held a 55–45 Senate majority. Many Democrats felt the system was fixed against them; even when they got more votes, they lost.

The extreme gerrymandering of recent years had only made things worse. The party in power in each state had always drawn congressional districts to benefit itself, of course, but computers had made gerrymandering much more effective. Democrats were just as eager to gerrymander as Republicans, but because Republicans held power in more key states, they had ensured that the nation's political map was drawn to their

advantage. Voters were increasingly locked into districts that were immov-
ably Republican or unshakably Democratic. That is why analyst Charlie
Cook, among others, wrote in his newsletter in February 2005 that he
doubted fifteen Republican seats even existed that could plausibly flip to
the Democrats.

For Emanuel, the first step in trying to overcome these obstacles was
recruiting good candidates. Most voters, even those who followed politics
avidly, tuned in only during the final stages of a campaign, when candidates
were furiously hurling charges at each other. But the most important part
of a race was who actually ran, and party leaders invested extraordinary
energy trying to persuade local figures—a charismatic mayor, an up-and-
coming county commissioner—to run for Congress. Emanuel would be
judged in large part by his success or failure in recruiting. His oft-stated
goal was to recruit fifty credible challengers in the 232 Republican-held
House districts. That would not guarantee anything, but it would position the Democrats to take advantage if Republican fortunes fell. Each
of the lawmakers on Emanuel's team was responsible for a section of
the country, and they received assignments at every meeting: Call a potential recruit in Ohio, contact the Iowa governor to ask about promising
Democrats there. They would report on their recent conversations with
recruits—who seemed close to a decision, who might be swayed by a call
from Barack Obama. "Basically it was strategizing about how to get our
top-tier candidates into these races," said Wasserman Schultz.

Emanuel had one criterion for candidates: he wanted people who could
win. That may sound obvious, but it's not. Many Democrats did not
believe in recruiting candidates who were so conservative they were pale
reflections of Republicans. In the past, candidates who opposed abortion,
for example, had not been welcome in the party. In 2005, many Democratic activists wanted only staunchly anti-war candidates. That was not
Emanuel's approach. "This is not a theoretical exercise," Van Hollen said.
"The goal is to win this thing. In dealing with candidates, we don't have
an ideological purity test. If you believe in the basic gut principles of the
Democratic Party—opportunity, fairness for all—we're not going to hold

people to a litmus test on a checklist of issues that different interest groups may have an interest in." That reflected a change taking place throughout the party, but Emanuel's approach earned him hostility from the party's liberal wing.

Emanuel and Van Hollen tried for months to persuade Patsy Madrid, New Mexico's popular Democratic attorney general, to jump in the race against Republican congresswoman Heather Wilson. Wilson was moderate and savvy, but her district in Albuquerque included many Hispanics and Democrats, so Madrid, a Hispanic and a Democrat, would have a good shot at knocking her off. But Madrid, who was considering running for governor or U.S. senator, was leaning against a House race. Emanuel started calling Madrid, not just occasionally but every two or three days. He knew she was a die-hard Democrat, and he spoke emotionally of how Bush and Cheney were destroying the country. Playing on her fondness for basketball, Emanuel said he was putting together a team, like a great basketball team, of candidates across the country.

Flattering as this was, Emanuel did not rely solely on his own persuasiveness. He enlisted Senator Hillary Rodham Clinton to call Madrid and urge her to run, as well as Pelosi, former senator John Edwards, General Wesley Clark, and various Hispanic House members. Madrid was especially taken aback when Hillary Clinton phoned her at Madrid's ranch in Mora, in the mountains of New Mexico. "I got a call from Hillary in the most remote place," Madrid said. "So I knew that Rahm was serious." Madrid was worried that if she won, she would have to move to Washington and be apart from her husband of thirty-three years, attorney Michael Messina. Emanuel stressed that members of Congress generally stayed in Washington only Tuesday through Thursday and then returned home. He arranged for husbands and wives of current House Democrats to call Messina and assure him that they spent plenty of time with their spouses. DCCC members even introduced Messina to members of the Washington legal community, so if he decided to move to D.C. he knew he'd have a job.

At a staff meeting in early October, Emanuel's top aide, John Lapp, offhandedly told him, "I talked to Madrid. She's in." Emanuel could barely contain his glee. "You're lying to me," he said. "Why don't you bury the fucking lead?" Emanuel was not the only one elated. "This is excellent news," one Democrat wrote on a liberal Web log called Our Congress. Even Republican spokesman Carl Forti acknowledged, "It's a good recruit for them. It's going to be a tough race, because it's a fifty-fifty district," evenly split between Democrats and Republicans.

After expressing his profane delight that Madrid had agreed to jump in, Emanuel immediately instructed his aides, "I'll tell you what—cut her a check for $5,000." Someone reminded Emanuel that Madrid did not even have a campaign committee yet, so there was nowhere to send a check, and wisecracks followed about Emanuel's overeagerness. He half mockingly aimed a middle finger at the room, something he seemed to do at least once a meeting. He also noted proudly that he had sent Madrid a cheesecake. Emanuel's district was home to Eli's Cheesecake, a Chicago institution, and when he was courting a candidate especially ardently, he sent them a cake. "I'm five for five on cheesecakes," he said.

Bringing in Madrid had been one of Emanuel's top priorities. "We worked it hard," he said. "Everybody has got their own particular issues. She needed certain things, she needed certain confidences, and I hung with her. . . . You've just got to work these people and you've got to stay with them. And one more thing: You can't be scared that they're going to say no. You just have to be at them all the time."

Emanuel called dozens of potential recruits in early 2005. John Callahan, the attractive, up-and-coming mayor of Bethlehem, Pennsylvania, had never spoken to Emanuel when he got his call. "Are you tired of being fucking mayor yet?" Emanuel asked without a preface. Callahan, who had no problem with salty language, was amused, and he responded in kind. "It's better than being a fucking congressman," he said. Callahan added that he did enjoy being mayor, and he had young children, so this was not the right time for him to run. The entire conversation lasted a few minutes.

Emanuel was always strategizing, trying to figure out the right angle to reel in an appealing candidate. If a potential candidate was worried about raising enough money, Emanuel would get several donors to call him and promise to raise $25,000 each. Then he would call the candidate and make sure he'd gotten the calls. Emanuel also hounded other Democrats to call recruits, so they would feel they were being invited to become part of a team or family. "He is on me every five minutes to call [potential recruits]," said Representative Steny Hoyer of Maryland, the number two Democrat in the House. "He is a laser. He is tenacious. He is unstoppable." Emanuel joked, "Sometimes I feel like a personal valet. You have successes, you have failures. This is like sand. This can fall right out of your hands if you don't do it right."

Emanuel kept an elaborate file of his potential and actual recruits. "Right now we have forty good races," he said on September 5. "Some are total As, some are A-minuses, some are B-pluses, and some are double Bs. But I'm going to get to fifty."

When Emanuel found an A prospect, he pursued his quarry relentlessly. Emanuel exercised many mornings with Congressman Bob Etheridge, a North Carolina Democrat. One day in the House gym, Etheridge mentioned a businessman named Heath Shuler, who he said might be willing to run in a conservative North Carolina district. "He is a football hero from the mountains," Etheridge said. "And he can win." Emanuel was enthralled by Shuler, a former University of Tennessee quarterback who had played professionally for the Washington Redskins. Emanuel enlisted Democratic stars from Barack Obama to John Edwards to call Shuler and urge him to run. Edwards even visited Shuler for three hours to make a personal appeal. Roughly fifty Democratic House members— one-fourth of the House Democrats—were prevailed upon to call Shuler. And there was more. One day Shuler was driving through Jackson County, coming from his father's house, when his cell phone rang. Seeing it was a 202 area code, meaning the call was from Washington, Shuler rolled his eyes—he'd received dozens of calls from congressmen by this time—and ignored it. Then he realized the caller was former president Bill Clinton, so he hastily pulled off into a parking lot and returned the call. Clinton joked with Shuler about the times when both were being pilloried for their performances in Washington, Clinton as president and Shuler as

Redskins quarterback. "Heath, I was so glad sometimes when I would look at the papers and I would see that you had made the headlines instead of me," Clinton chuckled. Only after this banter did Clinton get around to making his pitch. "Hey, look, Heath, it's an honor to give back to your country," Clinton said. "It's important to do the right thing, to be a part of making a difference in your community."

Emanuel asked Congressman Ron Kind of Wisconsin to take a leading role in courting Shuler, since Kind had been a college football star as well, having played quarterback at Harvard. Kind called Shuler every few days, listening to his questions about whether serving in Congress would destroy his family life. Emanuel stayed on top of Kind, making sure he was keeping in touch with Shuler. "I would be home, and Rahm would call me and say, 'Hey will you give Heath a quick call about such-and-such?'" Kind said. "It was 24-7."

Shuler was impressed with the attention. "Almost every congressman I spoke with said, 'Here's my phone number. Call my wife. Have your wife call my wife,'" Shuler said. But he was still worried that as a congressman he would rarely see his wife and young children. To prove to Shuler once and for all that congressmen do get to spend time with their kids, Emanuel began calling Shuler whenever he was with his own family. Shuler would pick up the phone and hear, "It's Rahm. I'm at a soccer game with my kids. Just wanted you to know that." Or "It's Rahm. I'm at a kindergarten play now. Talk to you soon." Shuler received perhaps ten such calls. Of course, this arguably also illustrated that whenever Emanuel was with his family he was working. Perhaps aware of that, Emanuel later said, "It was half-time. I didn't call him during the soccer games."

In any case, the onslaught had an impact on Shuler. "I was recruited from high school to play college football, I was recruited by almost every college in the country, and then I was recruited into the NFL," he said. "I know all the angles that people use to recruit you. Nobody does it as well as Rahm Emanuel. He is unbelievable." The Republicans, for their part, immediately recognized the danger of Shuler's prospective candidacy, and President Bush, on a visit to the Smoky Mountains, asked to meet with Shuler to try to dissuade him from running. Shuler declined, respectfully refusing a meeting with the president of the United States. There was no way Bush was going to dissuade him. He declared his candidacy in a brief statement in July 2005.

Running for Congress costs an enormous amount of time, stress, and money, and many Democrats did resist Emanuel's entreaties. When that happened, Republicans trumpeted the news, and they issued a series of press releases on the subject, titled "DCCC Delusions." Republicans ridiculed Emanuel for saying he would recruit fifty top-tier challengers to Republican incumbents. Congressman Tom Reynolds of New York, Emanuel's GOP counterpart, delighted in distributing a list of potential candidates Emanuel had tried and failed to recruit. "The Democrats like to go out and tell you what they're going to do," Reynolds said. But he insisted the Republicans would do better "war to war, combat to combat." He added, "I think they've got recruiting failures and money problems."

Emanuel's efforts were more than just an attempt to attract the best-qualified candidates. Integral to his own style was a sort of macho strut, and that was reflected in his recruiting. Despite the incongruous fact that Emanuel for years studied ballet, he projected a masculine assertiveness— with his missing finger, his browbeating style, his cursing, his stint helping Israel during the 1991 Gulf War. Emanuel and John Lapp, his top aide at the outset of the campaign, delighted in finding candidates who fit the manly mold—military veterans, police officers, pilots. Among their most prized recruits was Brad Ellsworth, an Indiana sheriff, and there were many others. Emanuel bragged repeatedly about how many military veterans he'd recruited. "That's the stuff I love—tough, macho Democrats taking on the Republicans," Lapp said. Emanuel at one point described a Vietnam veteran he was trying to recruit, whom he did not name, by saying, "I don't know if he's going to win, but I'll tell you this: I don't want to cross the motherfucker. I think he would take out a knife and kill you. I think he would kill you." He seemed to view that as an asset.

Some saw this as a pose or worse. David Sirota, a liberal blogger, had had enough when he read an October 2005 *Rolling Stone* article quoting

Democratic consultant Paul Begala saying of his friend Emanuel, "He's got this big old pair of brass balls and you can just hear 'em clanking when he walks down the halls of Congress." Sirota posted his reaction on the Huffington Post Web log: "We have a name for talk like that: It's called B.S. Because here's what Emanuel never seems to answer: How is someone 'tough' if they are so wimpy as to refuse to push their party to take clear contrasting positions on the most important issues facing America?" That's what real toughness would be, Sirota argued—confronting the Republicans forcefully on Iraq, health care, union organizing.

But Emanuel was fighting a weak, feminine image that had long haunted the Democratic Party, in part from its ties to women and gays, in part from its perceived weakness on national defense. Republicans often promoted their strength, while Democrats promoted their caretaking. Television host Chris Matthews had famously called the Republican Party "the daddy party" and the Democrats "the mommy party." Republicans had effectively portrayed candidates from Michael Dukakis to Walter Mondale as effeminate. In the 2000 and 2004 elections, George Bush presented himself as a tough guy, a rancher, a cowboy; Gore and Kerry—both of whom served in Vietnam while Bush avoided the draft—were portrayed as effete. Gore was derided when an internal campaign memo came to light advising him to wear "earth tones." Kerry was painted as a French-speaking sissy who favored such dubious sports as sailboarding. These undertones of gender had been part of the parties' images at least since the Cold War, and at a time when voters were feeling fearful of terrorism, it was crucial for the Democrats to combat this perception. Emanuel and Lapp were determined to do so, not only in the candidates they recruited but in their own personalities. They presented themselves as men of action, like characters from an Ernest Hemingway novel. "There's so much in politics where people move too slow. It's never that [with us]," Lapp said. "If we make a mistake, it's going to be because we moved too fast. Like if we recruit too heavily and get the wrong guy. It's not going to be an omission or hesitation."

To get the right candidate, Emanuel was more than willing to fight with other Democrats. He was looking for a candidate in a tough district in North Carolina, for example, and Congressman Brad Miller, a North Carolina Democrat, pleaded with Emanuel to back a protégé of his. But Emanuel thought the man was too liberal for the district and refused to support him, leading to shouting matches between Emanuel and Miller. Instead, Emanuel recruited a more conservative attorney named Tim Dunn, who had served with the Marines in Iraq.

There was a flip side to finding good candidates—Emanuel also needed popular Republicans to leave Congress. Since sitting congressmen rarely lose, the more Republicans stepped down, the more opportunities Democrats would have. But unnervingly, only 12 of the 232 House Republicans had announced their retirement by early October 2005, far fewer than usual. It was a frustrating dark spot on the Democratic horizon. In a conversation on September 28, Emanuel ran his hands through his hair, looking frazzled. He was in his DCCC office, around the corner from the U.S. Capitol, whose membership he was struggling to change. "Here's what's missing for my best case right now: I need more Republican retirements," Emanuel said. He had gone from one cup of coffee a day to four since the campaign began, and he sipped one now, offhandedly denigrating those who drank mere tea. "Everybody tells me it's going to happen," he said of Republican retirements. "I know you find this hard to believe, but I'm very impatient. It hasn't happened."

Well aware of the stakes, Republican leaders spread the message that if any Republican quit to become a lobbyist, the doors of Congress would be shut to him. Reynolds, Emanuel's Republican counterpart, took every opportunity to urge his GOP colleagues not to retire, telling them, "I hate open seats. I don't want open seats. We don't want you to retire." Reynolds also reminded fellow Republicans that most of them had waited their whole lives for the Republicans to control the White House, Senate, and House; now that the dream was realized, they should stay and enjoy it. In a memo on October 7, 2005, Reynolds underlined the message: "The one vulnerability we have is open seats, so we must all work to make sure that we keep as many members in the House, running for reelection, as possible."

Emanuel was not about to wait and see. He outlined his technique for encouraging retirements: "Beat the shit out of them in the press all the time. . . . And if they're seventy years old, with $200,000 in the campaign fund, they might ask, 'Do I want to do this one more [election] cycle, in a [political] environment which looks like it's pretty shitty?'" One target was Congresswoman Nancy Johnson, a moderate Republican representing a middle-of-the-road Connecticut district. Johnson was a popular, grandmotherly figure, elected twelve straight times and winning 60 percent of the vote in 2004. But she was seventy years old and perennially torn between her moderate constituents and her party's conservative leadership. Johnson's district, comprising a number of small towns in northwest Connecticut, had voted for Al Gore over George Bush by 52 percent to 43 percent in 2000 and split its vote evenly between Bush and John Kerry in 2004. Democrats recruited State Senator Chris Murphy, an energetic thirty-one-year-old, to challenge Johnson. On Our Congress, a liberal blog, one correspondent wrote, "This is, pure and simple, an amazing opportunity for Democrats." But another participant followed with a more realistic assessment: "Do you really think we have a strong chance at this seat without Nancy Johnson retiring? I mean, she's represented this district since 1983."

In a stream of press releases, the Democrats attacked the congresswoman. "Johnson has two opposite positions on Social Security 'privatization.' Where does she really stand?" asked one. Another derided Johnson for voting against health benefits for the Reserve and National Guard. A third accused her of voting "against aiding the fight against amphetamine." In other Democratic statements, Johnson was accused of "gutting" veterans' health care, "jeopardizing" Social Security, "letting polluters slide," and being a handmaiden of Tom DeLay. At one DCCC staff meeting, Emanuel's communications director, Bill Burton, reported that when Johnson held a constituents' meeting the next day, Democrats would press her on why she had not signed on to a lobbying reform bill. "We'll be able to pop her good," Burton said.

Burton said afterward, "You try to make their lives as miserable as possible. You do things to make them think, 'Do I want to go through this for another 399 days, to be at the end of this punching bag?'" Democrats also went after Congressman E. Clay Shaw of Florida, who was sixty-six years old. They pulled back only when Shaw revealed he had cancer, "because we didn't want to look mean," as one staffer put it.

It was at the same time that Emanuel was doing this work, assembling his team and courting candidates, that Rove made his speech in New York that in essence described how those efforts were certain to fail and Republicans would hold power for decades. Rove invoked the broad philosophical currents that swept back and forth across the American landscape, but he might as well have cited more practical considerations such as money, incumbency, and gerrymandering.

In the course of his speech, Rove described the Democrats' recent demise and the Republican ascent. And he did it in a way that, given the coming campaign, was more prescient than he could know. The fall of the Democrats, Rove said, "is a cautionary tale of what happens to a dominant party—in this case, the Democrat Party—when its thinking becomes ossified, when its energy begins to drain, when an entitlement mentality takes over, and when political power becomes an end in itself, rather than a means to achieve the common good."

2

AN UNSTOPPABLE FORCE

Rahm Emanuel once was so furious with an associate that he sent him a dead fish. That story had long circulated among Emanuel's friends and enemies. It was absolutely true, but there was more to it than that.

The event occurred when Emanuel was a senior staffer at the DCCC in 1988 and was fighting constantly with an outside pollster named Alan Secrest. They were unable to get along on any level. Secrest accused Emanuel of unethically steering business to other pollsters, and the two strong-willed men argued repeatedly over strategy. The DCCC was slow to pay Secrest, who responded by withholding polling information. That, in turn, made campaign staffers frantic as Election Day approached, since they needed Secrest's polls to make strategic decisions. DCCC staffers were upset by Secrest's approach and attitude. "It drove myself, Rahm, and all of our peers insane," said Joe Sinsheimer, who worked at the DCCC at the time. In the heat of a close campaign, Emanuel and Secrest frequently shouted at each other. "There were horrible phone fights, screaming matches, and so on," Sinsheimer said. For Emanuel, the final blow involved a Secrest poll in a Buffalo-area House race. As Emanuel recalled the story, Secrest's firm actually conducted a poll partly in the wrong district, producing misleading numbers that cost the Democrats the election. Secrest dismissed that account, saying no polling was ever done outside the district. "Our data processor made an analytically insignificant error which was corrected in a matter of hours," Secrest said. "It did not impact the analysis or the outcome."

The anger simmered on both sides, and two days after the election, Sinsheimer read an item in *USA Today* about a Massachusetts company called Creative Revenge that, for a fee, would send someone a dead fish in a beautiful mahogany box. "Let's send a fish to Secrest," Sinsheimer proposed. Emanuel and a third staffer, Jim Crounse, agreed to join the prank. The company would not send the fish unless it was clearly intended as a joke, not a serious threat, so the trio wrote a halfheartedly humorous note saying, "It's been awful working with you. Love, Jim, Joe and Rahm." That was enough to persuade the owner that the prank was meant in good fun, and the fish was dispatched through the mail.

Secrest, however, did not see it as a good-natured prank. Blaming Emanuel for the malodorous fish, Secrest wrote a long letter bitterly criticizing his conduct of the campaign. "I'm not interested in becoming a political whore like you, and I will not succumb—or let my staff succumb—to measuring ourselves by the approval or disapproval of the likes of you, Rahm," the letter said. "You had become a pathetic caricature in people's eyes early on." Emanuel responded by faxing Secrest's letter to leading Democrats around Washington, believing it showed Secrest to be unhinged. At the time, the three DCCC staffers were in their twenties, and not all their colleagues were thrilled with their prank. "I thought it was silly and sophomoric," said Richard Bates, then the DCCC's executive director. Emanuel claimed that he realized only later that Mafia members were known to send their targets a fish as a death threat—meaning "you'll soon be sleeping with the fishes"—which gave the joke a more sinister cast. As Emanuel's career progressed, the episode was often cited as evidence of his outrageous, no-limits behavior, and it has appeared in virtually every media profile of Emanuel. Even *The West Wing*, an NBC television show based on the Clinton White House, featured an episode in which a character received a dead fish.

Given Emanuel's upbringing, it was not entirely surprising that he would become a hard-charging political operative. Born in Chicago on November 29, 1959, Rahm Israel Emanuel at first was lethargic and slow to talk. As the middle son, he was a peacemaker between his two brothers—the older Ezekiel, who was hard-driving and excelled in school, and the younger Ari, a fighter and wrestler. "Of the three, he was the calmest," Ezekiel said. "Ari was incredibly hyperactive and always in trouble. I was the firstborn and always rushing." Ari and Rahm shared a bunk bed, and Ari got the top bunk even though he was younger. "I was physically stronger," Ari said.

The young Emanuel often pirouetted around the house while listening to music. "Ari would be wrestling, Zeke would be pondering deep thoughts, and Rahmmy would be leaping down the stairs and doing ballet dance twirls," said his mother, Marsha. Thinking he might have talent, his parents sent Emanuel to ballet class, forcing his brothers to go, too, so he would not be the only boy. He was to study ballet well into his adulthood, and the idea of Emanuel performing delicate jumps and twirls always created a curious contrast with the rest of his personality, a contrast he used to throw listeners off balance. President Bush once told Emanuel he looked fit, apparently trying to make a macho connection between two athletic men. "I study ballet, Mr. President," Emanuel explained (though by that time he had not danced in years), hoping to give Bush a jolt. Emanuel enjoyed his lessons, his mother said. "Every article I see, he says, 'My mother forced me to dance,'" Marsha Emanuel said. "Forgive me— you little shithead, I didn't force you, I forced your brothers."

For all the pirouetting, an unusual intensity began to surface as Emanuel grew. Gerald Noskin, who coached Emanuel's intramural basketball team in junior high school, said the undersized, scrambling player would scream in protest when he was pulled from a game for a substitute. "He was a little spitfire; I guess he grew up to be a big spitfire," said Noskin, a dentist in Skokie, Illinois. "In those days they gave children reasonably equal playing time. He just wanted a little plus. He just didn't want to sit on the bench." Emanuel's ballet teachers described a similar intensity, saying he was not especially talented but practiced with a striking discipline. "Intense would be a word I would have used even then," said Kerry Hubata, who taught at the Evanston School of Ballet. "He worked hard. And when we're looking at kids at that age, that is the big talent in dance—the talent for hard work. I've seen kids with physical talent who didn't work as hard. Others, who weren't as gifted physically but had the desire and didn't mind the pain, succeeded more. He had the drive." Larry Grote, Emanuel's high school advisor and soccer coach at New Trier High School, reaffirmed the picture of Emanuel as a youngster who used his intensity to compensate for average ability. "He wasn't one of our top players, so when he got in, he took advantage of it by playing as aggressively as possible," Grote said.

Emanuel did not initially have a clear direction or passion. He was a gregarious, popular student in high school with a B-plus average. At the end of his senior year, Emanuel was working at Arby's, the fast-food restaurant, when a meat slicer cut deeply into the middle finger of his right hand, literally reaching the bone. But this was prom weekend and Emanuel had no intention of missing the festivities, so he simply bandaged the finger and went off to party with friends, including a night swim in nearby Lake Michigan. The finger became infected with water-borne bacteria, making Emanuel critically sick. He lay near death in Children's Hospital in Chicago for weeks, as his fever reached 106 degrees and special antibiotics from Japan were pumped into his body. Nothing initially seemed effective, and a hand surgeon was brought in to evaluate how much of Emanuel's hand to amputate in hopes of saving his life. Eventually doctors cut off only a portion of Emanuel's finger and the infection subsided. That partial finger was to become part of Emanuel's image; rumors even circulated that he'd lost it fighting for the Israeli army. As he grew up, Emanuel regularly flashed his middle finger, and the effect of the half digit could be jarring. He joked that on occasion giving someone half a finger was exactly the sentiment he was aiming for.

But at the time, the accident was hardly humorous, and Emanuel's parents were distraught. "Ben [Rahm's father] was busy with the medical team, and I was busy holding my child in my arms and praying that he doesn't die," Marsha Emanuel said. "It was really ugly for three weeks. We nearly lost our child." Emanuel has described the accident as an important event in his life, and to family members he immediately seemed more focused. "That was a big turning point in Rahm's life, to be honest," his mother said. "It was touch-and-go, and finally when he came out of it he was more serious. . . . I honestly think that was his existential moment of near death and realizing that you have to do something with life." After six weeks, Emanuel got fed up with being in the hospital, pulled the IV tube out of his arm, and checked himself out. "Afterwards I was worried that the fever might have affected his mentality or his intellect," his mother said. "But the first time he woke up I realized he was cursing, and it was, 'He's going to be okay.'"

All three Emanuel brothers ended up reaching the pinnacles of entirely unrelated professions. The oldest, Ezekiel, is a leading bioethicist at the National Institutes of Health. A brilliant student, he received an M.D. and a Ph.D. in political philosophy from Harvard. He served on the faculties of the Dana-Farber Cancer Institute and Harvard and wrote a book on medical ethics called *The Ends of Human Life*. His articles—on everything from euthanasia to the doctor-patient relationship—appeared in the *New England Journal of Medicine* and similarly prestigious publications. Emanuel's younger brother, Ari, became a multimillionaire Hollywood agent. He is a forceful, successful figure in Hollywood, much as his brother is in Washington. Ari Gold, the foul-mouthed agent on the HBO show *Entourage,* was based in part on him. (Another television character, Josh Lyman in *The West Wing,* was based partly on Rahm.) Ari Emanuel has not shied away from conflict, and he was one of the few influential Hollywood figures to publicly attack the actor Mel Gibson when Gibson unleashed an anti-Semitic tirade at a police officer. "People in the entertainment community, whether Jew or gentile, need to demonstrate that they understand how much is at stake in this by professionally shunning Mel Gibson and refusing to work with him, even if it means a sacrifice to their bottom line," Ari Emanuel wrote on the Huffington Post Web log.

When Rahm Emanuel was thirteen, the family adopted a girl they named Shoshana. Her story created a darker, poignant counterpoint to the Emanuel dazzle. Shoshana's mother had come into the hospital where Emanuel's father was head of pediatrics, wanting to give the girl away, and after a discussion the family decided to take the child in. The Emanuels protect Shoshana's privacy, but she clearly has had a troubled life. By the middle of 2006 Shoshana had moved from the Chicago area and was studying to be a pharmacist's assistant, and the family will not discuss her location.

It is tempting to search for a revealing formula or revolutionary child-rearing secret that paved the way for the brothers' accomplishments. But the Emanuels apparently were raised much like any other upper-middle-class kids in the Chicago suburbs. In 2006, Benjamin and Marsha Emanuel lived in the same modest two-story house in Wilmette they had occupied when Rahm was in high school. Photographs from the Clinton presidency decorated the living room. In one picture, Clinton held Emanuel's son, Zach, then a baby, who in turn was grabbing the president's ear. Clinton autographed it for the Emanuels, "Your grandson has a grip." In the kitchen, decorations included an embroidered design featuring Hebrew letters and an "Emanuel for Congress" refrigerator magnet.

Emanuel's parents clearly are strong personalities. Benjamin Emanuel was born in Jerusalem and served in the pre-state Jewish underground. He joined the Irgun, an extremist right-wing group, rather than the mainstream Haganah, explaining that this was because his relatives had joined it, not because he subscribed to its ideology. Benjamin's brother, Emanuel, died in the Arab insurrection of 1936, and Benjamin changed his last name from Auerbach to Emanuel in his brother's memory. Benjamin traveled to Czechoslovakia in an abortive attempt to clandestinely buy guns for the Zionist cause. One of his jobs in the underground was to put up anti-British posters, and while he was doing so a British officer smashed him on the head with a baton, leaving a dent still visible on his balding head. Wanting to practice medicine, Benjamin settled in Chicago and became a successful pediatrician. He never lost his strong Israeli accent, and he transmitted his no-nonsense style to his sons. "He was notorious for seeing twice as many patients as the next guy on this list," Ezekiel said. "He would be personable, but just 'get to the meat of things and get it done.' That is obviously a trait that people can see in Rahm, and it's quite clear where it came from, in my opinion."

Marsha Emanuel, a proud leftist and impassioned civil rights activist, is equally forceful. She took her young children to civil rights marches if she judged there would be no violence. She herself was occasionally attacked, and the children knew she might not be home some nights because she had been arrested. Sometimes Marsha miscalculated the danger; she took a young Ezekiel to Martin Luther King Jr.'s famous march in Cicero, Illinois, and they were pelted with tomatoes and eggs. At another protest racist bystanders tut-tutted that she had brought her children to march alongside blacks. "I remember some women standing on the street corner saying, 'Oh, take those babies home, they don't belong here with those niggers,'" Marsha Emanuel said. "I didn't want my kids to hear it, but that was the reality."

As parents, Benjamin and Marsha did not push their children relentlessly to succeed; if anything, they let them follow their own paths. One winter the brothers wanted to build an igloo, so Marsha hauled out the family's pots and helped the boys freeze large blocks of ice. Another time the boys wanted to create a computer, so the parents drove around looking for switches and wiring. Ezekiel, the oldest son, had a fascination with dissection, so his parents bought him frogs, and his grandfather obtained a cow heart and lung from a butcher shop. The organs remained in the kitchen freezer for weeks.

In the fall of 1978, barely recovered from his amputation, Emanuel headed to Sarah Lawrence College in New York, which had an excellent dance program. Emanuel was an RA, a resident advisor, enforcing order among other students in the dorm, and his forcefulness reemerged. "I told everybody RA stood for 'resident asshole,'" said Meryl Rosen, one of his students. "He was like Napoleon, basically—this sort of dictator." Rosen felt affection for Emanuel, however. He was sophomore class president, and he encouraged Rosen to run for freshman president and even managed her victorious campaign. "He was like, 'Don't worry, we'll get you elected and then you'll just vote the way I do,'" Rosen said. Sarah Lawrence, which had only recently begun accepting men, remained overwhelmingly female. The few male students generally fell into two camps, Rosen said—gay men who were there for the school's well-regarded artistic programs and straight men who wanted to sleep with as many women as possible. "Rahm marched to his own drummer and was not in either category," Rosen said. "He was definitely his own flavor. He always had a big following. The dining room was a meeting place, and he would always have a big group of people and he would be carrying on and pontificating."

Emanuel did not hesitate to voice his opinions in class. "He was challenging, not in a hostile way, but he wanted to know why," said H. H. Kleinman, professor emeritus of literature at Sarah Lawrence. "I would alternate between amusement at his energy and admiration for him. He was a very tough character, yet he had a certain softness." Emanuel's advisor, or "don," as they were called at Sarah Lawrence, died in his senior year, and Emanuel spoke at the memorial service, breaking down in sobs. His replacement don was Jefferson Adams, a history professor who was in the process of leaving the Democratic Party under the spell of Ronald Reagan. "A lot of Democrats were making fun of Reagan, and I remember warning Rahm, 'Don't be a typical Democrat and start caricaturing and dismissing him,'" Adams said. "Rahm seemed to pick up on that." Emanuel was starting to become politically active, flying to Chicago on weekends to raise money for Paul Simon, then a congressman. He would visit a store near campus called Buyers Factory Outlet, where he could buy suits at a discount for his fund-raising activities. Adams and Emanuel debated politics in a good-natured way. "I didn't recognize him in the Clinton administration and later, where he has this reputation for being ferocious and swallowing people alive," Adams said. "That is not the Rahm I knew."

Politics had been the background music at Emanuel's home growing up. His grandfather was a union organizer who talked about the old days of grand labor victories. His mother was active in Chicago politics. As early as high school, Emanuel stuffed campaign literature in mailboxes for Abner Mikva, then a liberal Chicago congressman. In the final summer of his college years, Emanuel worked unsuccessfully to defeat Republican congressman Paul Findley, who was notorious in the Jewish community for his criticism of Israel. After college, Emanuel's first job was handling publicity for the consumer group Illinois Public Action, and he went at it with his usual single-mindedness. Trying to persuade *Chicago Tribune* reporter David Axelrod to write an article on his organization, he called Axelrod repeatedly, finally tracking him down at Rush-Presbyterian-St. Luke's Medical Center, where Axelrod's wife had just given birth. "Is it a boy or a girl?" Emanuel asked. "A boy," answered a euphoric, exhausted Axelrod. *"Mazel tov,"* answered Emanuel. "Now when do you think you'll be back at work to write that story?"

Emanuel's aggressiveness was especially suited for political fund-raising, which, at its core, involves shamelessly and relentlessly asking for money. Emanuel was hired to raise cash for Paul Simon's 1984 Senate campaign, where he showed no embarrassment about calling up wealthy individuals, asking them for a lot of money, and berating them if they did not come through at a level he deemed sufficient. "The first word that comes to mind is *chutzpah.* He has redefined the term," said Axelrod, who by then had left the newspaper business and was running Simon's campaign. Emanuel then landed a job at the DCCC, overseeing House campaigns first in the Midwest and then across the country. It was while at the DCCC that Emanuel sent the fish to pollster Alan Secrest. He also wrote an article during this period for *Campaigns & Elections* magazine called "How to Beat a Republican," explaining how after outlining his agenda a candidate could start "dredging up dirt" on the opposition. "And even if your early ventures fail to pan out, keep digging," Emanuel advised. "The untainted Republican has not yet been invented." He also traveled the country frequently to visit various campaigns. On one trip to Raleigh, North Carolina, Emanuel showed visible embarrassment for one of the few times in his life. He and his colleagues were eating dinner at a restaurant and Emanuel was cursing loudly. "I forget the topic, but he was 'Fuck this, fuck that, I can't believe these fucking assholes,'" said his colleague Joe Sinsheimer. "In the middle of the dinner, this sixty-year-old North Carolina man walks over and says, 'I'm trying to have dinner with my wife, and your language is not very polite.' He knew he had really offended somebody. He apologized and he was very chastened by it."

Chastened or not, Emanuel continues to spice his conversation with an inordinate number of curse words. He uses *fuck* like a combination of comma and semicolon, to punctuate and highlight his thoughts. In one conversation, he referred to Washington as "Fucknutsville." Apparently unsatisfied with the derogatory power of the word *knucklehead,* he commonly describes people—including, on one occasion, former Republican congressman John Hostettler—as a "knucklefuck." Emanuel once articulated his prescription for his party in presidential elections as "Let's not nominate fucking idiots." He once asked a reporter preparing a story, "You guys aren't going to ratfuck me, are you?" After his election to Congress, Emanuel was known to welcome a guest to his office with a friendly "Scumbag! Come in." At a roast of Emanuel in September 2005, Senator Barack Obama observed that when Emanuel lost half of his right middle finger, "this rendered him practically mute." Asked about her son's language, Emanuel's mother, Marsha, buried her head in her arms in exaggerated distress. "My fault," she said. She had never forbidden her sons to curse, she acknowledged. "We said, 'If you want to say those words, it just shows that you're uneducated and uncouth. The words that you can't say is to hurt people's ethnicity, religion, how they look, how they're shaped. Those are curse words and you dare not say them as an Emanuel.'" There is a tradition, of course, of politicians swearing profusely in private while speaking elegantly in public. One of the revelations in President Nixon's White House tapes had been his obscene language, and when the transcripts became public the phrase "expletive deleted" became a national joke. By the time then-candidate George Bush called *New York Times* reporter Adam Clymer a "major league asshole" in 2000, or Vice President Cheney told Senator Patrick Leahy to "fuck yourself" on the Senate floor in 2004, the public shrugged it off. But Emanuel's prolific swearing is a jolt to the unprepared.

Emanuel returned to Chicago from the DCCC as chief fund-raiser for Richard Daley, who was running for mayor in a race that bitterly divided the city along racial lines. Former mayor Harold Washington, the city's first black mayor, had died unexpectedly of a heart attack, and his would-be successors had little time to prepare for the campaign. Emanuel was ferocious. He told contributors who usually gave $1,000 that this time they were expected to give $5,000. Those who usually gave $5,000 were expected to provide $25,000. Emanuel told one donor that if he was not prepared to donate a certain amount he should keep his money, and he slammed down the phone. The angry contributor called William Daley, the candidate's brother and campaign chairman, demanding, "Who is this asshole?" Daley walked over to Emanuel and asked him, "What are you doing? This guy has been giving to Rich for twenty-five years." Emanuel answered, "Don't worry, he'll come through." The tactics were obnoxious and initially seemed counterproductive. But the Daley campaign raised an astonishing $13 million in seven weeks.

Emanuel's reputation was growing in the small world of political professionals. When Bill Clinton launched his improbable presidential run in late 1991, he chose Chicago political operative David Wilhelm to head it, and Wilhelm—believing an aggressive fund-raiser was critical to Clinton's success—called Emanuel every night at eleven o'clock until he agreed to become Clinton's finance director. Emanuel had recently opened a consulting business helping Democrats unearth dirt on Republicans, and his father questioned the idea of closing a promising business to work for an obscure candidate. "We never thought he would win," Benjamin Emanuel said. "He had no chance in hell." But Emanuel liked Clinton and wanted to work on a presidential campaign. "He was then a little more brash and less polished than now, but he clearly had loads of ability and drive," Clinton said. "My first impression was, 'This guy is going to help us win.' And he did. I doubt we could have done it without him, especially in those critical early months."

Clinton had intelligence and charisma and had mesmerized many of the reporters covering him. But he also was a little-known, scandal-prone governor of a small state, and it was far from clear at first that he had the credibility to win. Emanuel believed the key to persuading influential politicians and journalists that Clinton was viable was to raise as much money as possible. He fought with others inside the campaign to get Clinton to spend more time asking for money and less time doing ordinary campaigning. Clinton himself hated the idea. "I was on the [campaign] plane, and I knew for a fact that Clinton was unhappy that we had to fly through the night to pick up twenty grand instead of being in New Hampshire," said Richard Mintz, an early Clinton staffer. "Clinton complained. But he always did it." Emanuel's initial goal was to raise $3 million by the end of 1991, a pittance by today's standards but back then an amount that would establish Clinton as a serious candidate. To accomplish that, Emanuel jumped on a table to urge his small staff to work harder. He repeated his by then familiar tactics, telling donors who contributed $250 that they should be embarrassed to give such a small amount. When supporters organized a fund-raiser in one city or another, Emanuel would push them to get more money. "I remember him yelling into the phone, 'We're not flying the next president of the United States to fill-in-the-blank for $500!'" Mintz said.

Such tactics led to a $2 million surge in December 1991, and the Clinton campaign exceeded Emanuel's goal by bringing in $3.3 million total for the year. That proved critical a month later when a former lounge singer named Gennifer Flowers called a press conference to claim she'd had a twelve-year affair with Clinton and played tapes that she said proved it. The Clinton campaign was in danger of collapse, and it was more important than ever to keep the money flowing in. Emanuel organized a massive fund-raiser in New York and dragged in James Carville to speak to the donors, over the protests of those who thought the campaign's chief strategist should be in New Hampshire, where a critical primary was approaching. But with his funds, Clinton was able to buy an hour of New Hampshire television the weekend before the primary, and he came in second, a good enough showing that he could describe himself as "the comeback kid."

Emanuel's tactics did not consist solely of screaming and cursing, or he would not have achieved what he did. He deployed those weapons selectively. When he yelled at a donor, it was because he thought that approach would be effective with that particular person. Emanuel also was highly organized and built a sense of loyalty among Clinton's donors by giving them information such as poll results that made them feel like insiders. "You aren't as successful as he is if you just leave a lot of bodies everywhere," said Dee Dee Myers, who worked with Emanuel on the campaign. But there was little question that Emanuel's overall style was scorched earth. The night after the election, about twenty top Clinton campaign workers gathered in a back room at Doe's Eat Place in Little Rock, Arkansas, a down-home restaurant they had frequented throughout the campaign. Most of the staffers were weepy with the magnitude of their accomplishment, electing a president of the United States, and they were telling each other, "I love you" and "You're a genius." Not Emanuel. He stood up and began reciting the names of people who had, as he put it, "fucked us" during the campaign. With each name, Emanuel jabbed a knife in a table and yelled, "Dead man!" It was a roll call of revenge—recalling a scene in the movie *Animal House*—as Emanuel named people such as Cliff Jackson, an Arkansas friend who had turned on the Clintons, and Maryland governor William Schaefer, the only Democratic governor to endorse President George H. W. Bush. "Cliff Jackson—dead man!" Emanuel screamed, stabbing his knife into the table. "Schaefer—dead man!"

The Clintonites' euphoria was quickly tempered by the realities of holding office. The new presidency was immediately rocked by controversies over everything from Clinton's pledge to allow gays in the military to a costly haircut he received on Air Force One. Emanuel's pushiness backfired for the first time in his life, as he clashed with other staffers and was quickly demoted from his initial job as White House political director. His precise offense is murky, but he seems to have angered everyone from U.S. senators to First Lady Hillary Rodham Clinton. Emanuel himself blamed Susan Thomases, a friend of the Clintons' with whom he'd fought, but Thomases said in an interview she'd had no problem with him. In any case, White House chief of staff Thomas "Mack" McLarty approached Emanuel several months after Clinton took office and told him the president wanted him out of the White House. Adding to the humiliation, Emanuel's fiancée, Amy Rule, had moved to Washington that very day to be with him. Emanuel handled the embarrassment by simply refusing to leave, telling McLarty he would not quit the White House unless Clinton personally asked him. The president, unable to fire the man who arguably had saved his candidacy, relented, instead demoting Emanuel to "director of special projects." "I could have had self-pity and anger, and trust me, there were a lot of emotions that I was being hung out to dry for other people's failures," Emanuel said. "But I went out to prove myself." It was Emanuel's first professional setback. "It was a huge experience," said Emanuel's mother, Marsha. "Rahm told us he had to sit back and rethink his methodology. He was devastated by what happened."

Emanuel was assigned the thankless job of pushing the North America Free Trade Agreement, or NAFTA, through the Congress—a tricky political challenge since the trade pact was supported by far more Republicans than Democrats. At the outset, a total of five House Democrats publicly supported the trade deal out of the roughly one hundred the White House needed. Clinton badly needed this victory, and he summoned William Daley from Chicago in August 1993 to join Emanuel in running an intensive three-month campaign. Illinois congressman Dan Rostenkowski, a savvy politician if ever there was one and an old friend of Daley's, asked Daley why he was wasting his time, telling him, "It's dead." Emanuel and Daley set up a war room in the Old Executive Office Building next to the White House, convening representatives from various cabinet agencies. They pursued House members one by one, figuring out what approach was likely to persuade them—a call from the president, an appeal from a powerful business leader in their district, a promised favor. At one point, Emanuel felt Congressman Robert Torricelli of New Jersey had misled Clinton about his position on NAFTA, and he took revenge. "I leaked the fact he had told Clinton one thing and then gone the other way," Emanuel said. "And we screwed him on something later, I forget what it was." (Torricelli disputes this story.) One by one, House Democrats began announcing their support for NAFTA. As momentum gathered, more Democrats came along, so that by the November 17 vote, Clinton was expected to win. And he did, with 102 Democrats joining 132 Republicans to provide a 234–200 margin. It was an early example of what was to be one of Emanuel's great strengths—the ability to count votes. It was also Clinton's first good news in some time.

The new president faced equally bleak prospects with his $30 billion crime bill. The legislation, featuring Clinton's signature program to put 100,000 police officers on the street, had something for everyone to hate—an assault weapons ban, drug treatment programs, death penalty provisions. About twenty staffers piled into Emanuel's tiny White House office each week in the middle of 1994 to plot strategy for passing it. The White House had assumed the bill would squeak through, but on August 11, the House voted 225–210 to block it, in what the *Washington Post* called the "biggest legislative defeat" of Clinton's young presidency. The White House staff was stunned. But Emanuel spoke forcefully of not giving up and pushing for a new vote. "That was Rahm's great moment," said Jose Cerda, a White House aide. Emanuel argued for playing up how strongly police groups supported the bill, since it would be hard for Republicans to oppose the police. The next day, Clinton went on the offensive, traveling to a Minneapolis police convention to portray the vote against the bill as a vote against America's cops. "To all the police officers in this country who walk out there for us every day—Washington cannot just walk away from you," he said. At the same time, House Democratic leaders were making changes in the bill to win the support of moderate Republicans, and ten days after the initial defeat, the legislation passed 235–195.

The twin victories restored Emanuel to favor, and he became Clinton's senior advisor. The two have been close ever since. A hint of their relationship can be gleaned from an inscription on a photo the president gave his aide on his thirty-eighth birthday, signing it as though he were Emanuel. "Now Mr. President, how many times do I have to tell you, say it this way?" Clinton wrote. "And, by the way, wish me a happy birthday. Always gently, Rahm 11/29/97." By all accounts, Emanuel did not sugarcoat his advice to Clinton. "Rahm could be about the same with the president as he is with most people," John Podesta, Clinton's chief of staff, said. "Maybe pull it back ten degrees, but only ten degrees." Clinton added dryly, "I found his candor refreshing."

In the force of his personality, more than one observer compared Emanuel to another tempestuous character in U.S. politics, Lyndon Johnson. The differences between the gangly, deceptive Texan and the slight, hard-hitting Jew from Chicago were obvious. But both had an instinct for politics that was almost animalistic, an encyclopedic knowledge of the political scene, a gift for hard-hitting and creative methods, and a raw, elemental energy. Johnson would put one arm around an interlocutor and, grabbing the man's lapel with the other, thrust his face at the listener as he made his case. Emanuel used gestures and obscenities, but the feeling of all-out force was the same. "He has some LBJ genes," said political scientist Larry Sabato. "He's the Jewish LBJ. That's pretty impressive; even LBJ couldn't conceive of a Jewish LBJ. They are both driven animals, with the base instincts needed to overturn the status quo."

Like Johnson, Emanuel was criticized on occasion for caring more about winning than any higher cause. Emanuel could be seen as an operator, someone who excelled at the deal making and tactics of politics but not the visionary part—a Lyndon Johnson rather than a John Kennedy. Some of his policy initiatives, such as championing school uniforms when he was in the White House, were superficial. The criticism bothered Emanuel deeply, and he was at pains to showcase his policy ideas and emphasize that the only reason he wanted to win, in all his political campaigns, was to help change the country. Emanuel did know a lot about policy and had developed proposals on everything from lobbying to drugs to tax reform. He wrote a book in the spring of 2006 with his friend Bruce Reed outlining an agenda for the Democrats. "He doesn't give a shit about power," said his brother Ezekiel. "He gives a shit about doing something." The truth was probably somewhere in between. Emanuel was competitive beyond imagining and obsessive about winning. But he also had come up with an array of policy ideas, underscored by the idea that the unwritten contract between middle-class Americans and their society had been shredded. Yet many of his proposals were small-scale, politically deft initiatives in the Clinton mold, designed mostly to ease the financial burden on the middle class. "Rahm really understands the value of ideas in politics and the value of ideas of moving the country forward and changing things," said his friend Podesta. "But he likes the Cliffs Notes version. Rahm was made for the Internet. It's kind of like, whatever you can learn on Google."

Emanuel's years at the White House undeniably matured him. When he started he was thirty-three years old and had just helped elect a president. When he departed in late 1998, he was turning thirty-nine and had suffered through his own demotion and resurrection, as well as the turbulence of a scandal-ridden administration. "He has taken all that fury and energy and he has focused it," Begala said after the 2006 campaign. "In the 80s he was a shotgun, spraying a thousand pellets. Now he is a rifle, with one very powerful bullet that comes at you faster than the speed of sound. They are both useful, but a rifle is much more deadly." It's not that Emanuel started avoiding fights, to be sure. But he no longer sought them out. If he had sent a fellow Democrat a fish in 1988, by 2006 he was sending them cheesecakes.

Emanuel also got married while he was at the White House. In 1990, a friend arranged a blind date with Amy Rule, who had an MBA from Wharton and worked at the Art Institute of Chicago. The two hit it off and married four years later. Rule converted to Judaism while Emanuel was working at the White House, and he attended virtually all of her conversion classes, though he was exhausted and sometimes fell asleep during a session. It was a mixed marriage in more ways than one, since Rule came from an actively Republican family. Her father attended the 2004 GOP convention wearing a "Rahm Emanuel for Congress" button.

Emanuel was among the last of the original Clintonites to leave the White House, departing in 1998 for a brief, lucrative stint as an investment banker. In the two and a half years before he ran for Congress, Emanuel made $16.2 million working for Bruce Wasserstein, a Wall Street deal maker who had also been a major Clinton fund-raiser. As Emanuel put together sizable mergers and acquisitions, many of his clients were corporate leaders he'd known while raising money for Clinton. Emanuel was continuing to work at the nexus of money and politics, just from a different angle. In addition to taking advantage of his contacts, Emanuel's timing was good; a flurry of deals were coming together in the late 1990s and there was money to be made. By all accounts, Emanuel also worked hard for his clients. In any case, his quick fortune enabled Emanuel to jump back into politics less than three years after leaving it, his finances more than secure as he campaigned for a House seat in the middle of 2001.

Emanuel's district, covering most of Chicago's North Side and northwest suburbs, was heavily Democratic, which worked in his favor, and heavily Polish, which did not. Its previous representatives had names such as Rostenkowski and Blagojevich, and Emanuel did not fit comfortably on that list. Although eight Democrats ultimately entered the race, it quickly settled into a contest between Emanuel and State Representative Nancy Kaszak. From the beginning, Kaszak played up her Polish American roots. Emanuel tried to reach out to Polish American voters by appearing at community events and speaking on Polish American radio stations. The campaign quickly grew hostile. Kaszak portrayed Emanuel as a slick Washington operative out of touch with the district's needs. When she held a press conference to announce her support for crime-fighting measures, Emanuel's aides infiltrated the event and passed out documents showing that Kaszak had voted against harsher penalties for criminals. The stunt drew a sharp rebuke from Kaszak's campaign operatives, who denounced Emanuel for engaging in negative politics and distorting Kaszak's record. Two weeks before the vote, the campaign erupted as Kaszak supporter Edward Moskal, president of the Polish National Alliance, claimed wrongly that Emanuel was an Israeli citizen, adding that Israel "defiles the Polish homeland and continues to hurl insults at the Polish people." Emanuel called the comments anti-Semitic, and Kaszak herself criticized the statement and severed her relationship with Moskal. The two candidates had been neck and neck for much of the campaign, but Emanuel pulled away at the end, ultimately winning by 50 percent to 39 percent, with 11 percent going to other candidates.

Emanuel had been a tireless campaigner, constantly shaking hands at grocery stores, train stations, and other locations. He was helped by his ability to raise money and by the endorsements of high-profile Democrats such as Bill Clinton. But Emanuel's real weapon was Chicago mayor Richard Daley, who endorsed Emanuel, got his labor allies to do the same, and even cut a commercial for Emanuel. "Rich was a big supporter of Rahm's, and he is very popular in that district," said William Daley, the mayor's brother. "The mayor was a strong, strong ally of Rahm's." Daley's support, however, had a darker side. The mayor's political operation dispatched city patronage workers to help Emanuel with his campaign, and that get-out-the-vote operation became part of a federal investigation that was still ongoing when Emanuel took the helm at the DCCC.

Many who had crossed Emanuel's path during his rise felt he bullied people to get what he wanted. In the summer of 2006, Emanuel was trying to persuade Congresswoman Nita Lowey, a New York Democrat, to hold a press conference on a certain topic. He took her head in his hands, stared into her face, and said, "You have to do this press conference." The gesture was a strange one for two middle-aged adults, and Emanuel held her face for an uncomfortably long time until Lowey agreed. In the mid-1980s, when Emanuel was a staffer at the DCCC, Patsy Madrid, then a young candidate for the House, visited him to seek support. "He was extremely rude," Madrid recalled. "I was a nobody. It was demoralizing." Even Podesta, a friend and admirer, said, "He can be mean. He's kind of dismissive, highly dismissive. . . . Rahm could be pretty nasty with people and cut them to the quick with a biting comment—and not do it behind their back."

But Emanuel also had a large group of friends, and he spoke to many of them almost daily. In part that was because of his loyalty, and in part it was because his passion and drive could be compelling. "He is the ultimate alpha male in some ways. He is a rooster, he struts around, he will come in to your office and let you know if something really good happened to him," said Dee Dee Myers. "But he will also be the first one in your office if something good happened to you. Or if somebody did something bad to you, he'll come in and say, 'Let's kill him.' That counts for a lot in the trenches of political warfare."

One of Emanuel's friends even asked him to officiate at her wedding, surely not a role easily envisioned by his political adversaries. Anna Greenberg, one of Emanuel's pollsters, was Jewish, and she was engaged to a government investigator named John Delicath, who was not. They agreed to have a Jewish wedding and asked Emanuel to preside. "You can't swear," Greenberg warned Emanuel when they met to discuss the ceremony. Emanuel took the job seriously, speaking to rabbis and consulting sacred texts to prepare. "Jews do not just blindly observe their traditions only to keep them going," he said at the ceremony. "We relive them and breathe new life into old traditions. Reinventing and rethinking the meaning of our traditions is as old as the traditions themselves." Emanuel made a few political jokes—many of the attendees were partisan Democrats—and finished up by saying, "See, I didn't swear."

As that episode suggested, Judaism played a big role in Emanuel's life. His family had often spent the summer in Israel as he was growing up, and during the 1991 Gulf War Emanuel spent two weeks sorting brakes in a warehouse for the Israel Defense Forces. For the right audience, he would sprinkle his campaign talks with Yiddish phrases. Emanuel was close with Jack Moline, the rabbi at Agudas Achim Congregation outside Washington. When Emanuel worked at the White House, he asked Moline to come to his office every two weeks and study Jewish texts with him. They managed to get in about twenty-five minutes of studying at each session; the rest of the time White House staffers were barging in and reporters were calling. On one occasion Clinton himself showed up while Emanuel and Moline were discussing Jewish texts. "It scared the shit out of me," Moline said. "Rahm was sitting with his legs up on a table. I had a mouthful of sandwich. Clinton said, 'Did you see that basketball game last naht?'" Between such interruptions, Moline and Emanuel discussed the meaning of leadership in the Jewish tradition.

Emanuel got especially upset at any disapproval of his policies by Jewish authorities. One year during the Jewish High Holidays, Moline gave a sermon criticizing Clinton's welfare reforms, in which Emanuel had played a central role, as "criminal." Emanuel hounded Moline for weeks to change his mind. Finally Moline heard Emanuel speak to a group of rabbis about welfare reform and told him afterward, "I've got to say, you were pretty persuasive." Emanuel responded sharply, "I want that in writing." Moline assumed he was joking. But a few days later, Emanuel called and said, "I'm putting my wife, Amy, on the phone. Tell her I was right about welfare reform." Moline heard Emanuel's wife say, "Leave the man alone." But Emanuel insisted that Moline tell his wife he'd been right. Then he insisted Moline fax him a letter confirming that the rabbi believed Clinton's welfare reform had some merit. "He just needed that affirmation from me," Moline said. "He takes the tradition and the people who represent it very, very seriously. It was far more important that he convince me that welfare reform was a good idea than that he convince half the people in his party."

As the 2006 midterm campaign heated up, Emanuel would have to draw on all that forcefulness. He faced great pressure because the Democrats had been so completely shut out of power. Even among those who followed the news, it was easy to underestimate the power accumulated by one party when it controlled the White House and both chambers of Congress. Democrats had lost virtually any say in the lawmaking process. They were blocked from offering amendments. They were excluded from conference committees—the small, all-important meetings between senators and House leaders to hammer out a bill's final version. Complex pieces of legislation were handed down hours before a vote, so Democrats had no chance to study them. In one especially egregious incident, Bush's Medicare drug bill was about to go down to defeat, so Republicans simply stretched the vote from the standard fifteen minutes to almost three hours, pressured lawmakers to switch sides, and shoved the bill through. With at least two other important bills, one on free trade and another on energy, the Republicans again ignored the rules and held the vote open as long as it took to browbeat enough members to change their minds. House Speaker Dennis Hastert decided at one point he would let a bill come to a vote only if a majority of House Republicans supported it—all but decreeing that only Republicans were legitimate members of the House.

Equally important, Democrats could not call hearings to focus attention on President Bush's problems, because a party must control at least one chamber of Congress to do that. In the Clinton years, Republicans scrutinized everything from the federal raid in Waco to allegations of Chinese espionage to the Whitewater and Lewinsky scandals. There were, in theory, many such opportunities for hearings in the Bush years. The administration secretly paid columnist Armstrong Williams to support Bush's No Child Left Behind law, for example. Official reports were edited to minimize the threat of global warming. Boondoggles were reported regarding Iraqi reconstruction contracts. But instead of spawning weeklong headline-grabbing hearings, each of these episodes faded quietly from view, with the Democrats unable to do anything about it. Republicans even used their control of Congress to order the capital's powerful lobbying groups to hire only Republicans if they wanted access to Capitol Hill—Tom DeLay's infamous "K Street Project." Those lobbying firms in turn channeled ever more dollars into Republican campaigns. The effect was a mutually reinforcing cycle that made the possibility of a Democratic comeback ever more remote.

Emanuel's colleagues were looking to him to break that cycle and restore them to a measure of power and dignity. The House was the cornerstone of GOP dominance in Washington. The Senate was a place of give and take, where leaders of both parties were relatively moderate and a single senator, even from the minority party, could influence the outcome, if only by gumming up the works. The White House, too, found itself compromising to keep up the president's popularity, and in any case a president could be voted out every four years. The House Republican leadership, in contrast, included only hard-line conservatives, and with rare exceptions could ram through any bill without accommodating alternative views. Weariness and urgency enveloped the Democrats in 2005 as they headed into yet another two years of minority status. Emanuel appeared to be the Democrats' best hope for regaining some say in Washington. Love him or hate him, he now seemed like their last chance.

3

CRACKS IN THE EDIFICE

In the summer of 2005, New Orleans was the nation's thirty-eighth largest city, with a lively tourist trade and a population of 454,863. When Hurricane Katrina struck the Gulf Coast on August 29, it seemed at first that damage to the city had been minor—"not the apocalyptic storm forecasters had feared," as one news report put it. But then the levees protecting New Orleans from the sea were breached, and by the next day 80 percent of an American metropolis was underwater. News broadcasts showed images of floating bodies and agonized survivors. "Thousands Feared Dead in Lawless City," read one headline. It was now clear Katrina was a disaster of historic magnitude.

Oddly, that point seemed to elude the Bush administration. The White House could not have responded more clumsily to Katrina if it had been actively trying to project indifference and haughtiness. On the day the hurricane hit, President Bush was at the Pueblo El Mirage Resort and Country Club in Arizona, talking about Medicare. As the floodwaters swallowed New Orleans the next day, he was photographed with a guitar in hand at the Naval Air Station in San Diego. Belatedly sensing political danger, the White House hurriedly released a photograph of Bush peering down anxiously at New Orleans as he flew above it, but that only suggested he did not care enough to visit the actual scene of the suffering. When Bush finally did go to the Gulf on September 2, after several days of misery the government had been helpless to alleviate, he stopped at a regional airport in Mobile, Alabama, and there he made his biggest mistake of all: He threw his arm around Mike Brown, director of the Federal Emergency Management Agency, and told him, "Brownie, you're doing a heck of a job."

The storm and Bush's response to it undermined one of the Republicans' strongest selling points—that they knew how to protect Americans and get things done. More than one commentator contrasted the president's reassuring performance after the September 11 terrorist attacks to his near paralysis following the hurricane. A *Newsweek* poll on September 10 showed that Bush's approval rating had fallen to 38 percent, the lowest of his presidency, and other polls showed a similar plunge. Half the registered voters in the poll said they planned to choose a Democrat in the upcoming congressional election, while just 38 percent said they favored a Republican—the biggest drop in the polls so far for the Republicans. Attempting to stanch the political bleeding, Bush flew again to New Orleans on September 15, where he took personal responsibility for the debacle and proposed a massive rebuilding program that contrasted sharply with his small-government philosophy. "There is no way to imagine America without New Orleans, and this great city will rise again," Bush promised. The White House sought to ensure good stagecraft for the nighttime address, as Bush wore a blue dress shirt with an open collar and walked along the green grass in New Orleans' Jackson Square, a setting meant to suggest rebirth. But the underlying trouble was symbolized by the White House decision to import its own floodlights and generators for the speech, given the uncertain state of New Orleans' electrical supply.

Rahm Emanuel sat in his office a short time later, eating banana chips and nibbling salad with the onions removed, trying to figure out how best to take advantage of Katrina. The Democrats had been starting to voice a campaign message that Republicans cared more about keeping power than helping ordinary Americans, and Bush's response to Katrina was like one long campaign commercial on that theme. "I think Katrina just did us a really big favor, to be crass about it," Emanuel said. He called Bill Burton, his communications director at the DCCC, and ordered him to find out which Republican congressmen from the Gulf region had voted to cut the budget of the Army Corps of Engineers. The Corps was responsible for New Orleans' levees, and given the levees' fate, such a vote would now look reckless. Emanuel told Burton to try to get the Associated Press to write about these Republicans' disregard for their constituents' safety. "Hey, look, if the AP doesn't do it, let's see if either the *[New Orleans Times-] Picayune* would do it or we can go to a blog," Emanuel said. "No fingerprints," he added curtly, meaning the news item should not be traceable to the DCCC. In a conversation after the phone call, Emanuel rejected the idea that there was anything ruthless about hammering Republicans for votes that might have seemed reasonable at the time. "What's ruthless about voting records?" Emanuel said. "What's ruthless is, I say you're out there fucking someone else. That's ruthless. . . . I consider going after somebody's personal life and fucking with that, that's ruthless. Voting record on the Corps of Engineers? That's a goddamn public policy."

Emanuel then took a call from Democratic consultant Paul Begala, who wondered how to respond to the Republican line that Democrats, in criticizing the Republican handling of Katrina, were playing politics with a tragedy that had killed hundreds. Emanuel suggested wrapping the criticism in a positive message that New Orleans could be rebuilt. "'Restore, rebuild, and have a retrospect'—that's what I'm saying," Emanuel told Begala. "When they say, 'You can't point fingers on something like this'— well, you can't say it worked according to the plan."

The Republicans were taking a big hit, but that did not mean the Democrats' prospects of retaking the House had improved. House districts had been drawn to guarantee big majorities for one party or the other. After the storm, Democratic districts became even more Democratic, and some Republican districts became less Republican—but not enough for any seats to change hands. On August 12, two weeks before Katrina, the *Cook Political Report* estimated that eighteen Republican seats were vulnerable, compared to fourteen Democratic seats. After the storm, the numbers changed to seventeen and eleven—a minimal shift and hardly reflective of a Republican collapse.

Experts still saw almost no chance the Democrats would retake the House. "There is a modest Democratic tide brewing, but it will take more than a modest Democratic tide," said Gary Jacobson, a political scientist at the University of California, San Diego. Kimball Brace, whose company created software programs for redistricting, echoed that the Democrats' chances were "not that great." Those inside the DCCC felt the same way. "I would consider it a victory if we gain seats, if we have a significant gain," DCCC executive director John Lapp said on September 23. "Honestly, with the redistricting the way it is, if we can get in the high single digits, that's a victory." Emanuel liked the overall trend but noted that the political winds could easily switch before the election. "We've got fourteen months to go," he said. "And maybe this is a twenty-year veteran of politics talking, or someone who was with Bill Clinton for seven years, but shit happens. Fourteen months is a long time. Anything can happen in politics."

Trying to influence those events as best he could, Emanuel wrote a memo at the end of September telling Democratic candidates that three themes had emerged from recent polls: Voters wanted change, they wanted independence, and they wanted a new direction. The candidates, Emanuel instructed, must "make this theme their own. . . . This theme should bleed through everything House Democratic candidates communicate. Whether a Democrat is talking about Social Security, Medicare, education, ethics, energy, jobs, or taxes, the message is the same: The Republicans have failed to make any progress, while Democrats represent change."

The Republicans played into this strategy in short order. A month after Katrina, House majority leader Tom DeLay was indicted for allegedly violating campaign finance law by funneling business donations to Texas candidates. Emanuel had long since settled on ethics as one of his big weapons. Republican congressman Randy "Duke" Cunningham had announced in July 2005 that he would not seek reelection after it was revealed he took gifts from contractors in exchange for steering government business their way. But the indictment of DeLay, the sitting House majority leader and personification of Republicans' hard-hitting approach to governing, raised the ethics issue to another level.

Bill Burton, the DCCC communications director, was in his office at 12:35 P.M. on September 28 when the DeLay indictment was reported by the Associated Press and almost simultaneously by CNN. Burton's tiny office, which he shared with press secretary Sarah Feinberg, was cluttered like a teenager's bedroom, with political maps attached to the wall and photocopies of the day's front pages taped to the front door. A half dozen televisions stacked near the door were tuned to various news networks. When CNN reaffirmed its report with a "DeLay indicted" statement at the bottom of the screen, Burton called Emanuel and said tersely, "It's Bill. Tom DeLay's indicted." Emanuel happened to be on the floor of the House of Representatives, where members are forbidden to talk on cell phones. He broke the rule by answering the phone and replied quickly and somewhat cryptically, "Okay, it's happening," and then hung up. Burton sent an e-mail to his "friends and family" list, which included everyone from journalists to lawmakers. "DeLay indicted," it said. "More to come." Many members of Congress got the big news from Burton's e-mail.

On the House floor, where lawmakers had gathered for a vote, ripples spread almost tangibly across the chamber—a wave of excitement through the Democratic side and a surge of anxiety among the Republicans. Within minutes Emanuel emerged from the House chamber and spoke to his team by phone again, ordering no one to comment to the press. That seemed at first to make little sense: Why not use DeLay's troubles to emphasize Republican corruption? But as with Katrina, Emanuel did not want to reduce the story to partisan bickering. "When someone is digging their own grave, you don't have to help them dig it," said Feinberg, the DCCC press secretary. "This is not a time when you need to push the news, or even say a word. The first time a Democrat opens their mouth, it becomes partisan. So you try to have the story that 'DeLay Was Indicted' instead of 'DeLay Was Indicted, Democrats Attack.'" Even so,

Democratic leaders such as Nancy Pelosi were quick to seize on the DeLay indictment to once again denounce Republican wrongdoing, to Emanuel's frustration.

By 3:25 P.M., John Lapp had e-mailed a message citing the charges against DeLay and asking rank-and-file Democrats for money. The indictment by chance came two days before September 30, the end of a financial reporting period. That meant the money the DCCC raised in July, August, and September would soon be reported and scrutinized by reporters as a sign of how the party was doing. Lapp wanted to use DeLay's problems to attract a wave of last-minute contributions. "Dear [donor], Today Tom DeLay's House of Scandal took a wrecking ball as he was indicted in Texas for—what else—criminal conspiracy related to illegal corporate fundraising," Lapp wrote. His note featured a photo of DeLay with the word *indicted* stamped across it and the caption "End DeLay's House of Scandal. Make a MATCHED Contribution Today." Feinberg dismissed the suggestion that it was crass to ask for money three hours after a criminal indictment. "When you are nearing the end of your quarter and the number one Republican has been indicted, you don't make gratuitous comments to reporters, but you don't pass up the fact that this is something your supporters believe should have happened a long time ago," Feinberg said.

The payoff the Democrats really wanted, and Republicans feared, was a Tom DeLay mug shot—a gritty-looking photo of the deposed leader, facing forward and in profile, that would evoke a classic image of criminality. If DeLay looked bad enough, the mug shot could be used in numerous Democratic campaign ads. DeLay was scheduled to appear in court on October 21 to announce his plea and be photographed. A few days before that, Burton and DCCC research director Christina Reynolds met in Burton's office to strategize. Reynolds envisioned DeLay being led in front of the cameras in handcuffs. "I'm going to cry like a little girl if there's no perp walk," Reynolds said, then asked, "You gonna cry?" Burton answered, "No, because there will be a mug shot." When that happened, they decided, they would issue two press releases, one geared to a national audience and one tying individual Republicans to DeLay. At a meeting soon afterward, Burton told Emanuel, "DeLay is being arraigned at the end of the week. We'll have a [film] crew at the courthouse. We're working to get the mug shot as soon as possible." Three days later, Lapp sent another e-mail to supporters saying, "Just wanted to give you an update on Tom DeLay's legal situation. Yesterday, he was issued an arrest warrant and in coming days, as hard as this is to believe, he will be booked, fingerprinted, and seen in a mug shot. That's right, the former Republican Leader, now twice indicted, will face the humility of a mug shot."

Democrats were not alone in sensing the explosiveness of such an image. *The Hill,* a congressional newspaper, said DeLay's arrest was "confronting the Republican Party with the cold, hard possibility that the former majority leader may soon be pictured in a mug shot and in handcuffs." But DeLay outfoxed the Democrats one last time. When he posed for his courthouse photograph, he made sure to wear a big politician's grin, as though he were at a ribbon-cutting ceremony, rather than the sullen expression that is the hallmark of such photos. There was no profile shot at all. DeLay was wearing a spiffy suit and tie and the lapel pin that marked him as a member of Congress. The sheriff's office in Harris County, Texas, did not force DeLay to hold a sign with his name or pose next to a measuring stick, other typical features of mug shots. The resulting image could just as easily have been an official portrait to be hung in DeLay's congressional office. The official handout from the Harris County Sheriff's Office did include information such as "Record type: Adult inmate," but it was not the powerful image Democrats had hoped for.

The Democratic decision to focus on Republican corruption was not obvious. It was a deliberately conceived plan, and it could have failed. Emanuel's key strategic decision in the 2006 campaign was to have a national strategy in the first place. The conventional wisdom was that it made no sense to have a single theme for 435 House races, or even for the several dozen likely to be competitive. Former House Speaker Tip O'Neill famously declared that "all politics is local," and congressional districts could be radically different from one another. In Michigan and Indiana, job losses were important. In places with military bases, treatment of soldiers and veterans was paramount. Ohio had its own special ethics scandal. Some districts were conservative and others liberal; one might be represented by a scandal-ridden firebrand, another by a quiet lawmaker with a high approval rating. So a single message was unlikely to resonate everywhere.

Emanuel gambled that 2006 would be different. Every so often an election comes along that breaks the rules. The public becomes so disgusted with one party that its disaffection transcends everything else. In 1974, voters went to the polls three months after Watergate forced Richard Nixon from office, and Democrats gained forty-nine seats in the House. In 1994, with President Bill Clinton at a low point in his presidency and his health-care reform plan in ruins, Republicans picked up fifty-four seats and seized control of the House. Even in a less-historic election such as that of 1982, voters unhappy with the "Reagan Recession" gave Democrats twenty-seven new seats. It was far from clear that 2006 would be a similarly pivotal year. But Emanuel was now betting on it, and it was a big bet, because if he was wrong his campaign would be singularly ineffective. His goal was to etch in the public's mind the idea that Republicans were entrenched, tired, incompetent, corrupt. "They [voters] may just say to the Republicans, 'You old fuckers, you're not going to listen? We're going to send you a fucking message,'" Emanuel said on September 7, 2005. "'We gave you the keys to the car, you fucking crashed it. All right, we'll take the keys away for a while until you learn your lesson. You get a five-minute time-out.' And we become the beneficiaries of that."

The hardest part of this strategy was persuading voters to vent their frustration on their particular congressman. Voters always tell pollsters they dislike Congress in general but are fond of their representative, whom they've come to know and trust. Emanuel's challenge was to tie even likeable, moderate Republicans to a GOP regime he depicted as corrupt and out of touch. From his perch at the Clinton White House, Emanuel had seen Newt Gingrich sweep to power on a message of Democratic corruption, ending his hopes that Clinton could achieve great things working with a Democratic Congress. Emanuel now sought to use Gingrich's tactics against the heirs of that same Republican revolution. As early as April 2005, he created a Web site called "Tom DeLay's House of Scandal," which named an individual Republican lawmaker the "GOP crony of the week" and invited voters to find out "how tangled up with DeLay is your member?" Emanuel frequently used the phrase "culture of corruption" to convey the idea that the problem was systemic and not tied to a single individual. He instructed his staff to attack any Republican lawmaker who had taken money from DeLay or contributed to his legal defense fund. In October, for example, the DCCC had issued a press release targeting Republican congressman Jerry Weller of Illinois. "Weller Gives to DeLay Legal Defense," it said. "Is He Happy With His Investment?" Another statement, this one on Congresswoman Virginia Foxx of North Carolina, said, "Foxx Takes Thousands of Dollars in Campaign Cash From DeLay; Puts National Party and DeLay Ahead of North Carolina Families."

The specifics varied, but the message was the same—the problem was not Bush or DeLay. It was all Republicans, who were part of a system that needed to be shut down.

Emanuel similarly crusaded against the "Rubber Stamp Congress," an attempt to link individual Republicans to unpopular Bush policies, from Social Security privatization to the Iraq war. A year before the election, Emanuel released a report claiming that House Republicans supported Bush 84 percent of the time, considerably more than Democrats had supported President Bill Clinton. His staff crafted a logo of a large rubber stamp that served as the backdrop for a series of press conferences. In January 2006, Emanuel visited a district outside Philadelphia to announce a Rubber Stamp Congress Web site and attack the local congressman, Jim Gerlach, for regularly voting with DeLay. "I never knew Tom DeLay had so many commonalities with suburban Philadelphia," Emanuel taunted.

All these messages were bolstered when ethics dominoes began falling in the fall of 2005. In the two weeks before DeLay's indictment, White House official David Safavian, who'd just resigned, was arrested and charged with lying to investigators. Federal investigators also began focusing on the stock transactions of Senate majority leader Bill Frist. That enabled the Democrats to say that Republican leaders in the White House, Senate, and House of Representatives all were facing corruption inquiries. At a December 1 political forum sponsored by the University of Virginia, DCCC staff director John Lapp talked so much about Republican corruption that moderator John Mercurio asked exasperatedly, "Do you get a reward if you mention *indictment* a certain number of times?"

As Bush's popularity sank in late 2005, Republicans began distancing themselves from the president. Republican congresswoman Heather Wilson, locked in a tough fight for her New Mexico seat, made a splash by demanding an investigation of Bush's domestic wiretapping program. She opposed Bush's Social Security plan. She said publicly that Vice President Cheney was wrong to describe the Iraqi insurgency as in its "last throes." She expressed "concern" about Bush's Medicare drug program. She voted against a Republican budget bill because it would cut Medicare. Other Republican candidates suddenly found they had "scheduling conflicts" and could not appear beside Bush or Cheney when they came to town. Congressman Gerlach, fighting for his political life in his district outside Philadelphia, began his television ads this way: "When I believe President Bush is right, I'm behind him. But when I think he's wrong, I let him know that, too."

Republicans fought back in other ways, too. DeLay blamed the DCCC for a vendetta against him, and although he did not name Emanuel specifically, there was little question whom he meant. Within the first few sentences of his press conference on the day of his indictment, he fingered the committee. "We all know what this is—a political witch hunt," DeLay said. "It is actually a predetermined campaign event on the DCCC Web site, and it's a campaign that's been going on for over two years." DeLay apparently was referring to longtime Democratic allegations about DeLay's corruption. Republicans were not used to being harassed like this. DeLay also appeared on the MSNBC television show *Hardball* that night, where he again blamed the DCCC. The indictment was clearly riling the Republicans. Congressman Tom Reynolds, Emanuel's Republican counterpart, called a press conference on October 7 to insist that things were not going as badly for Republicans as it might seem. But his first words were defensive: "I'm glad you could take time from writing about Tom DeLay."

Republicans pushed the argument that House races are won or lost on local issues, not on vague notions of a national ethics problem. Republican spokesman Carl Forti said DeLay's travails were "completely irrelevant" to individual House races. "The issues in competitive districts are whether the Democrat would raise taxes and how the Republican voted in Congress," Forti said. "People don't vote for Congress as a whole. They vote for their member of Congress. They believe in him or her. Democrats have to have a viable reason to vote against someone other than 'He's in the same party as George Bush.' You won't beat, let's just take [Republican congressman] Mark Kirk, because he took money from Tom DeLay or is in the same party as Tom DeLay or because George Bush is unpopular." Then, to cover his bases, Forti issued a series of press releases intended to create the perception that if Washington was sleazy, Democrats were just as guilty as Republicans. Republicans highlighted the case of Democratic congressman William Jefferson of Louisiana, whom the FBI said had hidden $90,000 in bribe money in his freezer. "Ethics is a losing issue for Democrats," said Republican spokesman Ed Patru. "Every time the Democrats want to raise ethics, we'll be happy to point the finger right back."

But with Republicans holding all the power, it was hard for them to blame Democrats for Washington's corruption. And it did not get any easier. Late on the afternoon of Thursday, October 6, the big-screen television in the hallway of the DCCC offices was turned to CNN's *The Situation Room*. The top story was the investigation into the leak of a CIA operative's name and the speculation about the imminent indictment of a top White House official. Among those targeted by the investigation, the news reports said, was I. Lewis "Scooter" Libby, Vice President Dick Cheney's chief of staff.

The buzz in the DCCC offices was palpable, and all the discussion seemed to be about the scandal. Feinberg literally rubbed her hands with glee at the prospect of indictments. "Will it be Scooter, or Rove, or both, or neither?" she said. Burton told Emanuel that ABC News reporter George Stephanopoulos—a former colleague of Emanuel's in the Clinton White House—was considering Emanuel's request to appear on his show to discuss ethics. Several staffers stressed the importance of not appearing jubilant when indictments came. "We put in the call to the [Democratic National Committee] to hold their horses and not go dancing in the streets," Feinberg said. "Don't hold your breath," answered someone else. Burton replied, "Actually, everyone seems to be on the same page about expressing sadness that our government has come to this point." That would be the official line: sadness over the turn of events, not gloating that an enemy had fallen.

When Libby alone was indicted a few days later, the Democrats were disappointed that Rove, Bush's closest aide, had been spared, but were nonetheless giddy. Despite some deviations, most Democrats followed the prescribed message of professing sadness. "It is a sad day for America when a federal grand jury indicts a high-ranking White House official," said Senator Richard Durbin of Illinois. Democratic Party chairman Howard Dean began his official statement, "This is a sad day for America." Internally, though, the mood was less restrained. In a message to supporters a few days after the Libby indictment, Lapp—while calling it a "solemn time"— wrote, "Last Friday we witnessed an explosion, an event that, like Watergate, will shape politics and the way we see government in America for years to come."

The DCCC's offices, in the Democratic National Headquarters building at 430 South Capitol Street, were nondescript, tucked away in a corner of Washington near the Capitol and facing a parking lot that seemed perpetually under construction. The warren of cubicles, surrounded by offices for senior staff, could have been housing a real estate firm. But a crazy, intense energy animated the place. Almost all the staffers were in their twenties, and when they were not on the phone or plowing through data, they tended to career around the room, yelling uplifting or dispiriting bits of information to each other. Most were only a few years out of college, making little money and often working late into the night. Every cubicle was decorated with posters and bumper stickers bearing messages like "Losing Sucks," "Be a Smart Ass—Vote Democratic," and "Stop Arnold— Serious Problems Deserve Serious Leaders."

Lapp, the DCCC's executive director, had been Emanuel's first hire and his most important. His entire interview of Lapp was three minutes long. Emanuel's longtime friend David Axelrod had worked with Lapp in Iowa and recommended him to head the DCCC. Emanuel and Lapp were the same type, Axelrod thought—aggressive, fast-moving, and hyperactive— although Lapp was a clean-cut Virginian to Emanuel's scrappy Chicagoan. Emanuel interviewed Lapp at the end of 2004, and Lapp barely had time to stress his belief that Democrats could win even in conservative states when Emanuel dismissed him. Lapp assumed the worst, but Emanuel had seen all he needed. That was Emanuel's decision-making style; he made gut decisions in an instant, preferring to move fast and make mistakes rather than get bogged down in agonizing. That quality could be unnerving to staffers. Sometimes a subordinate would go into Emanuel's office to make a suggestion; surprised when Emanuel immediately said yes, the staffer would continue explaining why his idea was a good one. "What's the matter with 'yes'?'" Emanuel would shout. "Are you going to sit there and tell me for five more minutes how smart you are?"

Lapp had made his name seven years earlier when he was twenty-seven and running the campaign of Democrat Ken Lucas in a conservative Kentucky House district that had not elected a Democrat in thirty-two years. In a preview of Emanuel's approach at the DCCC, Lapp emphasized Lucas' pro-life, pro-gun, pro-tobacco views, not worrying that they differed from national Democratic positions. Lucas won. Respected in political circles for his talent, Lapp was baby-faced and surprisingly sentimental. Like Emanuel, he was consumed by politics and seemed to work twenty-four hours a day, which by his own account was one reason he was divorced. "There is only one way to do politics, and that's 110 percent, but your family and personal life suffers," Lapp said. He was determined never to run another campaign after 2006 so he could spend time with his son, Truman. Lapp revered Emanuel and at times emulated his tough-guy style, though it did not seem as natural with him. Describing how he would go after Republicans, Lapp would say things such as, "You look for the old, tired people at the back of the herd, then you come in with a cheetah and you dig in your fangs" or "You've got to step on their vertebrae until you hear a crack."

Lapp brought in Bill Burton to head the DCCC's communications operation. Burton had gotten his start in politics working for Al Gore in Minnesota while bartending at night. If Emanuel interviewed Lapp for three minutes, that was longer than he spent on Burton, who received perhaps forty-five seconds. Burton handled the big-picture media operations of the campaign, waking every morning at five to read the papers and e-mail favorable pieces around the country. A large, jovial man, Burton had an African American father and a Polish American mother. He considered himself black, but to many he looked Caucasian, and that created some awkward moments. When black Democrats complained that Emanuel had few African Americans among his top staff, for example, it was not clear whether they realized that Emanuel's chief spokesman was African American. Burton worked closely with Sarah Feinberg, the DCCC press secretary, in a cramped office featuring a large doll of the cartoon ogre Shrek wearing a name tag that said "Press Shrekretary." Blond and blue-eyed, Feinberg was not Jewish, despite her name, as she had found herself explaining to many crestfallen Jewish men at the end of a date. Emanuel displayed more obvious affection for Feinberg than his other staffers, even giving her time off in the middle of the campaign to get married. Feinberg accompanied Emanuel on his grueling campaign trips, and other staffers quickly learned that when they needed to ask Emanuel to do something he was likely to resist, the most effective approach was to send in Feinberg.

Another key staffer was Christina Reynolds, who handled "opposition research," which meant finding dirt on Republicans. Reynolds put together a series of notebooks outlining GOP candidates' vulnerabilities for use by their Democratic opponents. The book on Iowa Republican Jeff Lamberti, for example, was fifty-nine pages long and began with the observation that "Jeff Lamberti leads a life of privilege and comfort, out of touch with Iowans' everyday challenges and very much in touch with the Republican Party's cronyism and corruption." Reynolds did not investigate candidates' extramarital affairs, which she considered unethical and ineffective. With her smoker's voice, Reynolds, who always seemed harried, projected a "tough broad" persona, but she also came off as warm, in contrast with the poisonous nature of her job. "I consider myself a positive person, but I do enjoy ripping apart Republicans," Reynolds said. She had worked for former senators Tom Daschle and John Edwards and was frustrated by their determination to run nice-guy campaigns. Emanuel lured her to the DCCC by promising that he had no such scruples.

It took a certain type to put up with Emanuel's yelling and badgering for two years. Karin Johanson—a savvy, experienced operative who took over as Emanuel's staff director in spring 2006 after Lapp moved to the DCCC's Independent Expenditure operation—would receive as many as fifteen phone calls from Emanuel in a day if he was not in the office. Emanuel also would call Burton and shoot off the names of congressional districts, looking for a status report: "Pennsylvania 6. Iowa 1. New Mexico 1." Burton would respond with quick updates—"We're doing a press conference there on high gas prices"—and Emanuel would keep going until he reached a district on which Burton did not have the latest information. Then, satisfied that he'd knocked Burton off balance and shown him he had more work to do, Emanuel would sign off, "All right, buddy. See ya." Johanson, who at fifty was four years older than Emanuel, grew tired of the harassment. "It's been a long time since I've worked for someone who harangued," she said. Emanuel's outbursts could be so dramatic, and so comical in retrospect, that the staff started compiling a list of his most colorful quotes. What had prompted them to start the list, on

March 29, 2005, was Emanuel's response to what he viewed as Lapp's excessive hand-wringing. "What I want to know," Emanuel demanded, "is how you became Jewish in the past twenty-four hours."

Emanuel expected his orders to be obeyed immediately. On a trip to the Northeast in mid-2006, he asked an aide about a fax the staffer was supposed to retrieve for him. "Did you get the fax I wanted?" Emanuel asked. "It wouldn't come through," the staffer said anxiously. "Fuck you," retorted Emanuel. "Rahm, I tried three times," the aide said plaintively. Emanuel fired back, "So don't you think you'd get it right? Why don't I just travel with an intern?" The pace was exhausting. "It's not for the faint of heart. It's an incredibly intense speed," Lapp said. "You've got to keep the pace up. When people come to work here, it's like, 'Okay, the pace is even more intense than you think it is. Whatever you heard on the street—more intense than that.'"

At a staff meeting on November 15, Emanuel seemed to kick into overdrive. The Republican troubles during the fall—Hurricane Katrina, the indictments of DeLay and Libby, and through it all a rising public dissatisfaction with the war—had made many Democrats suddenly hopeful, but that only scared Emanuel. Begala had been the first of his inner circle to predict, back in September, that the Democrats would take over the House, and Emanuel had told him, "Pauly, shut the fuck up." He was worried about overconfidence and was anxious to ensure that no one let up, even for a second. He wanted every House Republican attacked during Congress' upcoming Thanksgiving break. "Nobody gets a rest when they're home," he said. Emanuel was also frustrated that a potentially vulnerable Democratic congressman named Alan Mollohan, whose state of West Virginia was becoming increasingly Republican, seemed to believe he could not possibly lose and was running a lethargic campaign. Mollohan's team disputed this, but Emanuel ordered that a poll be conducted to show Mollohan he was in peril. Emanuel appeared jumpy, even for him. He harangued the staff more than usual, saying at one point, "Don't just stare at each other across the table. You know what you have to do." At another point he snapped, "Why don't we all get on one team and pull together. I'm serious." That prompted Lapp to shout, "We're pulling!" It was hard for anyone to complete two sentences without Emanuel interrupting.

Afterward, Emanuel invited a reporter into the men's room. Told he seemed more intense than usual, he said, "Gotta shake 'em up," meaning his staff. He pantomimed grabbing someone by the lapels and said, "Make sure nobody's sitting on their fucking laurels." Among the proposals Emanuel had dismissed that day was Lapp's request to highlight Emanuel's growing reputation as a warrior in the fund-raising appeals the DCCC sent out. Lapp mentioned a recent piece in *Rolling Stone* called "The Enforcer," which compared Emanuel to Newt Gingrich. That could be a perfect piece to attach to a request for money, showing the DCCC now had a killer at the helm. Apprehensive about raising it, Lapp said, "I'm just telling you, people are fired up about having a Newt Gingrich of the party. If you want to fire people up, that's a way to do it." "No," Rahm replied tersely. A frustrated Lapp answered, "Is that because you don't want to raise money? Is that why?" Emanuel explained later, "I don't want to do that. I have no interest in that. You think I'm egotistical, but these profiles just get my colleagues upset. You have to be careful. You have a lot of people around who think it's fine I'm doing what I'm doing but don't want me to get too big for my britches."

As 2005 drew to a close, the political climate had become worse for the Republicans than anyone could have expected. Journalists had taken to describing this as the worst year of Bush's presidency, and, if anything, that understated the situation. For four years, the Bush White House and Republican Congress had set the political agenda—cutting taxes, passing bills on terrorism and education, launching a war, and regularly being reaffirmed by voters. The fifth year of Bush's presidency, however, was a year of backlash and bills coming due. As its end approached, a handful of political analysts began saying, with all the requisite cautions and caveats, that the Democrats might have a chance to retake more than just a few House seats. But there was a year to go, the Republicans were sure to mount a counteroffensive, and it seemed that 2006 could not possibly go as badly as 2005. Emanuel, taking no chances, was trying to fight on every front. But it was not yet clear whether he could shake up the electorate.

What was clear, however, was that he was already shaking up his colleagues.

4

FEAR AND LOATHING

Before Emanuel, Democratic campaign chiefs did not attract much interest from Republicans one way or another. His predecessors, including Congressman Robert Matsui of California and Congresswoman Nita Lowey of New York, were gentler figures—largely fundraisers, removed from the nitty-gritty of daily politicking. Emanuel was different: a professional strategist, a proven fund-raiser, a skilled message crafter, and a cold-eyed political assassin. Right off the bat, he made Republicans nervous. "I think there is a lot of angst on our side," conceded Congressman Tom Cole, an Oklahoma Republican, after Emanuel's appointment. "A good politician is almost by definition a professional paranoid. When the [poll] numbers are this close, the president's numbers are not good, the war in Iraq is not popular, they sense the perfect storm out there, and they sense in Rahm someone who can take advantage of an opportunity."

From the office of House Speaker Dennis Hastert on down, Emanuel was viewed with a mixture of apprehension and contempt; he was a threat, remote but real. Hastert's staffers, notorious for their thin skins, spoke of Emanuel with loathing. One accused Michael Tackett, the *Chicago Tribune*'s Washington bureau chief, of being Emanuel's "agent."

Other Republicans, like Congressman Mark Kirk of Illinois, became Rahm experts, studying Emanuel's body language on the House floor to decode his relationship with fellow Democrats. At a roast of Emanuel toward the end of 2005, following the usual ritual of insults from friends and colleagues, Emanuel said, "I know it could have been worse. Some wanted a dunking booth. I'm told the Speaker [Hastert] actually suggested a firing squad."

The dislike was mixed with a grudging recognition of Emanuel's political skills. House majority leader Tom DeLay was no stranger to merciless politics, and when informed Emanuel had been chosen to head the DCCC, he responded, "Now they're finally serious." Cole, the Republican congressman, was campaigning to lead the Republicans' own election efforts for 2008, and he promised his colleagues he would be the Republicans' Rahm Emanuel. "He won't give us quarter or give us slack," Cole said. "The DCCC is his client, like Bill Clinton was his client. He was ferocious in defense of Clinton, and he is being ferocious on behalf of the DCCC." Republicans in swing districts especially disliked Emanuel. "If you are in a lead-pipe-cinch Republican district, it's easier, but if you are in a marginal district, it's tough," Cole said. "The shark looks beautiful when you are outside the tank. But inside, it looks a little different."

Republican congressman E. Clay Shaw of Florida was one of Emanuel's top targets. Shaw, sixty-seven, had served in the House for a quarter century and had no desire to lose his job in a humiliating defeat. On a hot Washington day, Emanuel was walking from his office to the Capitol for a vote when he passed Shaw. He nodded and said, "Clay," by way of greeting. Shaw stared ahead icily and kept walking. "See how he didn't say hello?" Emanuel said with a combination of excitement and agitation. Other Republicans exhibited a dark humor about Emanuel's attacks. Congressman Chris Shays of Connecticut, a highly vulnerable Republican, ran into Emanuel in the House gym and told him he'd heard Emanuel was planning to spend $3 million to defeat him. "I'll tell you what," Shays joked. "Just give me the $3 million, and I'll retire voluntarily."

Emanuel had no illusions about the loathing he inspired. He once concluded a meeting of Democratic lawmakers by joking, "I want you all to look around—you're my only friends left. And I know not even all of you like me." At another point he said, "Don't underestimate what happens when you do this job. You're trying to take away the jobs of colleagues. So don't kid yourself about the personal consequences, career-wise, that this job has. Look, this is not for the faint-hearted. . . . I have not done one low blow. But that being said, their job is important to them, and I am seen as a threat to their job security. And that's life. And I didn't come here to win a popularity contest with them. Now, the good ones know I've got a job to do. But when all is done, done is done, I'll be hurt politically for a while around here. My point is, this doesn't come free, okay. And I don't even give a shit. I've got to do it. I've got a job to do. And I'm going to do what I'm supposed to. I wake up some mornings hating me, too." Told on another occasion that he scared the Republicans, he replied, "I don't scare them enough."

The friction between Emanuel and his Republican counterpart, Tom Reynolds of New York, who was in charge of electing Republicans, was especially apparent. A ruddy, stocky fifty-five-year-old, Reynolds had risen through local politics in the Buffalo area. He was genial but tough, calling to mind a small-town sheriff. Reynolds affected a folksy manner reminiscent of a Midwesterner, and his sentences would often trail off into malapropisms. After making a statement, he might say something like "So I'd kind of have to stand on that direction." In response to reporters' questions about the election, he would regularly say something like "I don't have any idea" or "You'd have to ask the experts," once prompting an exasperated journalist to shout, "You *are* an expert." But underneath the down-to-earth affectation, Reynolds was bitingly competitive, and he, like Emanuel, wanted to be Speaker of the House one day, preferably sooner rather than later. Reynolds' campaign office, down the street from the U.S. Capitol, was dominated by a poster of two buffalo crashing into each other over the caption "Bring on the Competition." On another wall, behind Reynolds' desk, hung a poster of an angry elephant about to charge with the label "Serious Warning." Still another wall showcased a famous series of photos of Lyndon Johnson browbeating a hapless fellow senator; in each successive picture Johnson leaned more threateningly

over the man, who in turn leaned farther back, cowed by the sheer force
of Johnson's personality. This tableau of belligerence and threat was completed by a framed photo and creed from Vince Lombardi, the football
coach who said, "Winning isn't everything, it's the only thing." The effect
was reminiscent of the tacky motivational posters on the walls of tele-
marketing firms, but it also fairly reflected the fearsome drive under
Reynolds' affable demeanor. Ultimately, Emanuel and Reynolds were two
ambitious men whose success depended on the other's failure. If Emanuel
retook the House for the Democrats, that would end Reynolds' hopes of
rising in the Republican Party. But if Reynolds was able to minimize the
Republican losses, he would be a hero to his colleagues and tarnish
Emanuel's reputation.

Under Reynolds, the National Republican Congressional Committee,
or NRCC, issued press releases attacking not Democrats in general but
Emanuel in particular. One was headlined "Read Rahm's Lips," and
another was titled "Say It Again, Rahm," both deriding Emanuel for
ostensibly proposing tax increases. Republican spokesman Carl Forti
acknowledged that the goal was to calm a somewhat panicky fear of
Emanuel among Republicans. "Rahm has brought a new energy to the
DCCC you have not seen in the past few [election] cycles," Forti said in
the fall of 2005. "Attacking him shows the Republican conference that
there's not a lot there. He may talk a good game, but he hasn't done much
to back it up yet."

Emanuel dismissed the banter between himself and Reynolds as
gamesmanship. "It's just two jackasses jacking off at each other, that's
all," he said on September 28. "We were sitting there in the hall yesterday
having fun. Last week, I said, 'Tom, reporters keep calling me and telling
me you respect me. The difference is, I'll remember your name in the
morning.' We laughed hysterically. To tell you the truth, I am probably
unintendedly helping him in his district. We totally get along." He added,
"You want to know something? When all is said and done, neither Tom
Reynolds nor I control our fate. . . . At the end of the day, Tom didn't control how the president responded to Katrina. Tom wasn't the one who got

us into a war without a plan. [When it comes to] the context in which this race will be fought, neither one of us has a bucket to piss in or a window to throw it out of."

If Emanuel talked about Reynolds with some affection, Reynolds seemed to truly detest his Democratic counterpart. That was due partly to the fact that Emanuel violated protocol by going directly after Reynolds' own seat, which forced Reynolds to air campaign commercials early. Reynolds sometimes flinched visibly when Emanuel's name was mentioned. "I respect his hard work. I respect the fact that he is one that understands, wide-eyed, the responsibilities of being a campaign commit-tee chair, and particularly one that's in the minority," Reynolds said in fall 2005, with a notable lack of warmth. "I talk to him on the street, I talk to him in the hallway. He is a fellow colleague and kind of an amicable chap." At another point he said, "If this was a tennis game, I would say he's a good tennis player and he makes my game better. He's a good pol. He's from Chicago." Then Reynolds added that he was a good pol, too—and from New York.

Emanuel taunted the Republicans, trying to throw them off their game like a trash-talking basketball player. He reveled in whatever fear he could instill. For six years Karl Rove had persuaded Democrats that he had their number, that whatever they did he would figure out a way to beat them. That psychological edge could be invaluable, and Emanuel had the same effect on Republicans. One of his great pleasures was pick-ing a vote by a GOP House member that would not play well in his dis-trict, such as supporting a Bush budget cut. Such a vote might ordinarily get little attention, but Emanuel would make a point of issuing a state-ment criticizing the vote and sending it to the Republican's hometown newspaper. Then he would send it directly to the lawmaker's office, "to fuck with their heads," as he put it. Emanuel also spent precious money on radio ads, unusually early in the campaign, to criticize specific Repub-licans for violating ethics rules or opposing veterans' benefits. It was another way to throw his opponents off stride, to convey the message that this time the Democrats would be attacking in ways Republicans were not accustomed to. "Even if it wasn't a big radio buy, the fact that there was this purchase was picked up in the local papers and it created some heat," explained Congressman Van Hollen. "That's new. I don't think you had seen that early response to different issues, focused on what we perceive as vulnerable members of Congress."

To Cole, it was Emanuel's decision to focus on the GOP's "culture of corruption" that earned him the greatest dislike from Republicans. "That personalizes things," Cole said. "If you are in a political battle over Social Security or taxes and you recognize the basic decency of the opponent, that is one kind of fight. If the message is, 'You are a no-good sleaze bucket and corrupt,' that is a different kind of battle. That is causing the greatest anger in the Republican caucus. Even if you find a case or two where that is correct, when you try to paint the whole side that way, that really, really hurts." Reynolds was among those who felt that way. "Apparently a campaign decision—maybe a policy decision, but a campaign decision—has been, 'Let's just tear the place apart, break up the institution,'" Reynolds said. Almost identical complaints had been leveled at Gingrich as he was leading the Republicans to power in 1994.

Emanuel's aggressiveness, and the anxiety it caused Republicans, put enormous pressure on Reynolds to show his fellow Republicans that he was fighting back, matching Emanuel blow for blow. Hence the flow of Republican press releases with headlines such as "Emanuel Hypocrisy Goes National" and "Emanuel Stands up for Corruption." "One of the reasons Reynolds goes after me is to show their guys, 'We're protecting you from Rahm,'" Emanuel said. "Nobody knows who the fuck I am outside the Fifth District of Illinois. But they are so possessed, they have to show, 'We're taking on Rahm for you.'"

Many voters, even those who follow congressional races fairly closely, are unaware of the enormous influence of the party committees. The DCCC and NRCC have not always been powerhouses. Their influence has grown over the years. The biggest change occurred in the 1990s. For decades the Democrats had seemed positioned to control the House forever, and neither party thought much about running national campaigns for the House. That changed with the Republican takeover in 1994, when suddenly the House was in play in every election. In the late 1990s, the parties discovered "soft money"—unregulated funds that, while supposedly for "party building," could be used to influence elections directly. The DCCC spent a mere $42,000 per congressional race in 1994, but by 2000 it had raised $50 million to spend around the country. With those newfound resources came power. The committee chairmen could bend candidates to their will by bestowing or withholding financial largesse as well as expertise, information, and other resources. In 2004 Congress eliminated soft money, but fund-raising only increased and the committee chairmen retained enormous influence.

When he took over, Emanuel reexamined virtually every aspect of DCCC operations with the cold eye of a former staffer. He introduced a rapid-response operation to pounce early on potential Republican candidates. He forced candidates to sign agreements promising to build up their campaigns or he would cut them off. Candidates had faced such demands before, but Emanuel was far more rigorous about it. He was relentless in getting lawmakers and donors to call potential recruits, and once candidates began running, he was relentless in pushing them to raise more money, hold more press conferences, stage more rallies. A more typical DCCC chairman, to take one example, was Congressman Patrick Kennedy of Rhode Island, who headed the committee in the 2000 campaign. As a member of a famous family, Kennedy had extensive connections and did an impressive job of fund-raising. But he spent little time on strategy or tactics, nor did the Democratic leader at the time, Dick Gephardt, expect it of him. Emanuel was in another category altogether. "It's different from any other model," said Karin Johanson, a senior staffer under Emanuel who had also worked at the DCCC in previous elections. "In the past, the chairman has been a fund-raiser, not an operative. The operatives were the staff and the consultants. He's unique. . . . He worked at the DCCC, then he worked at a much higher level in the White House. No one ever works at that level—with what he learned about fund-raising, rapid response, the press—then comes back and works on House races."

As he surveyed the nation's political map, Emanuel was methodical in choosing which Republicans to target for defeat, determined not to let sentiments such as personal loyalty or dislike factor into his decisions. First he focused on every district where Al Gore or John Kerry had received at least 45 percent of the vote, meaning the district had a good number of Democrats. Then he scrutinized every open seat where a Republican was retiring. Finally he targeted all Republicans facing ethical questions. Together, this amounted to close to eighty districts. Emanuel did not contest every one, but the DCCC ultimately ran television ads in forty-eight districts, a good indicator of where it put up a strong fight.

As the campaign progressed, Emanuel began seeing the battle in terms of four distinct "footprints." Most promising was the Northeast, from the Philadelphia suburbs through Connecticut and New York. Next came the Ohio River Valley, including Ohio and Kentucky, where the state Republican parties faced major ethics problems. A "snake" of open seats ran through Indiana and Illinois, plus Colorado. And in the Southeast, Emanuel hoped to pick off seats in Virginia, North Carolina, and Florida. But the larger story of the 2006 campaign was the revolt of the moderates. Since 1994, the Republican Party had become steadily more Southern, evangelical, and conservative. Its leaders were Texans and Georgians, and the party was in thrall to the religious right. Republican positions on issues such as stem-cell research alienated many of the same moderates who had once been attracted to the Republican reputation for common sense. The party's tone became ever more harsh, conservative, religious, judgmental. It had taken a while, but by 2006, many moderates were ready to bolt. In 1994, there had been a long-anticipated swing of Southern conservatives from the Democrats to the Republican Party. Twelve years later, there was a pent-up surge of moderates in the other direction. That was especially true in the Northeast and in suburban areas across the country. And that is where Emanuel directed many of his resources.

For all the energy he was devoting to winning back the House, Emanuel's relationship with his fellow Democrats was complex. If he succeeded, many Democrats would become committee or subcommittee

chairmen, gaining immense power literally overnight. Most felt apprecia-
tion for his efforts. But despite the increasing partisanship on Capitol Hill,
many Democrats were also good friends with Republicans, and a Democratic congressman might find himself guiltily helping a Republican colleague in a tough reelection battle. Emanuel was furious when he worked
hard to recruit a strong challenger against a vulnerable Republican, only
to find that some Democratic congressman was refusing to endorse that
challenger for fear of antagonizing his Republican colleague. Emanuel
had Republican friends himself, but in his view, Democrats either wanted
to retake the House or they didn't, and politely refusing to attack Republicans was not the way to do it.

In early 2006, Congressman Alcee Hastings, a Florida Democrat, was
quoted in the *South Florida Sun-Sentinel* speaking sympathetically of Congressman Shaw, one of Emanuel's top Republican targets. Hastings,
because of his friendship with Shaw, also refused to endorse Shaw's Democratic challenger, Ron Klein. In the *Sun-Sentinel* article, Hastings even gave
Shaw strategic advice on how to defeat Klein, advocating that he knock on
doors to connect personally with voters rather than relying on television
ads as he had in the past. Then, in a closed meeting of Democratic House
members, Hastings chastised Emanuel and the DCCC for not recruiting
more candidates across the country, saying the Democrats needed to run
a respectable candidate in every House district.

It was not entirely surprising that Hastings and Emanuel would clash.
Hastings was a colorful figure. A former federal judge, he had been
impeached and removed from the bench by Congress in 1989 for corruption and perjury, making him only the sixth U.S. judge in history to suffer
that fate. He took his revenge by running for Congress himself, winning
a seat from southeast Florida in 1992. Hastings was a forceful speaker and
strong personality, and his diatribe against the DCCC in the closed session
was eloquent and cutting. It enraged Emanuel, who saw Hastings as typ-
ifying those of his fellow Democrats who were content to criticize but did
nothing to help the cause. "He's great on lectures," Emanuel said of Hastings. "Phenomenal lecturer. I'm getting a lecture on recruitment when A,

you haven't done a goddamn thing and B, we've got a [Republican] target and you're out there kissing his ass in the press?"

But Hastings refused to back down, repeating to friends that Emanuel had not done enough to recruit candidates in every congressional district, particularly blacks. "I think Rahm Emanuel is a brilliant strategist, a super fund-raiser," Hastings said. "But I have a total disagreement with him. . . . There are too many races where we could have found a candidate who may not have been the best candidate in the world, but they could have been on the ballot. That is what Newt Gingrich understood." In 1994, Hastings recalled, an unheralded Republican named George Nethercutt defeated House Speaker Tom Foley. "How in the hell could George Nethercutt ever have thought he would beat Tom Foley, the Speaker of the House?" Hastings said. "But Newt Gingrich knew he had to have somebody in the race. And when the wave came, fifty-four [Democratic incumbents] were gone. Rahm and I disagree, so we have had the 'You can't beat somebody with nobody' conversation on numerous instances."

As for the Shaw-Klein race, Hastings said he was close to both Shaw and Klein and could not in good conscience take sides. "Ron Klein is my friend. I have known Clay Shaw for nearly forty years," Hastings said. "Far be it from me to insert myself in a race of that kind." He added, "My compliments toward Clay Shaw have not been in the context of this election. It carries over from other times. He and I have worked together, and I will continue my efforts to do things legislatively that benefit the community that I serve. But I won't do anything politically to harm Ron Klein or help Clay Shaw."

Hastings was not the only Democratic congressman Emanuel thought was not pulling his weight. "I've got hundreds of those," he said. "I've got hundreds of examples of members screwing us. I've got members telling our challengers, 'I won't help you to challenge that X Republican.'" Emanuel continued, "I did say to one colleague once, 'You have an interesting concept of the word *team*. But when they come after you, I'll remind you of what you said to me. Because they will come after you.' I can give you chapter and verse of people acting like knuckleheads." In one example, Congressman Adam Schiff of California, who served on the DCCC's recruitment committee, declined to recruit a challenger to a California Republican congressman. Schiff explained that he was seen as a bipartisan type and wanted to keep it that way. "I thought Rahm was going to strangle him," said the staffer who recounted the story. "I'm sure you've seen that look before." As one way to fight back—not against Republicans but against uncooperative fellow Democrats—Emanuel instructed his staff in early April to find a way to reward those Democrats who did help out, praising them on the DCCC Web site and in articles in their hometown papers. "Goddamn it, I want to shame the rest of them who sit on their ass all weekend," he told his aides.

Emanuel battled Democratic colleagues especially fiercely over money. Every Democratic House member, if he did not face a tough race himself, was expected to contribute dues to the DCCC. But raising that money was not always easy and many were slow to give up their share. On March 8, 2006, Emanuel sent fellow Democrats a letter whose courteous tone barely masked his frustration. "After careful review of our records, we have identified 100 Members who have yet to pay at least half of their dues for the 2005–2006 cycle," Emanuel wrote. "We must have 100% participation from the caucus in our Member dues program." In case anyone missed the point, Emanuel attached a list of all members, how much they owed in dues, and what they had given; Emanuel was one of the few who had given the full amount to the DCCC, in his case $400,000. Some Democrats had failed to pay any dues at all. Hastings had given $30,000 of the $150,000 he owed.

The frustration was mutual. Some lawmakers who campaigned for Democratic candidates felt Emanuel ignored their contributions and treated them dismissively. "He is universally admired. He's doing the fund-raising and the politics, and he's doing it better than it's been done," said one senior Democratic aide. "But there is jealousy of all the attention he's getting, especially from the older members. Others feel that they've done a lot, too. I think they know that all the things he's trying to get them to do, they should do. But here, as in life, there are people who are jealous. And he feels that if everyone worked as hard as he did, we'd be in the majority."

There was a deeper dynamic at play as well. Many Democrats were happy to have Emanuel fight their battles, to have him be the ruthless bully someone had to be if the Democrats were to win. It was fine with them if Emanuel was attacking Republicans, branding them all as corrupt, enduring the stares of colleagues whose careers he was trying to end. That allowed other Democrats to keep the high ground, maintain cordial relations with Republicans, receive praise for bipartisanship—even as Emanuel, the designated pit bull, did the unpleasant work of targeting individual Republicans. Emanuel's resentment of this ran deep.

If there was a gravitational center to the Democratic antagonism toward Emanuel, it was the Congressional Black Caucus, the group of all African American members of Congress. With thirty-seven members, the Black Caucus comprised almost one-fifth of House Democrats, and nothing rivaled it as a powerful bloc within either party. The caucus was well organized, convened regularly, and met with House Democratic leader Nancy Pelosi to press its demands. Top Democrats had a delicate relationship with the Black Caucus, needing to placate the group yet sometimes believing its positions hurt the party. In one sense, caucus members should have been Emanuel's biggest supporters. If the Democrats won back the House, the party would gain the power to name committee chairmen, and several black lawmakers would be in line for powerful chairmanships, a historic advance in African American political power. But as the campaign moved forward, black lawmakers were fighting with Democratic leaders such as Emanuel and Pelosi on various fronts. The FBI, for example, was conducting a bribery investigation of Congressman William Jefferson, an African American congressman from New Orleans. Investigators said in an affidavit that Jefferson had taken a $100,000 fake bribe from an informant, and the FBI had later found $90,000 of it stashed in various containers in Jefferson's freezer. Pelosi worried that this lurid story would interfere with the Democrats' attempts to brand the Republicans as corrupt. But when she tried to show that Democrats would not tolerate wrongdoing by removing Jefferson from the powerful Ways and Means Committee, the Black Caucus rebelled, some accusing Pelosi of racism.

Black lawmakers also complained that Emanuel had not hired enough black staffers at the DCCC. "I don't like the idea of always having to raise the issue: 'Where are the minorities? Where are the minorities? Where are the minorities?'" said Danny Davis, a Chicago congressman with a slow, deep voice. "But certainly you would want your Democratic Caucus, or your Congressional Campaign Committee, to be sensitive and amenable to these kinds of struggles." Black Caucus members protested formally to Pelosi and informally to Emanuel himself, and sometimes the talks erupted into shouting matches. Pelosi arranged for several African American lawmakers to meet regularly with Emanuel, but neither side was assuaged. "I hate to say it because it sounds whiny, but there is a general question of whether there is sensitivity at the DCCC to the fact of diversity," said Congressman Al Wynn of Maryland, who headed the Black Caucus' political action committee.

And when Emanuel harangued his colleagues to pay their dues to the DCCC, some black congressmen felt that he did not take into account how hard it could be for black politicians to raise money. Some African Americans felt they deserved a break, since they often represented poorer districts and did not have as many wealthy contributors. "If a person says, 'Danny Davis, where are your dues?' I may have a particular difficulty getting my dues that you don't know about or you don't relate to," said Davis. "Rahm don't take no prisoners." Congressman Mel Watt of North Carolina, the Black Caucus' chairman, said the friction between African American lawmakers and Emanuel was to be expected. "I don't think we have ever had a DCCC chair where there haven't been disagreements, family discussions, differences of opinion," Watt said. "We are always expressing ourselves on diversity issues, staffing issues, to which races money gets committed and to which it does not." No doubt Emanuel's personality helped make those discussions more heated. But Watt said, "Those are ongoing discussions. But they are family discussions, and I wouldn't overblow them."

Emanuel was privately contemptuous of the Black Caucus and dismissive of its concerns. He saw the caucus as one more group—like the conservative "Blue Dog" Democrats—that needed to be pushed. There were two blacks among Emanuel's roughly ten senior staffers. Asked about the complaint that he did not have enough minority aides, Emanuel waved his hand dismissively. "You know that every [DCCC] chairman has faced the same criticism?" he said. "Okay. So I don't give a fuck." He literally spat out this last sentence. Then he began shouting. "As I said to them, Blue Dogs—they hate me too, because I'm arrogant and pushy with them. I'm an equal-opportunity prick to everybody. Because they've never, ever *worked! Nobody! None of 'em!*"

But Emanuel's biggest clashes within the party were with Democratic Party chairman Howard Dean. The backgrounds of the two men could hardly have been more different. Emanuel was a party insider, close to power brokers and fund-raisers. Dean, a former governor of Vermont, had risen suddenly to national prominence largely on the power of the "netroots"—liberal activists who debated passionately on political Web blogs and ran an ongoing insurgency against the party hierarchy. It was those activists who'd poured money and energy into the short-lived Dean for President campaign of 2004.

Now that Dean was party chairman, his goal was to build a Democratic operation in every part of the country, what he called a "fifty-state strategy." Those efforts won him tremendous support from state Democratic chairmen. How could the Democrats ever become the majority, Dean asked, reasonably enough, if they did not try to establish themselves in areas that currently leaned Republican? Dean was voicing the argument, made by many liberal bloggers, that Democratic insiders were overly obsessed with winning the next election, in the process diluting the party's message and ignoring vast parts of the country. "We need to be everywhere. That was one of the mistakes this party has been making for a long time," Dean said on CNN's *The Situation Room.* "This party needs to be rebuilt. We're not going to do it by playing in twenty states." He elaborated in an interview with the *Chicago Tribune.* "Look, I think the

Republicans have been terrible for the country. They can't manage the deficit, they can't manage national emergencies, they can't manage Iraq, they can't manage national security, they can't manage anything," he said. "But they are really good at campaigns. We ought to adopt a lot of their business model for running campaigns, and that's what I want to do. I want discipline in this party. I want a long-term business approach to this party that's going to last for more than one or two election cycles. I want to include everyone on this team."

Dean spent resources building a far-flung field operation and hiring party organizers in every state, even in conservative fortresses such as Wyoming and Idaho. He went so far as to visit the Virgin Islands, which had no voting representatives in Congress, to the ridicule of some critics. Emanuel complained that the Democratic National Committee, the party's central committee run by Dean, should inject millions of dollars into competitive House races, and that Dean was spending the money instead to build an organization that might or might not pay off sometime in the distant future. The DNC had $5.5 million in the bank at the end of 2005, compared to the Republican National Committee's $34 million, and that desperately worried Emanuel. At one point Ken Mehlman, the Republican Party chairman, called Emanuel to tease him about Dean's refusal to help out. Emanuel was not amused.

But Dean insisted he was spending the money to build up a framework that would pay off not only in 2006 but also beyond. Too often, he felt, the Democrats hoarded their campaign money until an election was only a few months away and then spent it in one great rush—rather than assembling building blocks, such as reliable lists of Democratic voters, that could pay off for decades. Dean made it clear that while he wanted to win in 2006, he was looking far beyond the next election. "To find out if the fifty-state strategy is going to be successful, you'll have to wait for a couple of presidential cycles," Dean said at one point.

Emanuel and Dean were both explosive characters, and their clash undoubtedly was in part one of temperament. But Emanuel, for all his outbursts and cursing, was tightly disciplined and had contempt for

Dean's habit of making controversial comments that distracted from the Democratic message. In December 2005 the former Vermont governor told a radio station, "The idea that the United States is going to win the war in Iraq is just plain wrong." Republicans seized on the defeatist tone of that statement, featuring Dean's comments prominently on the party's Web site. Emanuel agreed with their criticism. "If you are trying to build a national message, 'We're going to lose' isn't it," Emanuel said. "No disrespect to history, but McClellan tried it in 1864 and he lost to Lincoln. Name me the last person who won on that kind of message." Emanuel got increasingly worked up as he warmed to his topic. "If you're building a national message, you don't build it around the concept that America's losing. How about, try this, when Bill Clinton was running for president: 'We can compete and win again.' That has not only a positive message, it's true, and it speaks to our culture. 'We're going to lose' is not a fucking rallying cry. Okay?"

One evening Emanuel uncharacteristically decided to watch *The Daily Show*, the late-night comedy program, instead of going to bed early as usual, and by chance Dean was the guest. The show's host, Jon Stewart, listed everything going well for the Democrats—Bush's plummeting approval ratings, the scandals enveloping Republicans, voters' preference for Democrats—then he asked Dean with mock earnestness, "How will the Democratic Party blow this?" Dean laughed and said he didn't think it would, mentioning that two weeks earlier Democratic volunteers had knocked on a million doors throughout the country. Dean mocked Washington insiders—Emanuel, watching at home, had little doubt Dean meant him—and touted his fifty-state strategy. "We have at least four organizers in every state," Dean said. "We haven't given up on Utah or Mississippi or Alabama, and we're winning races in those places. . . . Mostly, it's the inside-Washington folks that are upset. They want to spend money on getting themselves reelected." The next day, at a staff meeting, Emanuel seethed. "There he is, with his 'knocking on a million fucking doors,'" Emanuel said. "He says, 'We're going to win races in Mississippi and Utah.' They better have the best fucking organization in Mississippi and

Utah." With a historic chance to retake the House, Emanuel thought it was folly to throw money at deeply conservative states instead of concentrating on places where Democrats could win. He told *The New Yorker*, "If you think Mississippi and Ohio are the same thing, you're an idiot."

Emanuel was the most vocal, and certainly the most vulgar, of Dean's critics, but other top Democrats—including Pelosi, Senate minority leader Harry Reid, and Senator Charles Schumer of New York—shared Emanuel's frustration. Emanuel and Schumer met with Dean in early May to persuade him to back off his fifty-state strategy and direct money to House and Senate campaigns. For the first time in a decade, they felt, Congress was within their grasp, and their idiosyncratic party chairman was going to blow it.

At the meeting, Schumer told Dean that he and Emanuel needed the DNC's money to win congressional races. Emanuel pointed out that Ken Mehlman, the Republican chairman, was planning to pour money into the races, and that if Dean refused to do the same thing, the Democrats were unilaterally disarming. Dean reiterated that he was building a field operation in every state, deploying Democratic activists who could walk the streets and help candidates win. That infuriated Emanuel. As he crisscrossed the country, Emanuel said, he had seen no evidence of Dean's field operation. "No disrespect, but some of us are arrogant enough, we come from Chicago, we think we know what it means to knock on a door," Emanuel said. "You're nowhere, Howard. Your field plan is not a field plan. That's fucking bullshit." Emanuel slammed his hand on the table. "Look, Chuck comes from Brooklyn. I come from Chicago. It ain't Burlington, Vermont." Emanuel lapsed into sarcasm. "Now, we understand that Burlington knows a lot about grassroots politics and we know nothing. I know your field plan—it doesn't exist. I've gone around the country with these races. I've seen your people. There's no plan, Howard." Emanuel also threatened that if the Democrats failed to retake Congress, on the day after the election, when it was time to address fellow Democrats about what went wrong, Emanuel would not stand with Dean. He left the meeting cursing, and later he recounted, "Chuck was as hard as me. There was no good cop, bad cop. It was just two pricks in the room."

Dean, for his part, declined to talk about the meeting. "That was a meeting that happened. It got in the paper. It shouldn't have gotten in the paper," he said. "And I don't put that stuff in the paper. I'm trying to build a team here, and the best way we can build a team is to keep our disagreements private, and that's what I'll continue to do." He also declined to respond directly to Emanuel's criticism. "I don't believe in discussing private business in public, and I'm not going to make an exception now," Dean said. "Disagreements belong inside the party, not in the newspapers. I don't put them in the newspapers. I'm not putting this one in the newspaper." He would not even respond to whether he had a functioning relationship with Emanuel. "I'm not going to comment on that at all," Dean said.

Dean eventually offered to give the DCCC $20,000 for each competitive House race. "He's trying to give me money to clear his conscience and say, 'I helped in '06,'" Emanuel said. "No." In a curt letter, Emanuel responded, "This is less than one percent of the total budget for the DNC. . . . If we do not come close to matching the resources Republicans are going to devote to field operations, our historic opportunity to gain a Democratic majority in the House will be gone."

Dean also promised that his young field workers would make phone calls and knock on doors for Democratic candidates. But Emanuel complained to Nancy Pelosi that even this was not happening. "None of these kids are doing it," Emanuel told Pelosi in an urgent phone call. "They're not phone-banking, they're not doing anything. . . . They've burned cash. He wants me to keep quiet and stop bashing him in the press. . . . But he should be in for $150,000 per race, $200,000 per race. Every chairman has done north of $5 million for the party; he's the first chairman who hasn't. Four or five months ago, when I was in Florida, Hillary called me and said, 'You've got to do something about Howard Dean.' So I took it on. The only person to give him a tongue-lashing in the press is me. Nancy, we're letting this guy off dirt cheap." Emanuel also emphasized the fecklessness of Dean's activists. "I've met the kids. I've been in sixty districts. They couldn't find their ass with both hands tied behind their back," he said. "The kids are good, but they're clueless. I met a girl in New Mexico. I said, 'How many calls have you made?' She didn't know!"

Part of the conflict was institutional—Emanuel was narrowly focused on House races, while Dean's job was to think about the whole party, senators to state legislators. It was hardly surprising that Emanuel wanted more than Dean was willing to give.

Emanuel's fight with Dean was, by extension, a war with the liberal bloggers who supported Dean and his fifty-state strategy. Web sites such as Daily Kos and MyDD had, by the 2006 campaign, become dynamic debate centers and recruiting stations, dispatching money and troops to favored candidates and tearing down others. Their influence was significant if not overwhelming, and they were a volatile ingredient, outside the control of party leaders. "I think parties are important, but I think the blogs exist as much to beat up the party as to support the party," said Dave Johnson, of the liberal blog Seeing the Forest. Sharing information and deftly using the Internet, the bloggers constituted a new class of amateur political expert, comfortable citing polls in little-followed primary races and trashing the record of a political consultant who usually went unnoticed. The discussions of polling were sophisticated, full of the sort of analysis that until recently had been the sole province of professionals. One posting on the liberal blog Swing State Project in November 2005, for example, discussing the prospects of New Jersey gubernatorial candidate Jon Corzine, read this way: "The good news is that the Q-Poll also gives Corzine his highest mark so far, 52%, and SUSA's got him at 50 (though he's seen 51 before). Marist, which puts Corzine at +5, has also been pretty scattered. It gave him that notorious +2 a month ago, only to give him his first double-digit lead (+10) since early September two weeks later. Now they're splitting the difference. So I don't know what to make of their polling."

Blogs had become a locus of activity for the party's frustrated left wing. They allowed combative liberals, diffused across the country, to form a bloc that could not be ignored, and they presented a challenge to those trying to move the Democratic Party to the center. They frequently second-guessed the professionals and the party establishment. Emanuel tried to court the blogs while simultaneously pushing the moderate policies and candidates he believed were the Democrats' best hope. It was a delicate dance, part seduction and part deflection. Lapp voiced the mixture of frustration and amusement with which many Washington Democrats viewed bloggers. "Part of the appeal of the blogosphere and the progressive movement is to be anti-establishment. I think that's fine," Lapp said. "In some ways, the [party] committees are about as cool as your parents joining a rock band." The blogs served a purpose, he said, prompting the disaffected to give money to Democrats. "If they can get more money by ranting against the machine, that's fine," Lapp said. "I just want more money and more people and more resources in more races, and if the way to do that is to attack Mom and Dad, that's okay."

Emanuel was praised on occasion by bloggers for bringing a fresh energy to the party. When he persuaded Mary Jo Kilroy, a county commissioner in Ohio, to challenge Republican congresswoman Deborah Pryce, Tim Tagaris of Swing State Project was positively effusive. "I don't know how the DCCC did it, and they deserve a lot of credit I am sure," he wrote. But more often, bloggers lashed out at the DCCC as representing a muddle-headed centrism that would never rescue the Democrats or reignite the sweeping populism the country badly needed. David Sirota, who ran his own blog, Sirotablog, and also contributed regularly to the Huffington Post blog, was especially fierce. Reacting to a comment by Emanuel on November 17, 2005, that the Democrats would announce a position on Iraq "at the right time," Sirota wrote, "Try not to projectile vomit all over your computer screen." He added, "When, Rahm, is the 'right time'? Is it closer to the election when you think it suits your own personal political ambition better, even though hundreds—if not thousands—of more American troops will have been killed? How many more people have to die or be maimed, Rahm, before it is the 'right time'? And are you really so arrogant and out-of-touch to believe voters will swallow this kind of cynical politics on election day?"

Daily Kos, the leading political blog, conducted an online poll on Emanuel after his fight with Dean became public. The bloggers disapproved of Emanuel 59 percent to 28 percent, and some comments were scathing. "Rahm is pure slime," opined one blogger. "Rahm has NEVER been about changing things, only securing his spot in the Good Ole Boys Club," added another. "Rahm is nothing but another CORRUPT Chicago Machine HACK." But others approved of Emanuel's fierceness and his swaggering attacks on Republicans. "Rahm is doing a great job," wrote one blogger. "He's a hard ass, which is what the DCCC needs. He fights with Dean and Dean fights back. That's how it goes. Cut the brotha some slack, no?"

Sirota was among the most aggressive of Emanuel's critics. Living in Montana, Sirota affected the posture of an outside-the-Beltway heartland figure, a sort of electronic prairie populist. In a typical posting on Sirotablog in January 2006, he wrote, "It is quite possible that reporters, politicians and 'strategists' who spend more of their time in the cushy confines of Washington simply have no concept of what people out in the heartland really think." But until 2003, Sirota had worked as press secretary for the House Appropriations Committee Democrats, after holding other jobs in Washington's "cushy confines." So he hardly fit the profile of an anti-establishment rebel from the heartland. "The world's most unlikely cowboy," former White House chief of staff John Podesta once called him.

Sirota wrote for *The Nation* and co-chaired the Progressive Legislative Action Network, which promoted liberal laws on the state level. In 2006 he wrote a book, *Hostile Takeover: How Big Money and Corruption Conquered Our Government—and How We Take It Back*. He also was affiliated with the Center for American Progress, *In These Times,* MoveOn.org, and the *Al Franken Show*—key stations of the liberal community. Sirota's numerous postings could be vulgar—for example, accusing *Newsweek* columnist Joe Klein of "rectal journalism," which he defined as being "based on reporters and pundits simply pulling stuff right out of their ass and peddling it as fact." Sirota did not look like a rebel; he sported coiffed short hair and a clean-cut appearance. He wore a conservative suit and tie on his book tour. His demeanor was intensely serious, his blue eyes hooded by a slanting brow. Emanuel, he felt, personified a Democratic establishment afraid to present a strong alternative to Republicans. While Emanuel believed in recruiting conservative Democrats for conservative districts, Sirota and other bloggers often saw that as a dishonorable compromise that would never lead to a long-term majority. "For many, many years, the DCCC—under Rahm's leadership especially—seemed to think that having no ideology, no convictions, is a winning formula," Sirota said. "Even if you do win [in 2006] under that scenario, because the Republicans have screwed up so much, you have created an extremely tenuous majority, one that might set you back many, many years."

Attempting to keep bloggers in line, Lapp regularly posted messages on MyDD and Daily Kos and held online chats on the DCCC Web site. Bill Burton, the DCCC's communications director, kept in touch with Sirota via e-mail and even invited him out for a beer. Emanuel himself held conference calls every month with bloggers. At one such session, on an October night in 2005, the bloggers were for the most part painstakingly polite, in marked contrast to the way they tore into Emanuel online. Bob Brigham, of Swing State Project, courteously asked when Emanuel planned to distribute a list of all the Democratic House candidates. That prompted Burton, who was listening in, to explode, "Bob Brigham is such a pussy. He comes off as such a badass online but faced with Rahm asks an administrative question. Amazing." Emanuel, for his part, avoided antagonizing the bloggers during the conference call, appealing to them as part of the big Democratic family. He asked the bloggers to feature four specific candidates on their Web sites: Joe Sulzer in Ohio, Chris Carney in Pennsylvania, Tim Dunn in North Carolina, and Francine Busby in California. All were promising candidates, Emanuel said, but they needed a push to raise their profiles and improve their fund-raising. "I think the blogging community can really make a difference," he said. "You can lift those races to where they need to be."

Carping ensued. Several bloggers said they hated the latest Democratic slogan, "America Can Do Better." "It's really getting hammered," Johnson said. "The conservative blogs are seeing it as a large slow target, LST in military parlance. If this is in the trial balloon phase, it's taking a lot of fire." Emanuel answered carefully. "All these things are a negotiation," he said. "I'm not saying it's perfect, but everyone is buying into it—mayors, House members, senators. It's the first time I remember Democrats agreeing on something. I'll take unity and execution over getting something perfect." Another blogger criticized the performance of Joe Sulzer, one of the candidates Emanuel had praised, who was challenging Republican congressman Bob Ney. "I'm in Bob Ney's district, and I can tell you, Joe Sulzer is invisible," the blogger said. Emanuel seemed chastened, thanked the blogger, and promised to look into it.

Occasionally signs of accommodation surfaced between the bloggers and the DCCC. Some bloggers concluded that they could have a role different from that of the committee, and that it might make sense for Emanuel to emphasize a few key races while someone else—maybe the bloggers themselves—concentrated on a longer-term strategy. "The DCCC can focus on districts that are the most winnable," said Markos Moulitsas Zúniga, who runs Daily Kos. "We can do the others, every district, to spread the Republicans thin and to have a body there in case someone resigns. Some districts haven't seen Democrats in decades. That is where we can help them."

But the DCCC and the bloggers also continued to disagree, and their fight would echo through the 2006 campaign and beyond. One candidate in particular epitomized the clash between Emanuel, who was always looking for candidates who "fit" their particular districts, and the bloggers, who felt that unapologetic liberal populists could win almost anywhere. The candidate was an unassuming Iraq war veteran named Tammy Duckworth.

5

FRIENDLY FIRE

Tammy Duckworth arrived on a cold January evening for a campaign fund-raiser at the DCCC offices in Washington. Although she was new to politics, Duckworth's vivid biography was already attracting attention—she'd recently lost both legs when her helicopter was shot down in Iraq, then decided to run for Congress as a Democrat. Inside the drab building a few blocks from the U.S. Capitol, Democratic lawyers and activists clustered around a table laden with cheese, pita, and grape leaves, eager for a look at the new political phenom. A basket near the door held dozens of checks from attendees for $200, $500, or $1,000, many tucked inside envelopes embossed with the names of law or lobbying firms. Duckworth walked with a cane, her body bent from her horrific accident, an assistant pushing a wheelchair in case she tired. As she entered the room, an aide whispered, "Tell them your story. It's good if the first word out of your mouth is 'health care'—then tell your story. They want to hear that."

Duckworth did just that, creating a commotion as she stepped into the reception and was enveloped by supporters. "Every part of me that was not covered with armor basically was injured," she said. "In previous wars, I would have died." She was pressed for more details: how her helicopter was shot down, how she was pulled to safety by her buddies, how she returned to a painful rehabilitation. "What I do is neutralize the Iraq issue, the national security issue," she told one admirer, meaning no Republican could call her weak on defense. She confided to another, "I just got a new leg from Walter Reed, so I'm a little wobblier than usual. They're like new shoes, until you build up the calluses." A man whose name tag identified him as Charlie Smith rushed up and said, "I'm a Vietnam vet and I love you."

That reaction helped explain why Emanuel was so enamored of Duckworth. The election year had officially started, and reporters were paying a little more attention to the campaign for Congress, though it still seemed far off to most voters. Duckworth—bespectacled, wearing an American flag on her lapel, her dark hair streaked with blond—was one of Emanuel's dream candidates. An Asian American with a round, cheerful face, she was chatty and engaging, her demeanor contrasting with her evident difficulty in walking even short distances. She had already proved one of the irresistible news stories of the campaign: A brave woman volunteers to serve in Iraq, has her legs blown off by enemy fire, and comes back to run for Congress, calling the Iraq war a mistake but expressing a bond with her military comrades. She was instantly invited for a coveted appearance on ABC's *This Week with George Stephanopoulos*. She was profiled in front-page articles in the *Washington Post* ("After War Injury, an Iraq Vet Takes on Politics") and *USA Today*. Senator Barack Obama of Illinois, the brightest star in the Democratic firmament, filmed a thirty-second television ad for Duckworth, telling viewers, "Every so often you meet someone in public life who's truly extraordinary." The *Chicago Tribune* and *Chicago Sun-Times* endorsed her. Most candidates making an initial run for Congress, in contrast, felt lucky to earn a brief mention in their hometown newspaper. Duckworth seemed to symbolize something people were hungering for, perhaps an ambivalence toward the Iraq war, perhaps a desire to move beyond it without dishonoring the fighters.

For all the dazzle, Duckworth quickly became the center of a nasty fight over Emanuel's tactics. When Duckworth entered the race, another

Democrat, Christine Cegelis, was already running for the same congressional seat outside Chicago. Cegelis, a fifty-one-year-old single mother with two kids in their twenties, had run two years earlier, done surprisingly well, and built a loyal following for her willingness to take on a tough fight against Congressman Henry Hyde. This time, Cegelis' supporters thought she had a shot at winning and deserved the chance. But Emanuel, Illinois senator Dick Durbin, and other Democratic leaders did not believe Cegelis was working hard enough or raising sufficient money, and they settled on Duckworth as a more viable candidate. They used their clout to persuade her to run and to direct money, attention, and endorsements her way. That angered Cegelis supporters such as Connie Baker, fifty-one, of the small town of Elmhurst, who was appalled that the Democratic Party was actively undermining a deserving local candidate. "I will not support the Democratic Party ever again," Baker said shortly before the primary contest between Cegelis and Duckworth. "I am so angry, I cannot believe they are doing this. . . . We're very, very angry at Rahm Emanuel, and we feel very betrayed."

The contrast between the Duckworth and Cegelis campaigns was hard to miss. One had an abundance of glittery support, provided by Emanuel and his connections, while the other was run on a shoestring. On the same night Duckworth attended the Washington fund-raiser, co-hosted by Nancy Pelosi and other Washington dignitaries, Cegelis was home in Illinois, speaking at a modest session of the Independent Voters of Illinois—Independent Precinct Organization (IVI-IPO), a homegrown group of activists dedicated to "social justice through good government."

The Sixth Congressional District of Illinois, the setting for all this activity, had an illustrious history. Democrats as well as Republicans there had long prided themselves on their independence from the Chicago Democratic machine. The area had been represented for three decades by Congressman Henry Hyde, a lion of the House, who was respected by many Democrats despite his prominent role in the impeachment of President Bill Clinton. Having turned eighty-one in April 2005 and seen his health deteriorate, Hyde had reluctantly announced he would retire. The district leaned Republican, but like many suburban areas across the country it was gradually becoming more Democratic, and Emanuel thought he had a chance there. Giving the race a personal tone, the district was located directly between the home bases of Emanuel and House Speaker Dennis Hastert, who strongly disliked each other. Each badly wanted his party to win the seat.

Two years earlier, as President Bush was seeking reelection, Cegelis had decided to challenge Hyde. Cegelis, who worked for a software company, was an avid Democrat who in her youth had campaigned for Hubert Humphrey and George McGovern but had not been especially active in recent years. Cegelis was frustrated that no credible Democrat was taking on Hyde, and she described her decision to challenge one of the country's senior politicians as a sort of epiphany. "I was helping my mom pay for her medications when the Medicare bill passed, and I thought, 'What are they thinking?'" Cegelis said. "It got to the point where I felt this Congress didn't have a problem they couldn't make worse. You identified a problem, they passed a bill to make it worse. Basically it was, 'I'm mad as heck and I'm not going to take it anymore.'"

Cegelis was anything but smooth, especially at first. Pleasant-looking, blond, and bespectacled, she stumped through the district talking about how young adults could not find decent work, how jobs were fleeing overseas, how good health insurance was tough to come by. She held fund-raisers with a $20 admission fee, instead of the typical big-ticket events. She began attracting fervent support from the party's liberal wing—bloggers, Howard Dean supporters, union activists.

Greg Sweigert of the small town of Mount Prospect was a typical Cegelis fan. Sweigert, who worked in manufacturing and had lost his job, was attracted to Cegelis by her criticism of free-trade deals such as CAFTA, the Central American Free Trade Agreement. He held a coffee for her and invited her to speak at an industry gathering. "She talked about a lot of solutions, whereas a lot of other people were throwing slogans around," Sweigert said. "Most of the people are not thinking about their economic self-interest these days. They're thinking about God or guns or gays. And she was speaking to that."

The support Cegelis attracted, while not overwhelming, was painstakingly earned. "She cared so much about what was happening to the United States that she was willing to mortgage her house and quit her job to make a difference," Baker said. "Nobody came and asked her to do this. She made up her mind that nobody else was going to do it, so she was. She put together a grassroots Democratic campaign here in the Sixth District that didn't exist before this."

In the end, Cegelis won 44 percent of the vote to Hyde's 56 percent in 2004, an impressive showing against an established incumbent and the best performance against Hyde since the Watergate year of 1974. Cegelis became an immediate hero to liberal activists, who credited her with having the courage to take on a conservative icon. When Hyde a few months later announced his "difficult decision" to retire, Cegelis seemed well positioned. If she'd managed a respectable showing against Hyde in 2004, her supporters believed, she would have an even better shot against whatever lesser-known Republican sought to replace Hyde in November 2006.

On November 12, 2004, just ten days after Cegelis' loss to Hyde, Tammy Duckworth, a captain in the Illinois Army National Guard, was co-piloting a Black Hawk helicopter north of Baghdad. It was the end of a long day of missions, and Duckworth was happy to hand off the controls to co-pilot Dan Milberg, while she assumed overall command of the aircraft. Five minutes later, Duckworth heard the distinctive *tap-tap-tap* of antiaircraft fire, and a rocket-propelled grenade, one of the Iraqi insurgents' weapons of choice, struck the helicopter. Duckworth swore loudly, calling out to Milberg, "I think we've been hit!" Then she saw a giant fireball erupt from the helicopter. She grabbed the controls and tried to wrestle the aircraft to the ground, but the instrument panel was black and she could hear the awful sound of shrapnel being sucked into the engine. The helicopter was shaking, smoke was everywhere, and Duckworth searched desperately for a landing area. She had no idea she'd been hurt. Her legs were gone, but adrenaline had taken over and it did not occur to her to check her limbs. She felt as though she were pushing the pedals of the helicopter, but it was a phantom sensation. Milberg had retained control of the craft the entire time, and it was he, not Duckworth, who was piloting the chopper to the ground. Radio communication had been cut off, and the two were unable to talk through their headsets. When the helicopter finally bumped to the ground, Duckworth reached up, shut off the engine, and passed out. She was taken for dead by her comrades, who pulled what they thought was her corpse into another helicopter and took off. Duckworth woke up ten days later at Walter Reed Army Medical Center in Washington. It was only then she learned she'd lost both legs and her right arm had been shattered.

Two months later, Senator Durbin asked his staff to find two wounded soldiers from Illinois to accompany him to the U.S. Capitol for Bush's 2005 State of the Union address. Senators like to invite appealing guests to this glamorous event, and in wartime soldiers are an obvious choice. Duckworth was one of those recruited by Durbin's staff, showing up in a wheelchair and full uniform, an IV tube concealed under her clothes. "There she was, a big smile on her face, an impressive person," Durbin said. "I'm amazed—I can't believe this woman ten weeks before had been shot down." During the pre-speech festivities, a reporter from the *Chicago Sun-Times* asked Duckworth what she thought of protestors opposed to the Iraq war. "Isn't that why we're fighting this war—so people can speak out if they disagree with the government?" Duckworth asked. It was a far better answer, Durbin thought, than most politicians were giving at the time. Durbin and Duckworth stayed in touch after the speech, Durbin inviting her to testify before Congress, Duckworth notifying him about Illinois veterans who needed help.

Increasingly impressed, Durbin called her that summer with the off-the-wall idea that she run for Congress. He fully expected her to laugh dismissively and hang up the phone. But Duckworth, after a few days of pondering, agreed. An elated Durbin immediately called Emanuel and told him, "Rahm, I have an interesting opportunity for us." Emanuel did not believe it at first. "Are you serious?" he asked. Then Durbin called Obama, who was also excited.

Complications remained. Durbin wasn't even sure Duckworth was a Democrat, although it soon turned out she was. The military had to release her officially before she could become a candidate, cutting into her campaign time. Most troubling, Duckworth actually lived just outside Hyde's district, and she could not easily move into it because her friends had painstakingly fixed up her current house to accommodate her disability. Illinois law did not require a representative to live in her district, but voters were likely to look askance at an outsider seeking to represent them. Duckworth's opponents could portray her as an opportunist imposed on the district by powerful interests. On top of that, Duckworth faced more surgery to clean out an infection. The procedure would keep her in the hospital for two weeks and on an antibiotic IV for six more, hardly an ideal arrangement for campaigning.

But on December 18, 2005, Duckworth announced her candidacy. "As a soldier, I fought for my country," she said. "And I'm running for Congress to fight for my country, too, because I think we really need to change course." There was little in her background to suggest the makings of a candidate, but she quickly took to campaigning. "Four months in a hospital bed is a long time to be thinking about where the country is going. And I was in a hospital bed for four months," Duckworth said. "And I got more and more annoyed about where the country is going." As Duckworth campaigned, she spoke a good deal about the Iraq war. Her injury was in a sense her political calling card, giving her instant credibility. She wore a bracelet that read, "Defend Freedom/Pray For Our Troops." She framed even unrelated issues in terms of her experience, noting, for example, that while she had received an expensive artificial leg, others lacked decent health care.

Between the appeal of her story and the power of her patrons, Duckworth won the backing of nearly every influential institution in Illinois as the Democratic primary approached. In addition to Obama, Durbin, Emanuel, and the two Chicago newspapers, the Illinois AFL-CIO announced its support for Duckworth—even though it was Cegelis, not Duckworth, who was a former union member. Emanuel used his connections to get Duckworth an appearance on the Sunday talk show hosted by Stephanopoulos, his friend and former colleague in the Clinton White House. Another Emanuel ally, top Democratic strategist David Axelrod, became Duckworth's media consultant, and he helped bring other experienced Democratic operatives into the campaign. Durbin campaigned with her numerous times, later saying he'd worked harder on her campaign than any other besides his own. Cegelis could not compete with this onslaught, nor could a third Democrat in the race, a little-known professor named Lindy Scott.

As a veteran and an Asian American, Duckworth received support from still other quarters. Senator John Kerry, saying he wanted to ensure other veterans were not attacked as he was in the 2004 presidential campaign, solicited support for Duckworth in an e-mail and raised $147,000. Senator Hillary Rodham Clinton, an ally of Emanuel's, announced her support. Emanuel's staff contacted Congressman Mike Honda, a California Democrat and one of the few Asian Americans in Congress, and urged him to meet with Duckworth. After he did so, Honda posted a message on his Web site calling her "a vibrant rising star in the Democratic Party" and soliciting contributions. "Being Asian American is a big deal for me," Honda said at the time. "We need to have more diversity in this Congress. The more Asian Americans we can bring into this policy-making body, the better this country will be." The money Duckworth raised for the primary against Cegelis, mostly from outside the district, enabled her to overwhelm her opponent with well-produced television ads. One showed Duckworth meeting with senior citizens and talking about the cost of medicine as inspiring music played in the background. Another featured Obama in a dark suit looking into the camera and telling voters about Duckworth's "special connection with people."

The seduction of Tammy Duckworth was part of a broader strategy by Emanuel to field Iraq war veterans in as many House races as possible. For years, Democrats had fought the perception that they were not as committed to the nation's defense as Republicans and were out of touch with military culture. That might not matter in times of peace such as the

1990s, when Bill Clinton, whom critics labeled a draft dodger, easily defeated two decorated World War II veterans, George H. W. Bush and Bob Dole. But when voters were feeling insecure, as they were after the terrorist attacks of September 11, 2001, they turned to candidates they felt could protect them. Democrats tended to suffer in such times. This dynamic dated back at least to the 1960s, when anti-war protestors and peace activists found a home in the Democratic Party, alienating many in the center. In the 1988 presidential race, Democrat Michael Dukakis sought to combat this image by posing in a tank, but the image of the diminutive candidate looking uncomfortable in an ill-fitting helmet only compounded the problem, and was used by Republicans, not Democrats, in campaign ads.

The Democrats' anti-military image was so widely accepted that President Bush, who like Vice President Dick Cheney had openly avoided the Vietnam draft, successfully questioned the national security credentials of two Democrats who had volunteered to serve, Al Gore and John Kerry. In choosing Kerry, a certified war hero and Purple Heart recipient, as their presidential candidate in 2004, Democrats thought they had solved their national security problem, but they underestimated the public's willingness to buy the Republican argument that no Democrat was trustworthy on defense. A conservative group's television ads questioning Kerry's valor, although it had little basis in fact, managed to sully Kerry's reputation and challenge his integrity. Similarly, Georgia senator Max Cleland, a Democrat who'd lost three limbs in Vietnam, was defeated in 2002 by a Republican opponent who questioned his commitment to national security.

That was the tide Emanuel was battling. By late 2005 polls showed voters were increasingly disenchanted with the Iraq war, but it was not yet clear they trusted the Democrats on the subject. Emanuel believed that if a candidate such as Duckworth criticized the war, Republicans would be hard-pressed to question her patriotism. He had recruited eight Iraq war veterans so far to run for Congress as Democrats, while only one was running as a Republican. Democrat Andrew Horne in Kentucky, for example, had served in the Marines for twenty-seven years and taken part in both Gulf wars. Tim Dunn, in North Carolina, had served with the Marines in Kosovo as well as Iraq. Joe Sestak, a Pennsylvania candidate with a Harvard Ph.D., had been a vice admiral in the Navy. Never before had so many veterans run on what were essentially anti-war platforms.

As for their candidates who lacked military experience, Democratic leaders tried hard to teach them how to talk about defense matters. California congresswoman Jane Harman organized a training session in early 2006, flying thirty-one congressional candidates to Washington, where strategists urged them to advocate a "tough and smart" defense policy. This slogan sought to convey that Democrats were just as willing to use force as Republicans to protect America, but were unlikely to blunder into an ill-advised war as Bush had. The purpose of the session, Harman said, was to "frame our message in a way that voters hear better." Jeff Latas, an Arizona House candidate who had served in Operation Desert Storm and whose son was in the current Iraq war, wore a "Leave No Veteran Behind" button. "We Democrats have a surge of veterans running, and that shows we are strong on national defense," Latas said. "We're tired of seeing our kids sent to Iraq based on false and misleading information." Training binders distributed at the event included an "eight-step strategy on national security." "Voters will not respond to approaches that ignore fear, mock it or try to intellectualize it away, like calling Bush a 'fear-monger,'" the notebook said. "They need to know that you understand the dangers we face and that you have a tough, hard-headed focus on keeping them safe."

No seminar, however, could mask the Democrats' lack of a unified position on the war. Some candidates were calling for a quick pullout, while others simply urged more congressional oversight. Bush and other Republicans mocked the lack of a Democratic plan as further evidence of the party's incompetence on defense. Emanuel's hope was that voters were becoming so disgusted with Bush's conduct of the war that, if nothing else, they would turn to the Democrats as a check on the president. But Emanuel's veterans, like other Democrats, had to walk a fine line, criticizing the war without appearing unpatriotic or unsupportive of the troops. And some, it had to be said, were not particularly impressive as candidates. "It's not that an Iraqi veteran can't be a good candidate," said political analyst Stuart Rothenberg. "It's that there is no reason to think they will be." Several years earlier, when the Democrats were pushing health care reform, Rothenberg noted, they had fielded doctors and nurses as candidates, and most of them lost.

His point had been illustrated in an embarrassing television appearance the previous August by one of Emanuel's "fighting Democrats." Patrick Murphy, who had received a Bronze Star in Iraq and seen nineteen soldiers in his unit die, was a classic Emanuel candidate. Handsome and all-American, Murphy had been an altar boy in the Philadelphia area, where he was challenging Congressman Mike Fitzpatrick. But he stumbled when he appeared on MSNBC's *Hardball* and the host, Chris Matthews, asked if Fitzpatrick would have voted to authorize the Iraq war. "That's a tough question," Fitzpatrick said. But it didn't seem as though it should be a tough question for an Iraq veteran who was basing his candidacy on the war. Matthews asked again how he would have voted, and Murphy said, "It's a hard call." Matthews did not let up, saying, "You shouldn't run for Congress if you don't want to make that call." Murphy still refused to answer, falling back on pabulum. "Chris, I'm not pro-war or anti-war," he said. "I am pro-troops." Matthews pounced: "So you're running for Congress and you're running on the war issue—but you're not saying whether you would have voted for authorizing the war or not." "Well, Chris," Murphy finally blurted out, "I don't want to dishonor the guys I served with over there. So I am not going to say that."

But Emanuel persisted with his veterans strategy. And no one fit the profile better than Duckworth, the only seriously wounded veteran running for Congress.

When it became clear how much political clout was lining up behind Duckworth, Cegelis, her Democratic opponent, was stunned that her own party would treat her this way. "I'm a Democrat, but I obviously wasn't connected to the party," she said. "As a novice, I didn't realize how important it is that you have to be invited to the dance. People were upset I didn't call them and ask permission. I didn't realize I needed to. But in fact, that is how political parties work. You need their permission." Duckworth, she said, had no connection to the area she was seeking to represent. "It's not just that she doesn't live in the district, she's never been in or around the district," Cegelis said. "She is not from around here." Cegelis' supporters hoped Democratic leaders' heavy-handedness in dropping Duckworth into the campaign would backfire, galvanizing opposition to the Democratic machine. "Rahm Emanuel has done a great service by pissing the grassroots people off," Sweigert insisted. "He's moved the battle up to higher visibility. I think Christine would be the first one to say that she doesn't like to be ganged up on, but it's a good battle to fight. I don't want to reach too far and say it's a battle for the heart and soul of the Democratic Party, but it's a battle between the grassroots and the top-down. And it's about money, and Rahm being able to take all the resources of the DCCC and dump it into her campaign." He added, "It's like Vietnam. Rahm controls the air. He controls the airwaves, he controls the airpower. But we are like the Viet Cong. We control the street fighters. We are the street-level people, we have the shoe leather. It's the contrast of the big money versus the people who really want some kind of change in Washington."

Democratic power brokers responded with differing levels of contempt to such rhetoric. Durbin, always smoothly articulate, said he regretted having to steamroll Cegelis in order to launch Duckworth's candidacy, but he had little choice if Democrats were to field the best candidate. "That is the difficult, painful part of this," Durbin said. "I think Christine is a good person. I've never said anything bad about her." Emanuel, characteristically, was more acerbic. During a campaign trip to Philadelphia in late January, he became highly animated on the subject of Duckworth, both defiant and stung by the criticism. Cegelis was not working hard enough or raising enough money, he said, and his job was to find candidates willing to do what it took to win. "If she would only work as hard as she would goddamn whine," Emanuel said. "She's the only one who says, 'What can you do for me?'" He imitated a child's whiny voice. "She could absolutely win. She's just not doing it." The district, he added, was one Democrats had never contested before but could capture—if they had the right nominee. Leaving it to Cegelis, Emanuel said, would essentially cede the race to the Republicans. "Am I supposed to take a suburban district that is trending Democratic off the field?" he said. "Everyone says I'm supposed to expand the playing field. I try to expand the playing field, and then it's, 'Oh, he's bigfooting.' Do I have a few Internet blog people whining, who've never won an election? Yes. I said, 'I could do what all the other DCCC chairmen did, wring my hands.' But I didn't want to." He was not the only Democratic leader pushing Duckworth, Emanuel added. "You think Obama wasn't involved? Durbin? But who gets blamed? Me. Tough guy Rahm. No one wants to blame Barack, because he is who he is. So fuck you."

Emanuel's tireless engineering of Duckworth's candidacy exemplified what fellow Democrats either admired or detested about him: He wanted to win at all costs. He had no interest in a Democratic Party that was purer than the opposition if it lost. He did not care where a candidate stood on abortion or the Iraq war, or whether that candidate was displacing a "better" Democrat, if such purity cost a House seat.

Heath Shuler in North Carolina was another prime example of this. Shuler was running in a mountainous, rural area where Democrats had long been unable to win. The district contained the funky enclave of Asheville, a university town home to any number of artists, nature lovers, and former hippies. But Asheville was surrounded by the district's other fourteen counties, which were far more conservative and religious. The incumbent Republican, Congressman Charles Taylor, was deeply conservative. But Shuler was unlike the Democrats Taylor had faced in his previous eight elections. Thirty-four years old, youthful, and handsome, Shuler had grown up in the district on Toot Hollow Road. At Swain County High School, Shuler set every passing record in school history, scored 106 touchdowns, and led the Maroon Devils to three state championships. The most heavily recruited high school quarterback in America, Shuler had attended the University of Tennessee, where he again set passing records and was runner-up for the Heisman Trophy in 1993. After his college career, Shuler was snapped up by pro football's Washington Redskins, who planned to build their team around him. But the Redskins were terrible during that period and Shuler performed poorly, ending his stint in the NFL a few years later after being injured.

Despite his failed professional football career, Shuler was still a local hero in North Carolina, well known throughout the district. More important, he held all the conservative positions required of most Southern politicians. Shuler was an evangelical Christian who openly referred to Jesus as his savior, and he was comfortable, even eager, to talk about his faith. He did not drink soda because of the caffeine. He was against gun control, abortion, and gay marriage.

Shuler ran a campaign that emphasized his old-fashioned "mountain values." He often spent Friday nights at high school football games, where as many as fifteen thousand people were in the audience. Shuler's presence would be announced over the loudspeaker, and he would find himself surrounded by admirers and autograph seekers. He refused to campaign on Sundays, saying that was church and family time. He liked to tell homespun Christian-oriented stories on the campaign trail, such as one about the time he was starting high school and his mother left a message for him in his notebook. "She said, 'Heath, when you get to class, I've got something for you, something that I think you'll really like,'" Heath would recount. "I thought it was going to be a check or some extra money to get two lunches instead of one. It was a little note. It says, 'Heath, make each and every decision as though I am standing beside you. For when I am not, Jesus Christ always is.'"

The story was almost unbearably corny, but it sent the message that Shuler was not an ordinary Democrat but a local boy with strong Christian values. And he enhanced that image with his television ads. In one, Shuler was standing next to Victory Baptist Church, which he'd attended as a child. In another he drawled, "I was born and raised in the mountains of western North Carolina. From my family and church I learned the importance of faith and responsibility." That ad showed scenes of Shuler and his family around a dinner table and Shuler's son, clad in red cowboy pajamas, kneeling earnestly for a bedtime prayer as Shuler and his wife smiled from the doorway.

The situation was a little more complicated for Duckworth. While Shuler had grown up in his district and did not face significant primary opposition, Duckworth did not even live in her district and was trying to roll over a local Democrat with substantial grassroots support. Yet Emanuel believed that Duckworth, like Shuler, made a nice fit with a conservative area that Democrats otherwise would have difficulty winning over. Duckworth agreed, suggesting in slightly coded language that Cegelis was too liberal for the district. "I am the person who is most in touch with the voters in this district," she said. "I admire Christine for what she has done in the past, but I think I am more readily electable. When I made my decision whether to run, the numbers showed me I could win in this district. Christine was just a name to me at that time; I didn't know her personally. I realize I am the person who has the pulse of this district, who thinks like the people here."

On primary night, March 21, the Duckworth-Cegelis race was too close to call. By the next day it became clear that Duckworth had taken 44 percent of the vote to Cegelis' 40 percent, with the third candidate, Lindy Scott, receiving 16 percent. Emanuel was relieved. "We took on the communists in the party," he said sarcastically. "Thank God for the left. They're always there helping you when you need them." Cegelis, for her part, conceded defeat only when Duckworth took the initiative and called her. She refused to endorse Duckworth for about two weeks, doing so only after being urged by party leaders.

Duckworth now had to face Republican state senator Peter Roskam, a seasoned politician with the unified support of his party. Unopposed in his own primary, Roskam had nonetheless received more votes than the three Democrats combined, a stark illustration of the district's Republican leanings. A former aide to House Republican leader Tom DeLay, Roskam had the vocal support of the outgoing congressman, Henry

Hyde, as well as House Speaker Dennis Hastert. And with help from a visit by Vice President Dick Cheney, he'd raised $1.1 million before the race against Duckworth even began. Duckworth had raised $520,000 in a much shorter time—an impressive amount—but she'd had to spend $400,000 to win her primary, leaving her with a fraction of Roskam's war chest. For Duckworth—and Emanuel—the hard part was just starting.

6

SIGNS OF SPRING

If Republicans hoped the new year would bring a respite from their troubles, or a chance to regroup and launch a counteroffensive, they were disappointed. It was a bad January for the GOP. Hardly had the festivities of New Year's Day 2006 died down when Jack Abramoff, a well-connected Republican lobbyist, pleaded guilty on January 3 to conspiracy, tax evasion, and mail fraud. This set the stage for the coming year, the election year itself. It was hard to envision a more vivid embodiment of corrupt Washington than Abramoff: He admitted he'd tried to influence members of Congress by paying for their luxury trips and inviting them to meals at his upscale restaurant, Signatures. He also acknowledged defrauding Indian tribes who'd paid him millions to lobby for the right to run casinos.

Abramoff's plea, which raised the prospect that several Republican lawmakers could be indicted before the election, sent a tremor through the GOP establishment. Emanuel and Sarah Feinberg, the DCCC's press secretary, agreed in a hurried phone conversation to make no public statements on Abramoff, for the usual reason: It risked transforming a story damaging to Republicans into routine political bickering. But the next day, worried that reporters were not sufficiently emphasizing the connections between the disgraced lobbyist and the congressional Republicans he had courted, Emanuel convened a strategy meeting with top staffers. Emanuel wanted to be sure voters thought of this as a specifically Republican scandal, not an "everybody does it" scandal. It was agreed that DCCC staffers would quietly furnish reporters with lists of Republicans who had received donations from Abramoff and would urge Democratic candidates to declare their outrage at Abramoff's lobbying excesses. Lapp, meanwhile, capitalized on the scandal by sending out another fundraising appeal. "The Republicans are scared," Lapp wrote. "They know their time is up. But they are going to fight harder and dirtier than ever. We need to have the resources to fight back."

The Abramoff plea had a quick ripple effect. Three days later, Tom DeLay announced he was permanently quitting as House Republican leader. DeLay had provisionally stepped down from his leadership post after being indicted, but this made it permanent and allowed House Republicans to choose a new leader. DeLay and Abramoff were close, and DeLay had been facing pressure from Republican colleagues worried that he would be drawn into the scandal and endanger the entire party. Republican leaders' relief at DeLay's resignation was barely hidden beneath their laudatory statements. House Speaker Dennis Hastert called DeLay's move "an honorable decision," and Republican campaign chairman Tom Reynolds praised his "selfless devotion and unyielding dedication." Emanuel was worried that with DeLay's resignation, voters would believe the Republicans had put their scandals behind them. "Republicans have addressed a party problem, but not the institutional problem of corruption," Emanuel told reporters. "With the permanence of their special-interest philosophy, a change in the Republican cast of characters simply doesn't matter."

DeLay's departure gave Democrats an enormous psychological boost. With his ostentatious piety, his dubious tactics, his open hatred of liberals—and, most of all, his repeated tactical successes—DeLay was the embodiment of ruthless Republican power. A former exterminator, he had openly warned lobbying firms to hire only Republicans if they wanted access to Congress. He had enforced party discipline, earning the nickname "The Hammer" by ensuring that individual Republicans did not stray from the party's positions. DeLay had been a catalyst in the impeachment of President Bill Clinton, and when some House Republicans favored less drastic measures, DeLay had goaded them onward. His public comments reflected hostility toward not just liberals but also many of the realities of modern life. After the 1999 massacre at Columbine High School in Colorado, DeLay had hit back hard against the idea of reexamining gun laws. "Guns have little or nothing to do with juvenile violence," he had declared, saying the violence was due rather to parents who put their kids in day care, women who used birth control, and schools that taught evolution. In the midst of the debate over terrorism and Iraq, DeLay had opined that "the blame-America-first hate speech of the American left has infected the Democratic Party's national leadership to a dangerous degree."

But Democrats could not simply dismiss DeLay as a zealot, because he coupled such statements with a devastating effectiveness. Two of his moves in particular had reflected his ability to bend the rules with apparent impunity. DeLay had engineered a 2003 redistricting in Texas that gave the Republicans six additional seats in the House, even though the state was not due for a redistricting for seven more years. And when President Bush's Medicare bill was headed for defeat, DeLay had played a key role in stretching a fifteen-minute vote to three hours so GOP leaders could pressure Republican representatives to change their votes.

Even more important than the psychological boost of DeLay's departure, however, was the fact that the public was beginning to equate Republicans with scandal, if Jay Leno's *Tonight Show* monologues were any guide, and they usually were. "Because of the Jack Abramoff and Duke Cunningham bribery scandals, Republicans in Congress are now putting together what they call a sweeping reform package," Leno joked one night in January. "It's such a popular idea, they're charging companies a million dollars to sponsor it."

With the political winds against him, Bush hoped to regroup with his fifth State of the Union address and lay out a Republican agenda for the election year. Emanuel, after a quick campaign swing to Pennsylvania earlier in the day, joined his colleagues in the U.S. Capitol to hear the president's address on the night of January 31. To the extent the speech contained a surprise, it was Bush's criticism of America's "addiction" to petroleum and his proposal to cut oil imports from the Middle East by 75 percent. But for a speech that had been billed as outlining a new Republican message, it was surprisingly devoid of content.

The GOP missteps showed no signs of stopping. The White House struck a deal allowing the takeover of operations at six U.S. ports by a state-owned company from the United Arab Emirates. The notion of Arabs running American port operations proved politically explosive, and Republicans joined Democrats in condemning the deal until the administration dropped it. A few days later a bomb destroyed one of the holiest Shiite shrines in Iraq, setting off a wave of sectarian killing that moved the country visibly closer to civil war. Even a freak accident, in which Vice President Cheney shot a friend in the face while hunting in mid-February, symbolized the Republicans' inability to regain the offensive.

But Emanuel was not in the mood to lie back and hope the Republicans' troubles did them in. The campaign had become in many ways an interplay between the Republicans' missteps and Emanuel's countermoves. Sometimes, Emanuel found, the best course was to stay out of the way. In other instances, he seized on a Republican mistake and trumpeted it. And in still other cases, the campaign's hard work was being done behind the scenes and far from the news spotlight.

The campaign had entered a phase when small crises seemed to erupt every few days. In late February, Emanuel ran into trouble with Charlie Wilson, an Ohio state senator he was grooming for an open seat in a Democratic district. Other Democrats were running as well, but Emanuel had pinned his hopes on Wilson, a funeral home operator and popular figure, even writing a $2,000 check himself to Wilson's campaign. Wilson, sixty-three, was a folksy sort, a large, ruddy man with salt-and-pepper hair and broad shoulders who served as his own press secretary. His son Jason managed his campaigns, even while running the family-owned Wilson Furniture in Bridgeport, Ohio. This informality worried DCCC staffers, who had tried unsuccessfully to persuade Wilson to hire a professional campaign manager. But as the cutoff date approached for Wilson to file his official papers to run for Congress, including a petition with fifty signatures, everything seemed in order.

It wasn't. Wilson had gathered ninety-six signatures—almost double the number he needed—but it turned out only forty-eight were valid, because many of those who'd signed Wilson's petition lived outside his district. In a panic, Wilson tried to refile, but Ohio law did not allow this. "We had people that were eager to sign our petitions," Wilson explained later. "We checked them for being registered voters, but the area has been gerrymandered, so there are areas where one side of the street is in one district and the other side is not. So when we submitted our signatures, it was just a bureaucratic thing." That "bureaucratic thing," Democratic staffers joked ruefully, was called "the law." After intensive consultations, embarrassed Democratic officials realized Wilson would have to mount a write-in campaign to win the Democratic primary. If Wilson lost, the Democrats would be left with a weak candidate, essentially handing the seat to the Republicans. What should have been an easy race now would require time, effort, and money that could have been spent elsewhere. Worse, the episode gave Wilson and the DCCC an aura of incompetence. Professional politicians simply do not miss petition requirements, especially easy ones such as Ohio's. The Hotline, an online political diary, mused, "Did the DCCC just commit a blunder of epochal proportions? Or did they fall victim to the vagaries of complicated state ballot laws? Or to a stubborn candidate who let his son run his campaign? How did this happen?" In Ohio itself, political observers viewed the episode with interest. "This whole escapade involving Wilson's petitions is hardly fatal to his campaign," wrote Michael Meckler, an Ohio political blogger. "It does, however, create an impression that a certain coziness and lack of concern with ethics and the law permeates the politics of that region."

Emanuel was driven to distraction by the blunder, and he worried that Wilson would become shell-shocked. He urged aides to push Wilson to talk about substantive topics such as Medicare and national security. "I think he needs some issues," Emanuel said at one staff meeting. "I think he needs it psychologically, because all he's concerned with is how he fucked up." He turned to the practical aspects of running a write-in campaign, which no major party had done in recent memory. Voters had to be especially motivated, because they had to remember the candidate's name and spell it reasonably accurately. At Emanuel's request, former president Bill Clinton agreed to record a "robo-call," an automated telephone message urging Democrats to write in Wilson's name. Emanuel ordered his staff to focus on turning out African Americans and Hispanics, two groups with strong Democratic loyalties. The campaign by necessity would also feature old-fashioned electioneering touches, such as Charlie Wilson pens and a campaign song designed to burn his name into voters' brains. "I'm waiting for my song," Emanuel told his staff. "I'm waiting for my trinket. Make sure we find a fucking jingle about Charlie Wilson, something memorable on the radio." Sure enough, Ohio radio stations shortly began playing a catchy, country-style tune, complete with a fiddle part: "The second of May is Election Day / Charlie Wilson wants to be our congressman / But a technicality is keeping Charlie off the ballot / So now we're going to have to write him in." The song proved popular, and Wilson decided that if he won, he would use it in future campaigns with the words changed. Wilson's television ads, meanwhile, did not just promote his candidacy but were full-fledged voting primers that explained how to write in a candidate on Election Day.

The Democrats ultimately spent more than $440,000 on the write-in, money they had planned to spend elsewhere. Republicans, smelling blood, spent a similar amount in an attempt to knock off Wilson. But the Democrats' desperation not to lose the seat proved a strong motivator. Wilson and his supporters knocked on more than 40,000 doors and made more than 280,000 phone calls. The district was in steel country, and labor unions joined in, making more than 100,000 calls and distributing 35,000 leaflets urging their members to vote. And Clinton recorded his robo-call as promised. Voters around southeast Ohio picked up their phones and heard the former president's familiar drawl saying, "I want you to remember to write-in Charlie's name on May second. Charlie has the most experience, best ideas, and he's supported by me. Republicans are attacking him, and Charlie Wilson could use your help." When it was over, Wilson secured a comfortable victory with 66 percent of the vote. "We moved forward with real vigor," Wilson said afterward. "There was nothing casual about this." But the result was an enormous relief for Emanuel, even if it was painful to have to expend so many resources on a race that should have been easy.

At the same time, Emanuel was talking to Paul Hackett, an enigmatic figure who had recently lost a campaign for Congress, but just barely. Hackett was a tall, handsome, Democratic ex-Marine who, after serving in Iraq, had jumped into a special election in the summer of 2005 when a local Ohio congressman left for a position in the Bush administration. Hackett was in many ways a dream candidate. Over six feet tall, with sharp blue eyes, sandy hair, and a ready grin, he appeared at ease with himself and conveyed a sense that he was speaking from the heart. He had a booming voice that could become gravelly. After launching into an impassioned monologue, he would pause, grin boyishly, and say, "But what do I know?" Hackett's district, based in Cincinnati, was perhaps the most Republican urban area in the country, but with the credibility of a veteran who'd volunteered for Iraq, Hackett did not shy from attacking the war or expressing contempt for President Bush. "I don't like the son-of-a-bitch that lives in the White House, but I'd put my life on the line for him," Hackett told USA Today. When the remark prompted criticism, he retorted, "I said it. I meant it. I stand by it." Many voters had found Hackett refreshingly unpolished. Others saw in him a thin-skinned quality and an overdeveloped sense of his own purity. But there was little question Hackett had an openness unusual in politics. To the surprise of virtually everyone, Hackett had almost won that 2005 special election, taking 48 percent to his opponent's 52 percent, the best showing by a Democrat in that district in decades. That made him an instant hero to the party's liberal activists and bloggers. Hackett came to symbolize an unapologetic fearlessness that many Democrats felt their party had lost, and the leftist magazine *Mother Jones* called Hackett "that rarest of modern political animals—a fighting Democrat."

After an aborted campaign for the Senate, Hackett was now looking at running once more for the House seat he'd almost won. In late February, he called Emanuel, told him he was ready to run for the House seat, and asked for Emanuel's help.

Emanuel was happy to give it. Jean Schmidt, the Republican who'd narrowly defeated Hackett in 2005, had hardly distinguished herself in Congress. Her most infamous moment came when she essentially called Congressman John Murtha, a respected military veteran, a coward for advocating a troop pullout from Iraq, setting off a near riot on the House floor as lawmakers from the two parties surged toward one another. In a year with a strong Democratic tide, Emanuel felt Hackett could beat Schmidt. Emanuel's staff, at Hackett's request, spent several days talking to the press to pave the way for his renewed candidacy. But suddenly Hackett stopped returning their calls. Then he told the *New York Times* he was quitting politics altogether and would skip the House race. Hackett concluded his political career on February 14 by issuing a statement that cast him as a heroic outsider forced from politics by party hacks. "I made this decision reluctantly, only after repeated requests by party leaders, as well as behind-the-scenes machinations that were intended to hurt my campaign," he said. He had decided not to run for the House seat, he added, because he'd promised other candidates he would not do so. "I said it. I meant it. I stand by it. At the end of the day, my word is my bond and I will take it to my grave." That was news to Emanuel, since a few days earlier, Hackett had told the DCCC he was planning to jump in the race. Hackett concluded his statement, "Rock on."

If the Charlie Wilson episode was a nuisance and Hackett's decision baffling, a third problem threatened broader ramifications: Hurricane Katrina had eviscerated the Democratic city of New Orleans. That meant the party could lose House seats, but no one knew for sure. It was not clear whether the residents who fled the city would vote in New Orleans, in their temporary hometowns, or not at all. A civil rights group called

FairVote, even after studying New Orleans' electoral situation in depth, could not determine what the sudden population shifts would mean politically. "There has hardly been anything like this in American history," said Rob Richie, the group's executive director. "The only precedent is probably the Civil War, where we continued to have elections but there were some massive shifts in who was voting and where." Andrew Koneschusky, spokesman for the Louisiana Democratic Party, acknowledged that it was impossible to tell whether the situation would help Democrats or Republicans. "It depends who comes back, who doesn't, what absentee turnout is like. It's impossible to tell unless you have a crystal ball," Koneschusky said. "The whole thing is fluid."

Inside the DCCC, this uncertainty was causing anxiety. "One thing I don't have a handle on is, where did all the voters go?" Lapp said plaintively. The most obvious challenge was Louisiana's Second Congressional District, which encompassed almost all of New Orleans and had long been represented by William Jefferson, a cerebral Harvard Law School graduate and the first African American congressman from Louisiana since Reconstruction. Because the majority of those who died or fled New Orleans were poor blacks, the city had been left whiter, richer, and presumably more Republican. Complicating matters, Jefferson was the subject of a federal bribery investigation. If he was indicted or pleaded guilty and was forced to resign, that could throw his district into chaos, forcing a special election before either side was ready for it. "Any day we could wake up and Jefferson could have cut a deal behind our backs," Emanuel said. Other Louisiana districts were worrisome also, but the overriding factor was uncertainty. An internal memo prepared for Emanuel by his staff emphasized the need to find displaced Democrats and make sure they knew where to vote. Its most intriguing conclusion, however, was that Democrats who had resettled in upstate Louisiana could swing traditionally Republican districts to the Democrats. "An aggressive voter registration program in those districts could add thousands of Democratic voters to the voter rolls there and have a huge impact on Democratic performance on Election Day," it concluded. But the uncertainty was such that shortly after writing the memo, staffers admitted they were not sure it was accurate.

Even while troubleshooting, Emanuel worked to ensure that his broad message, that Republicans had lost touch with ordinary people, stayed before the public. A rare opportunity came along in April, when gas prices began soaring. Oil was hovering near $73 a barrel and prices at the pump surged toward $3 a gallon, then beyond. Many families were rethinking their summer vacation plans, and their dissatisfaction was a warning light for Republicans who had been counting on the economy as a bright spot in an otherwise bleak political landscape. Emanuel, who was out of town, phoned his staff and told them to push Democratic candidates to blame Republicans for the high gas prices. On Thursday, April 20, the DCCC sent a memo to its candidates titled "Rising Gas Prices—Some Suggestions on Addressing the Issue." It encouraged Democrats to connect high gas prices to a Republican Party beholden to an "excessively profitable" oil and gas industry. "Show voters that when you come to Congress, you will fight for changes in the way that Congress does business and a new set of priorities when it comes to energy policy," the memo instructed. "Hold an event at a gas station or other logical location where you call for a real commitment to bringing down gas prices and pledge that, as a member of Congress, you will fight for families in your district."

Several Democratic candidates—including John Cranley in Ohio, Patsy Madrid in New Mexico, and Ron Klein in Florida—followed the DCCC script and held press conferences criticizing the GOP's energy policies. With little other news, the Democratic offensive on gasoline attracted attention from television reporters. DCCC communications director Bill Burton was sitting in his office one day when Emanuel called in for a report. "Cranley, Madrid, and Klein are all doing gas price events today," Burton told him. "I sent CNN to them. We're getting calls from three network producers—NBC, CBS, and CNN. In fact, NBC is on hold right now." Burton then disconnected from Emanuel and switched over to the NBC producer, who was looking for a Democratic candidate he could film railing against high gas prices. Burton reeled off several candidates and urged the producer to send cameras to their press conferences.

A few days later, Emanuel teamed up with Senator Charles Schumer, who headed the Democrats' Senate campaigns, for a television-friendly event designed to hammer on the issue of gas prices even harder. Aides had erected a blue backdrop designed to resemble a gas station pricing sign. On the day Bush was elected, it showed, gas had cost $1.59 a gallon; on the day he signed the Republican energy bill, it was $2.23; and on April 27, the day of the news conference, it was $3.18. Cameras from NBC, CNN, and ABC were there. Schumer, wearing a dark suit and kelly green tie, looked soft and pale next to the small, dark Emanuel. "High gas prices are going to be the final nail in the GOP Congress' coffin this November," Schumer said. "The Big Five oil companies have their hands around the neck of the American people"—Schumer pantomimed choking himself—"and they're not going to let go."

A reporter asked Schumer and Emanuel what cars they had driven to the press conference, hoping to trap them into admitting they had used gas-guzzling limousines. Schumer answered happily that he had driven a Toyota Prius, a gas-efficient hybrid. Emanuel said he had come in a mid-sized Ford Taurus. But as he answered, Emanuel became increasingly annoyed at the gotcha-style question. He indignantly pulled fare cards for the Chicago and Washington transit systems out of his pocket to show that he used public transportation. "I'm not playing this game," he said with irritation.

Republicans, recognizing the political explosiveness of high gas prices, tried urgently to reshape the debate. They were now confronting the downside of holding absolute power in Washington: The opposition can pound you for anything that goes wrong, from the actions of distant rogue nations to troubling economic news. Bush quickly halted deposits to the Strategic Petroleum Reserve and authorized lifting some environmental regulations, more to show he was taking action than in hopes of actually driving down prices. The NRCC also issued a statement on gas prices, but rather than focus on the hardships facing Americans, it zeroed in on Emanuel, in what had become a near obsession. "Today's press conference is nothing but another slick Rahm Emanuel–led Democrat attempt at making political hay with the pinch Americans continue to feel at the pump," the statement said. It went on to list how Emanuel had voted on six energy bills, as though most Americans cared about Emanuel's congressional voting record or even knew who he was. From the beginning, Reynolds and his staff had been consumed by Emanuel, and it was starting to badly distort their communication strategy. Many of their public pronouncements missed a crucial point: As the party in power, the GOP could successfully be attacked on issues like corruption and gas prices, while the Democrats, who obviously had little influence in Washington, could not. Blasting Bush and DeLay was effective because they were well known; blasting Emanuel, still a relatively obscure congressman, was nearly pointless. Yet sometimes it seemed the bulk of the Republicans' press strategy was to provide a running commentary on Emanuel's performance. "Kids Running the Show at DCCC," one Republican press release was headlined, although most Americans had never heard of the DCCC. "Hey Rahm, do you still need 5 Kerrys?" began another statement, criticizing an obscure comment Emanuel had made supporting Senator John Kerry.

Seizing on the spike in gas prices fit nicely into Emanuel's message: Republicans, in power too long, were cozy with "special interests" such as the oil lobby, and hardworking Americans were paying the price. This quick hammering of Republicans was also an example of the new aggressiveness Emanuel had brought to the DCCC. Other campaign chiefs would doubtless have spoken out about high gas prices as well. But Emanuel did it with particular speed and directness, quickly shaping a national message and aggressively pushing his candidates to deliver that message. Indeed, the instructions on gas prices were part of a stream of directives the DCCC was sending Democratic candidates on how to speak on various topics. The memos often treated the candidates like novices to be led through the simplest political tasks. One memo, for example, advised candidates to attack Bush's Medicare drug program by criticizing it for containing a "complexity tax," which was another way of saying it was complicated. "One idea is to use a banner that says 'Let Medicare Be Medicare,'" the memo added helpfully.

As their joint press conference on gas prices showed, Emanuel and Schumer had developed a symbiotic relationship. Just as Emanuel's task was to retake the House, Schumer's mission was to win back the Senate. The two were not close friends, but in many ways the men leading the Democratic campaigns for Congress were remarkably similar. Both were tough, aggressive Jewish politicians who had risen to power through big-city politics. Schumer's desire for the limelight was so well known it had become a cliché on Capitol Hill. He and Emanuel spoke often, conferring on polling and the public mood, bouncing ideas off each other. Emanuel's daughter Ilana, eight, had begun imitating her father's phone conversations with Schumer. "Chuck!" she would say. A pause, then louder, *"Chuck!"* "They are like Batman and Robin," said Sean Sweeney, who was on Emanuel's staff and had worked for Schumer, "but each one thinks the other is Robin." Schumer had fewer races to worry about, but in many ways his task was harder than Emanuel's. Democrats needed six Republican seats to regain the Senate majority, but they seemed to have a good shot at just two—in Pennsylvania, where Republican senator Rick Santorum was highly unpopular, and Rhode Island, a heavily Democratic state. It was hard to see where the other four seats would come from. Even analysts who thought the Democrats had a shot at the House considered the Senate out of reach.

Emanuel and Schumer, two instinctively aggressive politicians, were running their campaigns in remarkably similar ways. Both believed in responding instantly to Republican attacks. Schumer had a rule that any GOP attack must be answered within twenty-four hours. Both were also prodigious fund-raisers. They tried to recruit conservative candidates in conservative areas—Schumer had brought in Jon Tester in Montana and Jim Webb in Virginia, for example, each of them to the right of the Democratic Party in many ways. And they were willing to steamroll Democratic candidates they viewed as likely losers in order to make way for those they considered more viable. There also were differences, of course. Schumer in public exhibited a comfortable geniality, while Emanuel was sharper and more restless. At their joint press conferences, Emanuel often fidgeted while Schumer was talking.

Because Emanuel and Schumer liked sound bites, their appearances could resemble two men reading off a series of colorful quotes. At one Emanuel-Schumer press conference on the Republican "rubber stamp Congress," the two campaign chiefs stood behind a podium adorned with an image of a rubber stamp. Schumer began. "The inclination of the Republican Congress is when the president says, 'Jump,' they say, 'How high?'" he said. "Republicans seem to be allergic to oversight." Then it was Emanuel's turn. "This is a Congress that has perfected the 'hear no evil, see no evil' approach to governing," he said. "Forget the compassionate conservative—some of us would settle for a competent conservative. . . . This election will be a rendezvous with their record. . . . They couldn't spot George Bush in a lineup right now, but they have five years of running as George Bush's partner. . . . Their mind-set is, follow the leader." Sometimes Schumer and Emanuel seemed to view each other with amusement, two political animals who acknowledged each other's skills but could see through each other's tricks. At another press conference, Schumer opened by saying the congressional Republicans had been marching so much in lockstep with Bush that they resembled "the Stepford Wives." Then he faced Emanuel and said, "Pretty good, huh?" Turning back to the audience in a theatrical aside, Schumer added, "I've sunk to Rahm's level."

Emanuel's relationship with the House candidates went far beyond memos on how to frame issues. He had persuaded many of these men and women to run, and he was enormously invested in their success. Emanuel called them frequently, going down a list of roughly fifty candidates every few days. "Hey, it's Rahm," he would say brusquely. "What's goin' on?" He made it clear he was always watching and judging. There would be consequences if they did not perform, from being yelled at to losing all support. Emanuel did make the occasional encouraging remark, but in a fierce style. His typical sign-off was, "All right, buddy. Fuck you. I love you."

In a conversation with Joe Sestak, a Pennsylvania candidate for whom he had high hopes, Emanuel delivered good news. "Joe Sestak—this is your rabbi, Rahm," he said. "Two things. Clinton—I'm close to having him do an event for you in Philly. And . . . he will do an event for you in New York City." Former president Bill Clinton was admired by many Democrats as the party's last big winner, and his ability to help a candidate was invaluable. "Clinton will put his arm around you and say, 'He's my man,'" Emanuel promised. In a later call, Sestak asked if there was any way Emanuel could direct more money his way. Emanuel agreed to ask Senator John Kerry, who was sending an e-mail to his supporters, to ask them to contribute to Sestak. "I'll try," Emanuel said. "I can't promise. You're doing well, and others don't have the same network. I'll try to get you on the Kerry e-mail." He concluded, "Don't fuck it up or I'll fuck you. I'll kill you. All right, I love you. Bye."

At another point Emanuel called Diane Farrell, the Democrat challenging Congressman Chris Shays in Connecticut. "Diane—it's Rahm," he said. "The Republicans haven't put any money down on your race. They may, but they haven't. So I want you to tell your campaign manager to get off my back. Second, I'll get you a date to have Mrs. Clinton come out there." Farrell then asked Emanuel how she should respond to the insistence by Shays, a moderate, that he had the same position on Iraq as she did. "No, you don't have the same position," he said. "He's given [the administration] a blank check." He recited what Farrell's message should be: "'For three and a half years, you haven't asked any questions. I'd ask questions. Our position is not the same.'" Emanuel often warned candidates to brace themselves for the Republicans' attacks. "They're going to come after you," he warned Pennsylvania candidate Chris Carney. "You haven't said anything stupid on the hustings, have you? . . . Well, don't waste your time with me. Go raise some more money."

He also had to deliver bad news. Nevada candidate Jill Derby called on one occasion to ask plaintively if Nancy Pelosi could host a fund-raiser for her. Derby's candidacy was not quite promising enough for that, Emanuel felt. "The notion that Nancy would host an event for you, given everything she's got to do, I don't think is real," Emanuel said. Then, in a bit of advice that sounded strange coming from a Democratic leader, Emanuel urged Derby to distance herself from the party, because of her conservative district. "There, you can't be a Democrat. You have to be an independent," he said. "My thing is, you want to own this word: *independent, independent, independent*. The more you look like a party member in a 39 percent [Democratic] district, it ain't cool."

Emanuel had an instinctive connection with some candidates. Chris Murphy was a young Connecticut state senator who, like Emanuel, had run tough campaigns before seeking office himself. Now he was trying to knock off Congresswoman Nancy Johnson, a popular figure in her moderate district. "Part of the reason I decided to [run] was based on my first meeting with Rahm," Murphy said. "As much as this game is based on numbers and polling, it is also having a hunch about the guy on the other side. I had a hunch about Rahm—that he is the kind of guy I wanted to go to bat for me in D.C. And I think he had a hunch about me, that I'm the kind of guy he wanted on the ground. I'm a young guy. I could have held on to my state senate seat for a while and run for Congress when it was open. So it was no small decision for me to run. But I was becoming convinced that this was a unique year and that the DCCC had their act together in a way that I hadn't seen before."

Emanuel also ignored many candidates. He had limited resources and he wanted to invest them wisely. John Laesch, who was trying to unseat House Speaker Dennis Hastert, was among those Emanuel believed had no chance. Laesch, a military veteran, had his strong suits—he had grown up on a local farm, been captain of his high school soccer team, served in the Navy, and worked as a carpenter. But Emanuel did not talk to Laesch, and even the midlevel DCCC staffer in charge of the Midwest could not find time for him. "Rahm Emanuel's job is to raise money so we can change the system, and he is doing a good job of raising money," Laesch said forlornly. "But I think they are not looking at the big picture. . . . Rahm has his own strategy, and apparently I will have to adapt mine."

If there was any candidate who should have been able to capture Emanuel's attention, it was Dan Seals. Seals was running to represent Emanuel's parents' district, and Benjamin and Marsha Emanuel had a

"Dan Seals for Congress" sign in their front yard. Seals was an attractive African American running in a Democratic, largely wealthy suburban area. Senator Barack Obama had hosted a fund-raiser for him. Seals, a longtime Democrat, had become frustrated after the 2004 election and begun attending local party events. His charisma was hard to miss, and soon Democratic leaders asked him to take on Republican congressman Mark Kirk. Seals refused, then reconsidered. "I had some late-night conversations with my wife—that's the first vote you need—and decided to do it," he said. Seals, a marketing director at GE Commercial Finance, began speaking in living rooms to groups of twenty to fifty voters, gaining momentum in a district that had voted for Al Gore and John Kerry. One of Seals' themes was that Kirk talked like a moderate when in Illinois but voted like a hard-line conservative in Washington. However, Kirk was popular, smart, and well-funded, and the polls suggested that Seals, for all his efforts, was not mounting a serious threat. So, unlike Emanuel's favored candidates, Seals had no Democratic congressman assigned to him as a "mentor." He did not qualify for the "Red-to-Blue" list, meaning Emanuel did not urge donors to give him money. DCCC staffers were helpful when Seals called to talk strategy, but that was about it. Emanuel told Seals bluntly that his candidacy did not merit help from the DCCC, at least not yet. "He was very direct," Seals said. All Seals could do was work hard and hope his campaign began to blossom. "Rahm helps those who help themselves," he said.

As Emanuel was picking and choosing between Democratic challengers, he was also prodding current Democratic congressmen who might be vulnerable. Some of them, he worried, were not doing enough to hold on to their seats. "They need to know someone is watching them, because they'll quickly take the off-ramp and sit at the White Hen Pantry for a year," he told his staff. While the Democrats were fighting to capture seats from Republicans, they could ill afford to lose many of their own. Emanuel and his staff sometimes seemed to feel more anxiety about saving these lawmakers' careers than the congressmen themselves did. It was an axiom of politics that any good politician was a professional paranoid, but in fact many came to believe the voters loved them too much ever to reject them. It was the job of Emanuel and Ali Wade, the staffer who ran the DCCC's "Frontline" program for protecting incumbents, to shake such members from their complacency and impress upon them the jeopardy they faced. Many of these congressmen represented Southern districts that had become increasingly Republican since they were first elected. "A lot of times guys who have been around a long time don't realize that if they are challenged in the right way they could be vulnerable," said Wade, a wholesome-looking Seattle native with long blond hair. "They're so used to winning easily. A lot of them have not had to run a campaign in decades."

Emanuel had forced these imperiled lawmakers to sign a "memorandum of understanding" requiring them to raise at least $1.8 million by March 31, 2006. The document also formalized such commitments as "The Frontline member agrees to acquire and/or employ the technology needed to run an effective and efficient campaign operation." Some long-time members of Congress considered this insulting, but Emanuel was determined not to have them lose through overconfidence.

These endangered incumbents came in all stripes. Congressman Leonard Boswell had for a decade represented Des Moines and its environs, an area almost evenly split between Democrats and Republicans. Boswell, seventy-two, had recently undergone stomach surgery, and the Republicans had recruited an energetic challenger for his seat. Congressman John Spratt, a South Carolina Democrat first elected in 1982, represented a district that had become increasingly Republican, and President Bush had won 57 percent of the vote there in 2004. His opponent, state legislator Ralph Norman, was a stronger candidate than Spratt had faced in a decade. The Republicans were gunning for Spratt, with Cheney and Karl Rove visiting the district to raise money. The DCCC was struggling to find a top-notch campaign manager for Spratt, who was not accustomed to competitive races.

But the most worrisome incumbent was Congressman Alan Mollohan. Emanuel had been trying for months to persuade Mollohan, who'd been in Congress for twenty-two years, that he could face a true threat this time. His home state of West Virginia, long a Democratic stronghold with its mining and union traditions, had been trending conservative for years. Even after a respectable Republican opponent, state delegate Chris Wakim, jumped in the race, Mollohan had been reluctant to raise much money, believing that would show voters he was scared. Emanuel was appalled by that sort of thinking. Increasingly concerned, he even called Congressman John Murtha, a former Marine whom Mollohan respected, and asked Murtha to urge Mollohan to pull himself together.

Then the news got worse. In April, the *Wall Street Journal* reported that Mollohan had directed more than $150 million in federal funds to non-profit groups he had helped create in West Virginia. That funding helped pay generous salaries for Mollohan supporters. For Republicans, the news was a gift. Not only did it provide powerful ammunition against a vulnerable Democrat, it helped offset the Democratic portrait of the GOP as the party of corruption.

The Democrats scrambled to control the damage. DCCC press secretary Sarah Feinberg, who happened to be from West Virginia, called reporters she knew throughout the state to insist that the allegations against Mollohan reflected a political vendetta. At the very least, the mini-scandal appeared finally to wake up the congressman. He began raising money and aggressively blaming Rove for the ethics allegations. The Republicans turned up the pressure also, sending Cheney to the district in late April to raise money for Wakim. The battle had now been joined at a higher level. Emanuel hated the idea that he might unnecessarily lose a longtime incumbent, and he ordered his staff to begin looking for dirt on Mollohan's opponent. A few weeks later, Christina Reynolds, the DCCC's research director, reported to Emanuel that Wakim seemed to have fudged his resumé—he claimed to have a Harvard degree and be a Gulf War veteran, but it was not clear that either was true. She was still looking into it. "Hopefully [we] can muddy the waters," she said.

At the same time he was prodding Democrats, Emanuel continued to goad Republicans in every way possible, from grand strategy to lowbrow taunts. He was in his campaign office one Friday when CNN correspondent Andrea Koppel appeared on the wall-mounted television to report on a brief speech Emanuel had given on the House floor that morning. Koppel showed footage of Emanuel reading a poem poking fun at the Republican Congress, based on Elizabeth Barrett Browning's "How do I love thee?" As the real Emanuel watched himself in amusement, the televised Emanuel read, "Dear K Street lobbyists, How do I love thee? Let me count the ways. I love thee to the depths of thy oil wells, For thou shall have $14.5 billion to drill them." This went on for several more lines. Koppel wrapped up by saying, "That's Rahm Emanuel, the tough talker from Chicago, having a Shakespearean moment." Emanuel was clearly pleased as he watched himself. A young staffer had come up with the verse, he explained, and he'd appropriated it for the floor speech. Emanuel's poetic reading prompted NRCC spokesman Carl Forti, ever fascinated with Emanuel and his ballet dancing, to issue a public response. "My curiosity was piqued today when I saw you on C-SPAN delivering a poem, and though I admit I was disappointed your presentation was not accompanied by an interpretive dance, I found your display quite inspiring nonetheless," Forti wrote.

All the while, the Republicans' fortunes continued to fall. John Lapp, the DCCC executive director, had just arrived at home on April 3, near midnight after a long day, when his Treo rang. It had been set to ring when news alerts came across with specific names, including "Tom DeLay." The news this time was that DeLay, succumbing to pressure from increasingly worried Republicans, was quitting Congress altogether. Six months earlier DeLay had been one of the most powerful figures in Washington; now he was gone. Lapp and other DCCC staffers tried to call Emanuel in Chicago several times, but uncharacteristically they could not reach him. They speculated that one of his children was sick or his cell phone was not working. In fact, Emanuel was spending the evening watching college basketball with his kids when his BlackBerry began vibrating. When he saw that DeLay had resigned, Emanuel decided to remain incommunicado, believing there was little useful he could do or say that night. So his staffers crafted a cautious statement without Emanuel and waited until the next morning to issue a comment over his name. Emanuel wanted to sharply dispute any sense that with DeLay out of Congress, the GOP had cleaned up its act. "National Republicans want you to believe they have turned the page, but the Republican culture of putting the special interests first does not revolve around just one man," Emanuel's statement said. He appeared on three television shows and a radio program on the night of April 4 to make that point.

The same day, Congressman John Boehner, the new House Republican leader, held a "pen-and-pad" briefing for reporters in DeLay's former suite, with the backdrop of a large plasma television screen displaying the seal of the House of Representatives. During the question-and-answer period, a reporter read Emanuel's statement aloud from her BlackBerry and asked for Boehner's response. "His job is to play partisan politics. Let him play it," said Boehner. "I don't have to get into that." But the real question for the Democrats was how to make the best use of DeLay's exit. Democrats denied it, but losing DeLay deprived them of a villain who was useful for energizing activists and raising money. "I think it's a good thing for our party," Republican congressman Ray LaHood of Illinois said of DeLay's departure. "I think it really neuters the Democrats' ability to use him in their fall campaign, making vulnerable members look like they were all in the same boat he was." Privately, many Democrats agreed. Emanuel ordered his staff to draw up a list of all Republicans who had taken money from DeLay or his former aide Tony Rudy, who had recently pleaded guilty to conspiracy charges. Emanuel also asked for the name of every House Republican who had voted to let DeLay stay on as majority leader even after he was indicted. "And just go after them," Emanuel told his staff. "I want them to have to answer questions this week back in their districts."

In DeLay's own district, his departure actually made it harder for the Democrats to win. This was a heavily Republican area that President Bush had carried in 2004 with 64 percent of the vote. Even so, DeLay had become such a villain that the Democratic candidate, Nick Lampson, himself a former congressman, had a legitimate chance to knock him off. But now, Lampson would face a fresh, presumably untainted Republican.

As spring drew to a close, the Republican disintegration and Emanuel's offensive came together to create a pivotal point in the campaign. The Iraq war was deteriorating, Bush's domestic agenda was unpopular, and Abramoff and DeLay had become symbols of Republican corruption. At the same time, Emanuel was riding herd on Democratic challengers and incumbents. Other Democrats were working hard also—Pelosi was campaigning and raising money, and grassroots activists were making calls and knocking on doors for their candidates. If the campaign had a turning point, a crossroads when the accumulated weight of Republican problems made it possible they could lose the House, not just hypothetically but actually, it was May 2006. Many figured the Democrats would still find a way to lose, but the notion of a Democratic victory no longer seemed laughable.

The polls in May showed Bush's approval ratings at record lows. Bush, in fact, had become about as unpopular as it is possible for a president to be, given that any chief executive will always have a certain bedrock level of support. And for the first time, Democrats were benefiting by comparison. Americans told pollsters they believed the Democrats would do a better job on Iraq, gas prices, immigration, taxes, drug prices, and civil liberties. A Harris Interactive poll showed Bush's approval at 29 percent and Congress' at 18 percent. President Richard Nixon's approval rating had reached 24 percent shortly before he resigned in 1974—after lying, breaking the law, and throwing the country into its gravest constitutional crisis since the Civil War—and Bush was only five points higher.

Most important, for the first time, the Republicans' popularity had sunk low enough to affect the number of seats in play. Until now, the Republicans' loss of support had changed the likely makeup of the House only slightly, because so many districts were firmly Democratic or solidly Republican. But now GOP seats were in jeopardy even in Republican areas, and even in districts represented by popular incumbents. And the identity of some of the vulnerable Republicans was equally surprising—

such as Deborah Pryce of Ohio, the fourth-ranking House Republican, and Thelma Drake of Virginia, whose district was a center of military culture and the evangelical movement. The depths to which Republican support had to sink for Democrats to have even a shot at those seats was a testament to the rigidity of the system, but the chances of a takeover were higher than they had yet been.

It was now almost exactly six months before Election Day, and Emanuel decided to summon fellow House Democrats to a DCCC meeting room. For a year and a half Emanuel had walked a fine line, hoping to excite Democrats for battle without unduly raising expectations. But the time had come to unleash whatever enthusiasm he could. As several dozen House members, accustomed to plusher settings, settled themselves into rows of hard plastic chairs, Emanuel began with a PowerPoint presentation on recent polls, which suggested that many voters in key districts were ready for a change. Then he rolled a video, which flashed quotes such as one from Republican pollster Tony Fabrizio confessing, "These numbers are scary." The soundtrack featured the pumping rhythm of the song "Another One Bites the Dust" as images appeared onscreen of Republicans recently felled by scandal, including DeLay and Duke Cunningham. DeLay was shown saying earnestly, "I have absolutely no fear about any investigation into me or any of my activities." Then the subject switched to the Democrats, and the music changed to a song called "Clocks," by the band Coldplay, chosen for its stirring melody. Democratic House candidates such as Francine Busby of California and Brad Ellsworth of Indiana appeared onscreen. The video concluded with the line "Together we will win this November." The lawmakers applauded as the lights went up.

Emanuel then went over the campaign race by race, making the case that a majority was within the Democrats' grasp. As he went from one candidate to the next, the gathering took on a certain electricity. "The majority is not in this room," Emanuel said. "The majority is outside this room. We have to get outside this room and help these candidates in every possible way." It began to seem at least plausible to many of these jaded congressmen, in a way it had not before, that enough races could tilt the Democrats' way to produce a majority. "But it's only going to happen if we work hard," Emanuel said. He urged his colleagues not just to give money but to mentor candidates, campaign with them, give them personal advice. He had rarely focused so directly on the part of his job that involved not just enabling the Democrats to win but making them believe they could. Sitting in the audience, Congresswoman Jan Schakowsky was struck by the change. "Rahm has been very measured in his predictions," she said. "He himself has been saying for a long time he is certain we will pick up seats and we will do well, but he hadn't really said much about taking the majority. This was a different tone on his part, that he could really feel it out there, and he believed that the opportunities were sufficient if we did everything we needed to do." Congressman Elijah Cummings of Maryland had gone into the room unsure whether the Democrats could capture the House, but he left a believer. "I've never seen him in what I call his 'general' mode," Cummings said. "He reminded me of a general about to lead his troops into battle who knew that if they simply kept the faith and worked hard they would win. I believe that this is our time. This is it, right here. And we have to take advantage of it."

The question, with six months left, was whether Republicans would find a way, as they had so often, to reverse the momentum, energize their troops, change the conversation, and pull out a victory.

7

A FAMILIAR FEAR

emocratic staffers gathered at the DCCC offices on the night of June 6 to watch the results of a special election to fill the seat of California congressman Randy "Duke" Cunningham. Cunningham had resigned six months earlier after admitting to taking bribes from a defense contractor, and San Diego area voters were deciding who would represent them until the regular election on November 7. It was the last time a Democrat and a Republican would face off until Election Day, and both parties were eager to scrutinize the outcome for any clues about what voters were thinking. The stakes were especially high for Republicans, because Cunningham's district leaned conservative and Republican, and a defeat by the GOP candidate—former congressman Brian Bilbray, who had represented a nearby district until 2000—could presage major losses in November. If Bilbray lost, journalists no doubt would predict a Republican catastrophe on Election Day, and those forecasts could easily become self-fulfilling. As for the Democrats, if they could not prevail in a district whose Republican congressman had just resigned after being bribed with a Rolls-Royce and an antique French commode, among other things, it would bode poorly for the success of their attacks on a GOP "culture of corruption." Unfortunately for the Democrats, their candidate, school board member Francine Busby, was a former women's studies professor whose folksy personality fit uneasily with California's Fiftieth District. Republicans outnumbered Democrats in the district by 55,000, many military families made it their home, and President Bush had defeated John Kerry there by 55 percent to 45 percent. Yet Emanuel knew he would have to capture tough districts such as this to have any hope of winning a majority in November. Bilbray and Busby had each spent $1.2 million on the eight-week campaign. That was a considerable sum, but it was dwarfed by the national parties' contributions: The Democrats had spent $2 million, while the Republicans had expended a remarkable $5 million.

The staffers gathering that night at Democratic headquarters were far from confident. The Republican Bilbray, a former small-town mayor, was tanned and coiffed in his public appearances, and he could appear tightly wound as he lashed out on immigration or ethics. The timing of the campaign had been good for him in one big way: Just as the race was starting up, an anti-immigration backlash swept the country. As it happened, Bilbray had publicly taken a hard line on immigration for a long time, and he had worked for a group called the Federation for American Immigration Reform, among other organizations, since leaving Congress. He adopted "Proven tough on illegal immigration" as his campaign slogan, planning to ride the issue all the way to the election. It seemed to be working; the *San Diego Union-Tribune* endorsed Bilbray based "on this vital issue alone." Throughout the campaign, Bilbray highlighted his support for penalizing illegal aliens and building a fence along the U.S.-Mexico border, and he accused Busby of backing "amnesty" for illegal aliens. The issue was complicated, however, by the fact that President Bush supported the same moderate approach to immigration as Busby, the Democrat. So did popular Republican senator John McCain, who even canceled a campaign appearance with Bilbray over immigration.

Busby, for her part, stressed corruption and integrity in her campaign, echoing the Democrats' national theme. She often called her opponent "Lobbyist Bilbray"—as though lobbyist were a title, like doctor or professor—referring to the work he'd done since leaving Congress. One Democratic television spot revisited a privately funded trip Bilbray had taken to Australia as a congressman in 1999. It featured a kangaroo saying things like, "G'day, Mr. Bilbray!" and concluded with the tag line, "Brian Bilbray. Such a good friend to lobbyists, he became one himself." Bilbray responded by also attacking Congress—"Congress has let us down," he said on his Web site—even though he'd been part of it just a few years earlier. As the campaign heated up, both sides sought every edge. Vice President Dick Cheney and House Speaker Dennis Hastert visited California to raise money for Bilbray, and Pelosi appeared on Busby's behalf. An NRCC ad for Bilbray, eventually withdrawn, claimed that Busby had praised a teacher arrested in a child pornography case. Democrats went beyond traditional advertising to run campaign spots in the middle of radio traffic reports. After hearing during one rush hour that "an overturned big rig on its side is blocking the number two, three and four lanes," San Diego commuters were told, "Did you know Brian Bilbray took over $300,000 from energy interests? And Bilbray lobbied for a company implicated in price gouging." Then it was on to the weather.

As the election approached, polls showed the candidates in a dead heat. The DCCC aired its final ad on May 31, less than a week before the special election, showing Bilbray's face juxtaposed with phrases such as "high gas prices," "special interests," and "bribery scandal" floating in the background. "Do we really want more of the same in Congress?" it demanded. The Democrats also launched a last-minute robo-call, a recorded phone message by Al Gore aimed at encouraging Democrats to vote. "This is Al Gore calling on behalf of the Democratic Congressional Campaign Committee. I urge you to vote for Francine Busby," the former vice president told voters. "What we don't need is another energy industry lobbyist in Congress." Republicans fought back with robo-calls featuring President Bush, First Lady Laura Bush, and McCain. The GOP left little to chance: The Republican National Committee sent 160 volunteers to California, including 65 congressional staffers, on the campaign's final weekend. They insisted these efforts did not mean they were worried.

"It's a special election, it's the only general election in the country, and we wanted to make sure we had the necessary ground support to get out the vote," explained Republican spokesman Tucker Bounds. "We're excited about the opportunity. It's an open seat and we have a competitive candidate there."

Then Busby's campaign was roiled by a last-minute gaffe. She was speaking at the Jocelyn Senior Center in Escondido, a city with a large Hispanic population, and toward the end of her talk a man said in Spanish, "I want to help, but I don't have papers." His comment was translated and Busby replied, "Everybody can help. Yeah, absolutely, you can all help. You don't need papers for voting. You don't need to be a registered voter to help." In a district whose voters were frustrated by illegal immigration, Busby seemed to be telling undocumented aliens they could help on her campaign and even cast a vote for Congress. DCCC officials publicly minimized the blunder, but John Lapp, asked privately if the mistake was serious, answered, "Big-time." Certainly the Republicans thought so. They launched a final radio ad just hours before Election Day. "Francine Busby's own words: 'You don't need papers for voting,'" the narrator said. "That's right, Francine Busby says you don't need papers to vote. Brian Bilbray disagrees. . . . The more we find out about Busby, the worse it gets." As Democratic staffers began filtering into DCCC headquarters on Election Night, June 6, that was not the note on which they had hoped to end the campaign.

Capitol Hill was dark and quiet, but the DCCC offices were full of fidgety activity. Someone had sent over several cases of Corona, and communications director Bill Burton had bottles of wine and Jack Daniel's on his desk, which he and others sampled regularly. Emanuel showed up at 9:30 after a day of fund-raising in New York—yawning, his dark suit rumpled, his face exhausted. Busby had no chance, he predicted fatalistically. "I'm going to bed," he said. "E-mail me. I'll have my BlackBerry on my pillow." At 11:07, the absentee ballot results came in. "Oh my God— Busby only lost the absentee ballots by three thousand," Burton said. Bilbray had been expected to build a lead of ten thousand votes among absentees, since many of them came from the military, and the narrow margin was good news. "The gap's seven thousand smaller than everyone thought it would be," Burton told reporters calling in, spinning the early results. Off the phone, he added, "This will require more whiskey," pouring some into a paper cup. The news provided a jolt of hope. "We're having a temporary moment of irrational exuberance," Karin Johanson, the DCCC's new executive director, said dryly. She told political director Sean Sweeney, "Rahm wants us to call a lawyer, but the lawyer is asleep." Since the Bush-Gore presidential election, every election showing a hint of closeness prompted both parties to immediately contact attorneys.

The night unfolded with an erratic rhythm—long periods of expectant waiting punctuated by jolts when results came in. At 11:55, Congressman Mike Honda of California wandered in. Honda appeared to be tipsy; spotting the bottle of whiskey on Burton's desk, he noted amiably that whiskey should be sipped with ice. "I never drink," he said, and after a pause for comic timing, added, "Water." Taking several pretzels from a bag on Burton's desk, Honda intoned, "Make . . . it . . . happen," extending his arms before him as if casting a spell to help Busby win. It took until 1:26 A.M. for the first non-absentee results to arrive, and they were a disappointment, putting Bilbray at 50 percent and Busby at 43 percent. An air of resignation set in, and Bilbray held his lead throughout the night. At 4 A.M. the Associated Press declared Bilbray the winner by four percentage points. Republican House campaign chairman Tom Reynolds issued a victory statement at 6:37 A.M., ridiculing Democratic hopes for an upset and predicting they would be equally disappointed on November 7. "National Democrats did not discover their shockwave in San Diego," Reynolds said. "National Democrats must come to terms with the fact that momentum for the midterm elections will not materialize simply because they preordain it in the media or because they ask their special-interest friends to buy it for them."

The results were galling for Democrats who had been hoping for signs of a Democratic tidal wave. Bilbray apparently had won with relative ease. For public consumption, Emanuel and the Democrats dismissed

Bilbray's victory almost contemptuously, noting that the GOP had spent $5 million to hold on to a heavily Republican district, something they could hardly do all over the country. "Despite the spin, CA-50 is a ruby red Republican district," Burton said in a written statement after the election. "If San Diego costs them $5 million, how much are Philadelphia, Columbus, Palm Beach and New London going to cost?" But privately, Emanuel was furious and scared. The results were close to calamitous, in his view—they provided no evidence that Democrats were having success attracting moderates or Republicans. Even their own Democratic voters had not been especially energized to vote for Busby. The outcome threw into question Emanuel's entire strategy of focusing on Republican corruption. Emanuel was especially angry that Bilbray had run as a critic of Bush and the Democrats had let him get away with it. And he believed in retrospect that it had been a mistake not to run ads against Bilbray for opposing an increase in the minimum wage. He was mad at himself and mad at his staff. The day after the election, Emanuel summoned his top aides into his office and screamed. "If anybody fucking steals our message again, I'm going to shoot somebody, *and I mean it!*" he shouted. He insisted that the Democrats redouble their efforts to tie every Republican to Bush and that they seize on the minimum wage and other populist issues with renewed zeal. The defeat in California instilled a fear into Emanuel and his staff that drove the Democratic campaign into an even greater frenzy.

Busby's defeat triggered a familiar fear among Democrats. Notwithstanding the disastrous Iraq war, growing corruption scandals, and Bush's low popularity, the Democrats wondered if they would find a way to blow it. That anxiety was compounded by events over the next few days. American forces killed Abu Musab al-Zarqawi, a notorious leader of the Iraqi insurgency, on June 8. That same day, Prime Minister Nouri al-Maliki completed his cabinet, finalizing the first popularly elected government in Iraq. The developments were modest, but it was by any measure the president's first good week in about a year. The Gallup poll showed Bush's approval rating at 38 percent, still dangerously low, but significantly higher than his abysmal 31 percent in May and a clear improvement. Then special prose-cutor Patrick Fitzgerald announced that Karl Rove, Bush's top advisor, would not be indicted for his role in the leak of a CIA operative's name, removing a cloud over the White House and freeing the feared Rove to help Republicans plot strategy.

If the public felt even slightly more hopeful about Iraq, the White House recognized, Democratic hopes of big electoral gains would prob-ably be frustrated. So President Bush seized the initiative. In a single week in mid-June, he convened a cabinet session at Camp David, made a sur-prise visit to Baghdad, and held a Rose Garden press conference, all to emphasize that Iraq had turned a corner. Upon closer scrutiny, much of the "good news" involved Republicans either dodging a bullet or accom-plishing things that should have been done a long time ago. When a pres-ident is celebrating the fact that his top aide has escaped criminal charges, he is hardly on the political offensive. The formation of an Iraqi cabinet and the killing of al-Zarqawi, who had been harassing American troops for two and a half years, were long overdue, and the real story was how long they took, not that they'd finally been accomplished. But perception can be reality, and reporters wrote numerous stories about Bush having a "good run." That, in turn, affected predictions about the campaign. "Sud-denly, a solid Democratic showing in November appeared less of a sure bet," political scientist Larry Sabato wrote in his Crystal Ball newsletter on June 15. "Fewer analysts today than ten days ago will say definitively that Democrats will take control of either house of Congress." Cam-paigns always had ups and downs. But the 2006 campaign had so far involved an almost uninterrupted downward spiral for the Republicans, and this was the first stretch in which their fortunes improved.

Not content to let Republicans make gains on their own, the Democ-rats quickly set about hurting their own cause. Congressman John Murtha, a seventy-three-year-old Pennsylvania Democrat, startled his colleagues by writing each of them a letter saying he would run for majority leader should the Democrats win back the House. Murtha, a decorated Vietnam veteran who had served thirty-seven years in the Marines, had received a good deal of attention for a speech tearfully urging Bush to pull U.S. troops out of Iraq. It was compelling to see a craggy, conservative ex-Marine, a recipient of two Purple Hearts and a longtime cheerleader for the military, become an outspoken war critic. More important, it allowed Democrats with fewer military credentials to challenge the war, and many were grateful. All this apparently persuaded Murtha he would make a good party leader. "If we prevail, as I hope and know we will, and return to the majority this next Congress, I have decided to run for the open seat of majority leader," Murtha wrote fellow Democrats. The move greatly annoyed Emanuel and other leaders. If the Democrats did take over the House, Democratic leader Nancy Pelosi would become Speaker and Congressman Steny Hoyer of Maryland was in line to become majority leader. Murtha's letter was a grenade tossed into the accepted order. More important, voters might see this intra-party squabbling as arrogant, coming five months before an election whose outcome remained in doubt.

Hoyer, the man most affected by Murtha's declaration, was a smooth, gregarious politician who'd been working his way up in the House since his election in 1980. With a deep voice and snowy hair, he resembled an actor playing a congressman. He was also given to playful acts such as sitting among reporters at a press conference and pretending to ask tough questions of his colleagues. Jolted by Murtha's insurrection, Hoyer had his spokeswoman issue a statement noting pointedly that he had "the support of the overwhelming majority of House Democrats." Hoyer also mobilized his friends in Congress. "Our battle must be to elect Democrats in a minimum of fifteen more seats in November," Congresswoman Jane Harman of California said in a prepared statement. "When that happens, Steny Hoyer, who has been a tireless and loyal advocate for the party, will be the right person to serve as our majority leader."

Democrats could ill afford to look like they were bickering over spoils the voters had not yet awarded. Tom Reynolds, the Republican campaign leader, issued a gleeful press release. "I would be remiss if I did not point out that in order to have a leadership race, Democrats would have to do something they have not done for several cycles now—even with Rahm Emanuel at the helm—and that is win," Reynolds said. Under pressure from fellow Democrats, Murtha suspended his candidacy four days after it began, but the damage had been done.

The renewed Democratic anxiety was reflected in a blunt memo by strategists James Carville, Mark Gersh, and Stan Greenberg, sent to Pelosi on June 19 with Emanuel's support. The strategists, based on polling and discussions with voters, were worried that Democratic momentum had stalled, that the party was benefiting modestly from the Republican melt-down but failing to excite voters in any larger way. "We are concerned that Democrats will gain seats in November, but in insufficient numbers to win control of the House," the memo said. "The Party's image has weakened, not strengthened, producing a growing alienation with poli-tics and the parties that could limit our gains to perhaps a net ten seats." The strategists argued that Democratic voters were not motivated enough, in part due to disappointment at John Kerry's crushing loss in 2004. Carville had traveled the country speaking to activists, but "even his best speech to raise the passions ran into a wall of complaints about the Democrats," the memo said. "Enthusiasm is not high." DCCC focus groups in a crucial Connecticut district had been disappointing. "These are jaded, frustrated voters, but without any sense of the Democrats, their mood is more 'why bother' than 'throw the bums out,'" the memo reported. It was an extraordinary private confession of pessimism from a party supposedly riding high. When it came to prescriptions, the memo was vaguer, though it said Democratic candidates needed to show more passion: "We are in an odd position where the voters seem angrier and more interested in change than do the Democratic candidates and politi-cians. This is about tone and style, but we lack the outsider feel that Republicans brought to this battle in 1994."

Those outside the party also picked up on the renewed Democratic anxiety, sometimes humorously. "Democrats Vow Not to Give Up Hope-lessness," read a headline in *The Onion,* a satirical online newspaper. The article had Pelosi saying, "In times like these, when the American public is palpably dismayed with the political status quo, it is crucial that Democrats remain unfocused and defer to the larger, smarter and better-equipped Republican machine. . . . If we play our cards right, we will be intimidated to the point of total paralysis."

The Democrats' stalled momentum and Carville's memo reinvigorated a question that had been the subject of debate within the party for months: Could the Democrats simply count on the Republicans to self-destruct, or did they need a compelling message to put before the voters? Insiders argued about the House Republicans' "Contract with America" and how significant a role it had played in the GOP takeover in 1994. A critical part of the Democrats' political mission had been achieved—voters were turning away from the Republican "culture of corruption" and "rubber stamp Congress" in growing numbers. But the second, equally crucial part—acceptance of the Democrats as a legitimate alternative—remained far from certain. Emanuel acknowledged that his party had to earn a minimal level of trust from the voters. "You have to clear the bar," he said. "We need an agenda." But he insisted this did not matter as much as some thought, because voters would focus on Republican mistakes and not Democratic promises. "This election is not about us—it's about them."

The difficulty for leaders such as Pelosi was pulling together the party's disparate factions. By midsummer, it seemed that every Democratic or liberal group—the Campaign for America's Future, Third Way, the New Democrat Network, the Center for American Progress—was holding a conference or releasing a paper on the party's message. This activity could be seen as the healthy ferment of a party groping toward a new philosophy, but more often it came off as floundering. Party leaders themselves had been meeting since early 2005 to craft a formal agenda. "It threatened to come apart, then it would come together, then it would threaten to come apart," said Congressman George Miller, a California Democrat who was involved. "It was a constant process of distilling." Consultants told the Democrats that to be effective their agenda should include exactly six items, and Emanuel came up with the slogan "Six for

'06." In late June the Democrats officially released the six items they pledged to tackle should they regain power: raising the minimum wage, reforming pensions, making college tuition tax deductible, negotiating for lower drug prices, investing in alternative energy, and adopting the recommendations of the September 11 Commission. Some ideas, such as immigration reform, were omitted because there was no way all Democrats would unite behind them. Few voters ever heard about the agenda, but it gave Democrats an answer when they were accused of having no plan.

Before and after "Six for '06," Emanuel constantly pushed Pelosi to highlight subjects he thought would play well for Democrats. He had privately sent her a memo in early 2006, for example, urging her to showcase two particular issues: stem cell research and the federal debt. Both showed how Republicans had lost touch with the public, he believed. The previous year, Emanuel wrote, had been a failure for Republicans because of the Iraq war, the stumbling economy, Bush's Social Security plan, and corruption scandals. But Republicans would now try to pass popular bills on pensions, health care, and similar matters, he predicted. The trick would be deciding which Republican ideas to back and which to reject. "We will be faced with the question of opposing or co-opting, while maintaining the image of an ineffective Congress," Emanuel wrote. In the meantime, pushing for House votes on stem cells and the debt was the way to go. The public solidly supported stem cell research, believing it could save lives, yet President Bush had promised to veto any bill expanding federal funding for it. And Republicans were quietly trying to increase the amount of money the government could borrow, which certainly would not play well with voters. "The stem cell debate and the vote on debt limit are issues that divide Republicans and illustrate how out-of-touch they are in addressing issues important to the American people," Emanuel pressed.

The memo in many ways reflected Emanuel's broader relationship with Pelosi. He was always pushing her to do more—implement a three-point plan, announce an agenda, arrange speeches on the House floor.

But while Emanuel was singularly focused on the goal of retaking the House, Pelosi had to satisfy the many constituencies of the sprawling Democratic Party. The friction was not personal; the two got along and had dinner together on occasion, and after all it was Pelosi who had appointed Emanuel to his post. But the hard-charging Emanuel chafed at what he felt was Pelosi's slow decision making and her rejection of his more aggressive suggestions. "I get along great with Nancy. Don't get me in a position that I'm fighting with her. I'm not fighting. That's not my role. I don't want to take on the leadership," Emanuel said. But he was frustrated that the House Democratic leadership did not move faster. "A lot of people are very comfortable with the world around here," Emanuel said. "You've got to want to throw the furniture around here. We've got a lot of people who like the furniture just as it is; they just want the furniture to be theirs."

Like a general restraining a talented but zealous subordinate, Pelosi adopted some of Emanuel's suggestions and rejected others. The Democrats made an issue of the debt, for example, but chose to wait before highlighting stem cell research. Shortly after his memo, Emanuel had sent Pelosi another paper listing four ways Democrats could get mileage out of Bush's unpopular Medicare drug program. He suggested a House motion condemning it, a debate on the House floor, town hall meetings by lawmakers, and a high-profile countdown to May 15, when the program fully kicked in. "I've given her this, and they're thinking about it," Emanuel said, his frustration evident. "It's still being analyzed." He added, "I'm interested in a leadership that thinks strategically—can we execute a plan?" Pelosi was not the only leader to be harangued by Emanuel. Senate Democratic leader Harry Reid of Nevada once told him, "Rahm, I'm not talking to you about stem cells anymore."

The conflict pointed up one of the big problems facing the Democrats: The party had no single leader. At one time a figure such as Adlai Stevenson could lose a presidential election and remain leader of the opposition, a respected position that enabled him to present an alternative to the Eisenhower administration and ultimately run for president again. But these times were less forgiving of losers, and statements by Al Gore or John Kerry, the Democrats' most recent leaders, were often dismissed as shrill or irrelevant. Competing comments from Reid, Pelosi, Emanuel, Gore, Kerry, Howard Dean, and others came off like a cacophony, not an orchestra. "It's a problem," Emanuel said. "Let me also say about Nancy, it's not like what I say she ignores; in fact, she implements a lot of it. But everything gets . . ." He struggled, seeming to suggest that his ideas were delayed or watered down, but not wanting to criticize Pelosi directly. "She implements what I suggest, when she can," he finished vaguely. At another point Emanuel physically slithered off his chair to the floor to illustrate Democratic leaders' slowness to act. He sometimes responded to this by waging a sort of one-man assault, launching campaigns on Medicare or stem cell research without the full weight of the party behind him.

Pelosi had more to gain than anyone if the Democrats regained power. She would become Speaker of the House, with all the power that came with that position. She would run half the Congress and be third in line to the presidency. Like Emanuel, Pelosi had labored as a political operative, chairing the California Democratic Party before coming to Congress. And she was working relentlessly to help retake the House. Many Democrats had felt great affection for the previous Democratic leader, Congressman Dick Gephardt of Missouri, but believed he had not worked hard enough to win back the majority. That could not be said of Pelosi. She was traveling the country and raising millions of dollars, taking advantage of her celebrity among Democrats as potentially the first female Speaker, which would make her the highest-ranking elected woman in U.S. history. Like Emanuel, Pelosi was willing to create enemies to get results. "I love people who are operational," she said of Emanuel. "They're there to get the job done." She also praised Emanuel for focusing only on races that were winnable. "The temptation is to spread yourself too thinly," Pelosi said. "Rahm won't be tempted by that. He's cold-blooded enough to make these decisions." Pelosi's own fundraising was methodical. She had laid the groundwork in 2003 and 2004 by traveling to places such as Atlanta and Tampa, second-tier cities from a fund-raising perspective, and establishing a network of donors there. That made it easier for her to bring in money from those places in 2006 with relatively little effort, while focusing her energy on the big-money cities such as Los Angeles and New York.

But fund-raising was only part of Pelosi's contribution. She called individual Democrats to persuade them to run for Congress, adding her celebrity to Emanuel's sales pitch. Pelosi and Emanuel often spoke several times a day—quick conversations in political shorthand—to confer on strategy. Pelosi backed Emanuel's plan to push a national Democratic message, rather than run district-by-district campaigns. While Emanuel was traveling the country and speaking to candidates, Pelosi spent hours strategizing with Reid on the Democrats' message. Pelosi, like DeLay, had managed to secure a remarkable unity in her party—unbroken opposition by House Democrats to Bush's Social Security plan, for example. Pelosi also was unafraid to enforce discipline on Democratic lawmakers. Sometimes a Republican who was being targeted by Emanuel would want to burnish his bipartisan credentials by joining a Democrat on a bill, and Pelosi would forbid the Democrat to go along. Given all this work, Pelosi and her staff were jealous of the attention Emanuel was getting. While Emanuel was being called "the enforcer" and "Rahmbo," few reporters focused on Pelosi's behind-the-scenes strategizing, traveling, and fund-raising.

With four months until Election Day, House Republicans, too, decided they needed to present an agenda of their own. In late June they unveiled an "American Values Agenda," an amalgam of proposals designed to stir the emotions of socially conservative voters. Many of the items were responses to recent court decisions. GOP leaders proposed, for example, discouraging legal challenges to Ten Commandments displays, guaranteeing condominium dwellers the right to show American flags, and stripping the courts of jurisdiction over the Pledge of Allegiance. In the interest of energizing the anti-abortion community, the agenda also included a bill requiring some women to be informed that a pending abortion "will cause the unborn child pain." In unveiling the program,

House Speaker Dennis Hastert explained, "Radical courts have attempted to gut our religious freedom and redefine the value system on which America was built." It was a message that had worked well for the Republicans in the past—the idea that powerful forces were waging war on ordinary Americans. The agenda even included a constitutional amendment to ban gay marriage, even though the Senate had already defeated the measure and it could no longer pass Congress that year. Clearly the "American Values Agenda" was not about producing legislation. It was about defining sharp cultural differences between the parties that would, the Republicans hoped, send conservatives to the polls.

It was at this point that the Republicans also made a risky strategic decision not to run from the war in Iraq but to embrace it. Democrats were struggling mightily with Iraq, looking for ways to criticize the war without sounding unpatriotic or as if they did not support the troops. At first, Democrats had criticized only the execution of the war—the lack of body armor, for example—rather than the war itself. Then they said the war itself had been a bad idea, but the troops were performing well. Finally they came up with an array of positions on withdrawing the troops altogether; some wanted to pull out immediately and some not at all, while others favored "phased" withdrawals. The Republicans mocked these varied formulations, saying they revealed, once again, the Democrats' irresolution on national defense.

In June, as American fatalities in Iraq hit the symbolic number of 2,500, the Republicans initiated furious debates in both chambers of Congress. House Republicans introduced a resolution urging completion of the Iraq mission and opposing an "arbitrary date" for withdrawal. The rhetoric grew nasty. Congressman Charles Norwood, a Georgia Republican, charged that many Democrats "lack the will to win. The American people need to know precisely who they are." He added, "It is time to stand up and vote. Is it Al Qaeda, or is it America?" Democrats were enraged. Pelosi called the war "a grotesque mistake," and Democrats pointedly asked for a moment of silence to recognize the 2,500 American dead.

The fight over Iraq continued on other fronts. In mid-July, the DCCC posted a hard-hitting video on its Web site aimed at attracting Democratic contributions. It opened with an ominous soundtrack and the words "Things have taken a turn for the worse." Viewers saw shots of a tank burning in Iraq, a gas station charging $3.55 a gallon, flag-draped coffins, a soldier mourning a dead comrade, a submerged New Orleans. The effect was apocalyptic, the mood eschatological. "Washington Republicans have sold America out," the video continued, followed by sinister photos of Cheney, Bush, Rove, and DeLay. Then the music turned bouncy and optimistic, accompanied by the words "But America is strong enough to change." Happy shots followed of an American flag, Emanuel and other Democratic leaders, and troops giving the thumbs-up. Bill Clinton was shown saying, "There is nothing wrong with America that cannot be cured by what is right with America." The film was posted on the DCCC Web site on July 2. It took conservatives a while to notice it, but when they did, they raised an outcry. The photo of military coffins—as well as a shot of a soldier mourning beside an upright rifle with a helmet perched on it—crassly politicized the deaths of American soldiers, they claimed. Conservative bloggers were among the first to react. "This is outrageous. This is disgusting," said a July 12 posting on RedState. "This is why the Democrats must lose in November. They refuse to hold sacred the lives of American soldiers. Instead, their dead bodies are instruments of fundraising for the DCCC."

The NRCC quickly jumped in, coordinating Republican candidates across the country to unleash press releases condemning the video. From Vermont Republican Martha Rainville: "I was painfully appalled that a political party would attempt to capitalize on our fallen soldiers." From Thelma Drake, a Virginia congresswoman struggling for reelection: "It is the height of cynicism and political opportunism to use pictures of our American fighting men and women after they have made the ultimate sacrifice for our freedoms." Republican leaders held a press conference in Washington. "For the Democrats, everything is about politics, but this crosses the line," Reynolds pronounced. Unable, as always, to refrain from naming Emanuel personally, Reynolds noted that Emanuel often read the names of the fallen on the House floor. "It takes a galling level of smug self-righteousness for Rahm Emanuel to invoke our honored dead one day and put their coffins in an ad the next," Reynolds said.

Democrats, of course, rejected the criticism. "I think it is despicable that young people's lives are being lost. Republicans are in denial about that," said Pelosi. "Yet they talk about politicizing war." Emanuel claimed the outcry actually worked in his favor. When the video had first appeared on the DCCC Web site, it had motivated a scant two hundred people to provide their e-mail addresses as contacts for future fund-raising. But after the Republicans created a national furor over it, thousands more people visited the DCCC Web site and provided e-mail addresses.

Around this time, an unexpected court decision produced a shot of good news for the Democrats. When Tom DeLay had quit Congress the previous April, Democrats sued to block him from withdrawing from his reelection campaign. This was a long shot at best. The Democrats argued that DeLay had already won the Republican primary, so he could not simply step aside for another candidate. Neither party remotely expected that argument to prevail. But on July 6, Judge Sam Sparks startled both sides by accepting the Democrats' argument and ordering DeLay's name to stay on the ballot. This was a major blow for the GOP. Texas Republicans had been planning to replace DeLay with a fresh-faced, unblemished figure, but suddenly that would not be possible—DeLay's name would stay on the ballot as the Republican candidate, even though he had made it clear he was leaving Congress and had no intention of campaigning. As a result, the Democratic candidate, Nick Lampson, was virtually assured of victory. Emanuel was driving through upstate New York on a swing through five congressional districts when Lampson called to tell him of the judge's surprising ruling. "I haven't read it," Lampson said. "But I can tell you something: My opponent will either be Tom DeLay or nobody." Emanuel kicked into his political strategist role, warning Lampson against public gloating. "The most important thing is, don't act presumptuous," he said. "Make sure you walk precincts tonight. You are going to earn it. Make sure you're seen being with people."

With DeLay's seat in hand, the Democrats now needed only fourteen more for the majority. Emanuel ordered his staff to send out a fund-raising appeal headlined "14 to Go," hoping to generate enthusiasm and donations. Two hours later, Emanuel had not received confirmation that the fund-raising message had been sent, and he turned on the aide traveling with him. "Can you call and see if they goddamn did that? Now!" Emanuel said. "If I don't see that, I'm going to go apoplectic."

That the seat of Tom DeLay, the embodiment of harsh Republican power, became the first seat captured by the Democrats in their quest for the majority was rich in irony. DeLay had used election law in an ingenious, even unprecedented way three years earlier by prodding Texas to redraw its congressional map and give Republicans six additional House seats. That, in fact, was why Emanuel faced the task of winning fifteen seats instead of the much more achievable mission of capturing nine. DeLay's maneuvering had led to his indictment, ultimately forcing him from Congress. And in departing Congress, DeLay had collided with election law and given the Democrats back a seat—his own. Nick Lampson, the Democrat poised to fill DeLay's chair, was one of the same Democratic congressmen he had ousted with his Texas redistricting scheme. For DeLay, there could be no more galling outcome than being replaced by a Democrat. The day DeLay had resigned from Congress, he had announced, with the sort of logic unique to him, that this was a terrible day not for him but for the Democrats, because he was depriving them of the joy of defeating him and retaking his seat.

Republicans, for their part, were tight-lipped; it was hard to spin this as a victory. When Republican spokesman Carl Forti was asked for his reaction to the DeLay decision, he answered uncharacteristically, "I don't know that I have one." Officials at the Texas Republican Party also declined to talk. Tina Benkiser, the state party chairwoman, instead issued a terse statement saying the court decision "effectively throws the federal election process into total chaos, and we will appeal this decision in order to protect the voters of Texas and their right to vote for a nominee of their choice." They did appeal, and they quickly lost.

Even with a seat in the bag, Emanuel was taking no chances. He worried that many of his campaigns did not have the high-caliber staff they needed. One of the DCCC's tasks was to help campaigns find talented operatives, or in some cases impose those operatives on campaigns that did not want Washington's meddling. It did little good for a campaign to raise money and craft a strategy if it lacked experienced staffers to put that strategy into effect. As Washington temperatures rose above 90 degrees in July, Emanuel invited twenty congressional press secretaries to Democratic headquarters. These young men and women worked for Democratic House members, and Emanuel's press team, Bill Burton and Sarah Feinberg, considered them among the best on Capitol Hill. Emanuel's goal was to persuade them to leave their jobs and join one of his campaigns, to act as a spokesperson for the candidate. It would be a hard sell; Emanuel was asking each of them to forsake the Capitol's comfortable confines for a remote location and work for an inexperienced politician who could very well lose. Emanuel delivered his pitch in the DCCC's first-floor all-purpose room, alongside tables covered with Miller Lite, Budweiser, Tostitos, and pretzels. Emanuel walked in at 7:15 P.M., went up to a staffer, and stuck out his hand, saying, "Rahm," by way of unnecessary introduction. "How long you been on the Hill?" he asked as he moved around the room. Finding someone who had worked for former Clinton aide John Podesta, a friend and a fellow Chicagoan, Emanuel volunteered with a smile, "The entire Podesta family has done many drugs."

After the small talk, the staffers gathered around Emanuel in a circle. "Here's the thing," he began, jamming his hands in his pockets. "I'm not going to bullshit you. It's not for the great quality of the beer that my staff brought you here. We need people out on these campaigns. A lot of you have great lives, you have great jobs. But we have great campaigns. But they can't get from here to there"—Emanuel raised his hand from a lower level to a higher one—"without a communications person." Emanuel praised the Democrats' chances, citing races such as Joe Sestak's campaign against Congressman Curt Weldon in Pennsylvania. "I've been around politics. You all have been around politics. I don't remember another time like this in the past eight years," Emanuel said. "But unless a lot of people start to get on the field, we're not going to seize all of these opportunities that we have. We wouldn't ask you here unless we had a real need. We didn't ask everybody to come. We only asked the people we thought were capable. I think we have a historic election and a historic opportunity here."

Someone asked why Emanuel kept mentioning Weldon, a harshly partisan Republican. "I just hate him," Emanuel said, before explaining what he thought were Weldon's weaknesses. "What's your bottom-line prediction?" another staffer asked, meaning how many seats he thought the Democrats would pick up. "Fuck you," Emanuel answered, to general laughter. Then, recognizing that "fuck you" might not be everyone's idea of friendly banter, he added almost apologetically, "In my house, when you say 'fuck you,' it's a sign of endearment."

Emanuel finished with a crescendo. "Guys—this is three and a half months. We are in a great place. We have recruited the hell out of these candidates. We are beating the hell out of the Republicans on fund-raising. We are in a great place. I am not asking you to start where we started twelve, or for some of us eighteen, months ago. I just need some more bodies on the field for the last three and a half months. You're here because Bill and Sarah and the rest of the team think you're capable. You wouldn't be where you are if you weren't. You're not only capable on the Hill, you're capable in campaigns. We need you. And if that ain't enough, your goddamn country needs you. Because these are bad people. And they deserve a two-by-four upside their head. And we're going to give it to them."

The staffers applauded as Emanuel exited. Burton stepped forward, gestured toward the drinks, and said comically, "Well, there's lots of shitty beer left." Outside, Emanuel climbed into his waiting car and sent Burton an e-mail saying, "Do not fuck it up now."

Emanuel also focused on turning a handful of hard-fought races into safe Democratic seats, so he could save precious funds and spend them elsewhere. "If I can alter these races and take them from being competitive and diminish the threat, you can save a lot of money and move it to targeted races," Emanuel said. "So that is the strategy we are working on right now. I'm trying to move dollars around. That's what the summer months are all about." Congressman Mollohan was perhaps the best example, now that he was confronting a serious challenge from West Virginia state delegate Chris Wakim. It frustrated Emanuel that he had to worry about a seat held by a longtime Democratic incumbent, and he wanted to put an end to the challenge. Christina Reynolds, the DCCC research director, had finally gotten to the bottom of Wakim's claims on his resumé. Despite calling himself a "Gulf War veteran," she discovered, Wakim had not actually served in the Gulf War. He had been in the military during that time, but without serving overseas. In addition, Wakim's official biography said he "earned his Master's Degree from Harvard University in 1991, graduating in the top 15% of his class." In fact, Wakim had attended Harvard's Extension School, a far less prestigious continuing-education program.

Reynolds tried to interest West Virginia reporters in Wakim's exaggerations but could not persuade them to write about it. Emanuel was frustrated. *"We need that story,"* he said at a July staff meeting. "It's all about Alan Mollohan, unless we come up with something." Reynolds provided the information to the scrappy publications that covered Capitol Hill, who were more than interested. Soon, a headline in *Roll Call* read, "Mollohan Foe Battles Resumé Charges," and a similar headline appeared in *The Hill*. The publicity had its desired effect. An angry Wakim held a conference call with reporters to rebut the charges. But before the call, DCCC press secretary Sarah Feinberg made sure reporters were armed with tough questions on Wakim's resumé, and the session turned combative. A local radio station then aired the contentious conference call, damaging Wakim further. "Part of our goal was, people know Alan Mollohan," Reynolds said. "What we needed to show was, not only do you not know Wakim, but he's lying to you about who he is." Emanuel pushed for similar scrutiny of other Republicans. Martha Rainville, a Republican running for Vermont's lone House seat, had taken $4,000 from a software developer, then pushed for a federal expenditure that

would help her benefactor. A GOP candidate in Colorado had once suggested that Social Security was "un-American."

Emanuel's opponents were playing a similar game, trying to cripple
Democratic candidates and make those races safely Republican. Most
worrisome to Emanuel was the U.S. Chamber of Commerce, a large business group allied with the Republican Party. The Chamber had much at
stake in the congressional races, and it plunged into them in earnest over
the summer, running a series of ads in key races. Emanuel fretted about
the group's clout and resources. "The thing that is scaring the shit out of
me is the Chamber of Commerce ads," Emanuel confessed. "I can beat
the NRCC, and our individual candidates can beat their individual candidates. What the Chamber is trying to do is what I am trying to do—take
competitive races and alter them." The first wave of Chamber ads praised
Republicans who had supported President Bush's Medicare drug program. That ad campaign was such a blunt instrument that some of the
commercials had to be changed because the Republican in question was
not even in Congress when the drug program passed. The Chamber ran
an ad for Republican congressman Dave Reichert in Washington State, for
example, saying, "Thanks to Dave Reichert, 713,000 Washington seniors
now benefit from drug coverage." But Reichert had not taken office when
the drug program passed in November 2003. Still, the ads were effective,
and for good measure, the Chamber announced a "Vote for Business
Bandwagon," a colorful bus that visited key congressional districts to
endorse Republicans.

At the final DCCC staff meeting in July, a cautiously upbeat mood
prevailed. The DCCC had just reported it had $32 million in cash on
hand, compared to $26 million for the Republicans—a major achievement
given the Republicans' traditional fund-raising edge. The staff broke into
impromptu applause for Brian Wolff, the committee staffer in charge of
fund-raising. Emanuel seemed stunned at the Republicans' low numbers.
"How did we get it so wrong?" he asked. He wanted the staff to take a
closer look, in case the Republicans somehow had more money remain-
ing than they seemed to. Emanuel also told the staff to stop directing

money to several formerly vulnerable House members, including John Salazar of Colorado and Charlie Melancon of Louisiana, whose campaigns were going well and who could handle themselves. "I want them off our payroll," Emanuel said. "I don't want to see them around. I think we're wasting money on them." A staffer noted that Republican congressman John Sweeney of New York had been accused of abusing his congressional mailing privileges, but it was unclear what consequences he would face. "As long as I get an article that he violated House rules, I'm okay," Emanuel said. "Just go at him on every level. No breath."

Emanuel ended the meeting with a warning. "To all your staffs—thank you for a great eighteen months," he said. "Tell them there's only three more. This is when people do stupid things."

8

IMPLOSION

Prince, Lobel, Glovsky & Tye was one of Boston's premier law firms, a fact that was instantly clear upon entering its quiet offices. The firm name, carved in metallic letters behind a receptionist's desk, was enhanced by a faint blue light, and deep brown paneling along the walls alternated with tasteful abstract paintings. The conference room provided a spectacular view of the city below; the décor appeared designed to subtly communicate power and wealth. The firm specialized in media, banking, and telecommunications, and its clients included such powerhouses as Cingular Wireless, Fox Television, and the Polaroid Corporation. At eight-thirty on the morning of August 16, 2006, a group of twenty lawyers settled into black leather chairs around a thirty-foot conference table to hear a congressional candidate from nearby New Hampshire ask for money. But mostly they wanted to hear Emanuel, who was only now becoming known among Democrats nationally as the brash Chicago congressman leading the charge for the House.

After brief comments from the New Hampshire candidate, Jim Craig— "I refuse to accept that we can't get this country back to where it needs to be"—Emanuel stood at a podium at one end of the room. His job was to extract as much money as he could from these wealthy Bostonians, to convince them that by giving they would be part of a historic event, the recapture of the House by the forces of good after twelve years of darkness. "People have gotten tired of this experiment in Republican control of government," Emanuel said. "There is a real, sensible, palpable frustration about what is happening in Washington." Emanuel was not a great speaker; often he did not finish one sentence before starting a new one, and he could lapse into a confusing shorthand when discussing legislation or politics. But his meaning was clear, and so was his intensity. His presence in this conference room was intended to signal that he was doing everything possible to win the House, so any contribution would be a good investment. "I've been in politics for twenty years. This is the first time I've seen the stars aligned like this," Emanuel said. "People know the party in power has messed things up."

Then came the hard sell. Emanuel held up a check in an envelope, saying he had given $12,000 to Craig. "I'm in for twelve, folks," he said. "I want you to reach deep down." He moved in front of the podium, closer to the audience around the conference table. "For the first time, this is within our grasp." He made a slow grabbing motion. "And we should not become Democrats who fumble the ball. We have eighty days to make our case to the American people. This is a historic election. This is a national election waged on whether we want George Bush to stay the course, and the American people are ready to reject it. The question is, do we give Jim Craig the resources to make the case?"

This fund-raiser for Craig, a decidedly second-tier candidate, was one of dozens Emanuel was attending around the country. He was also meeting privately with numerous wealthy donors who could afford the $26,700 maximum contribution to the DCCC. Emanuel was raising money simultaneously for the committee, which functioned as a central clearinghouse, and for individual candidates. The task was monumental. A campaign could be likened to a multimillion-dollar corporation that rises from nothing, raises and spends enormous sums, and collapses back into oblivion until the next election season. Emanuel spent more of his time courting cash than doing anything else. No matter how attractive a candidate or appealing his message, it meant little if he could not advertise on television, print brochures, or pay campaign workers to knock on doors. "The first third of your campaign is money, money, money," Emanuel once told a group of staffers. "The second third is money, money, and press. And the last third is votes, press, and money." By that calculus, a campaign should spend six times as much effort raising money as directly seeking votes.

Money had a psychological effect as well as a practical one. If Emanuel could show he was raising lots of cash, activists would be energized, journalists would write of the Democratic momentum early in the cycle, and promising candidates would jump into races. Emanuel, of course, had long been known as a hard-hitting fund-raiser. After his stint as Bill Clinton's money man in the 1992 campaign, when he had relentlessly prodded the candidate to make fund-raising calls, Clinton autographed a photo for Emanuel, "I give up. I give up. I'll make 500 more calls. Thanks for making my life more interesting."

In the 2006 campaign, Emanuel and his staff were judging candidates almost exclusively by how much money they raised. If a candidate proved a good fund-raiser, the DCCC would provide support, advertising, strategic advice, and whatever other help was needed. If not, the committee would shut him out. At one staff meeting in primary season, talk turned to a Pennsylvania Democrat named Andy Warren, who had raised a meager $38,662 in the previous three months. Emanuel ordered the staff to drop Warren and back his Democratic opponent. "Eliminate him," Emanuel said curtly. "Cut him off," chimed in executive director John Lapp. As for other candidates who had not raised what they promised, Emanuel said at the same meeting, "We'll just take three hours tomorrow and I'll call the idiots who need to be pushed." Lapp confided later, "He'll scream at them. Literally."

Candidates who were otherwise outstanding—articulate, impassioned, honest—but had trouble raising money were out of luck. "You wouldn't think that a requirement for being a good congressman is that you be a good telemarketer, but the fact is you have to be," said Illinois candidate

Dan Seals. "You are calling people and asking for support for hours each day. And as I'm told by my team, it doesn't ever really end. It's a lifestyle choice. I think that's unfortunate. I don't think it's good for anybody." Emanuel's emphasis on money was ruthless. But if a candidate could not raise money, he felt, supporting him was a waste of time, and the support should go to a candidate who had a chance. Emanuel's critics thought he was too quick to dismiss those who did not meet his fund-raising criteria, and that as a result he ended up with individuals who were establishment-friendly but lackluster, such as Tammy Duckworth.

Emanuel was fighting a constant battle of perceptions with Tom Reynolds, his Republican counterpart, over whose fund-raising was going better. Republicans almost always raised more than Democrats, and Emanuel faced pressure to show that the Democrats were at least staying close. At a DCCC staff meeting in late 2005, Emanuel's fund-raising team had reported raising $33 million in the year's first three quarters. That was good but still less than the Republicans, and Emanuel did not want reporters to focus on that gap. "You'll have to get ahead of it and spin it," Emanuel said. His aides did just that, issuing a press release four days later that announced, "Best ever fund-raising in an off-year." By the middle of 2006, fund-raising had picked up along with the Democratic prospects, and the DCCC's total had risen to $76 million compared to $103 million for the Republicans.

Several factors accounted for the Republicans' built-in money advantage. Many people who had the resources to write big checks favored the GOP. The Republicans had been in power a long time, so it was logical for businesses to give them money. And the Republicans had the White House; however unpopular President Bush might be with the public at large, loyal Republicans would always flock to fund-raisers where he appeared. Bush had raised an astounding $27 million at a single June event at the Washington Convention Center, with $15 million going to Republican House campaigns and $12 million to Senate campaigns. Emanuel spent hours strategizing on how to fight back. He was afraid the Republicans would in effect build financial walls around key districts, shielding them from the national anti-Republican winds.

To breach those walls, Emanuel tried to schedule his own stars to appear at Democratic fund-raisers, scrambling to get commitments from Bill and Hillary Clinton, for example. "We've got to resolve this right now," he had told his staff in April 2006. "I know the Clintons. I love them both, but we're never going to get a date [unless we push hard]. He [Bill] told me at lunch two weeks ago, 'I'll do whatever you want.' I want to get it resolved." Former vice president Al Gore was another big draw for Democrats—one of the biggest, in fact, to the surprise of many. Gore had been held in low regard after losing to Bush in 2000, since many Democrats felt he had given away a race that he should have won easily, and as a result subjected the nation to the Bush presidency. But Gore had recently reemerged as one of the party's most popular figures. He had been featured in *An Inconvenient Truth,* a successful film about global warming, and had received good reviews for a humorous appearance on *Saturday Night Live.* Many Democrats felt Gore was finally showing the impassioned, likeable qualities whose absence in 2000 had cost him the presidency. This was not lost on Emanuel, who wanted to harness Gore's newfound appeal to raise money for the DCCC. "I want to nail down a Gore strategy," he said. "I think Gore is going to have a resurrection, and I want to be first in line to take advantage of it." Gore later told Emanuel he would help raise money for any House candidate as long as the candidate had a responsible position on global warming.

Emanuel had initially set a goal of raising $94 million by Election Day. But as the Democratic momentum built and a victory seemed possible, more people made contributions, and Emanuel had increased the goal to $105 million, more than House Democrats had ever raised. The money came from three sources: dues from Democratic House members, small contributions from ordinary voters, and gifts from wealthy donors who paid $10,000 or more. Most of Emanuel's fund-raising time was spent meeting with wealthy lawyers or financiers, telling them this was the year to give, even as Nancy Pelosi and other Democrats also were raising enormous sums.

Emanuel met privately in mid-August with Alan Solomont, a longtime Democratic fund-raiser in Boston who'd made a fortune in the elder-care business. Solomont, wearing a light beige suit and salmon-colored tie, began by observing, "Political fund-raising is like adolescent sex: It's awkward, impatient, intense, and over quickly." The comment made Emanuel visibly uncomfortable, a rare occurrence for him. "Maybe your adolescent sex," he said agitatedly. "Fuck you."

Solomont moved on to his real point, which was the need for better coordination between the various Democratic candidates who were scrambling for money in Boston. Democratic candidates for the House, Senate, governors' mansions, and state legislatures were competing for the same dollars, and the party had to handle this delicately. "We have it," Emanuel insisted. "We've raised $300,000 or $400,000 more in Boston than we have in the past." Solomont was not convinced. "We can get a lot more out of this, Rahm, if we can figure out a way to do this together," he said. The two agreed to look for ways to improve coordination. Then they discussed upcoming fund-raisers in Boston, at which Emanuel hoped to raise $250,000 for the DCCC and $250,000 more for individual House candidates. "We can get at least that much," Solomont promised.

Solomont had done a lot for the Democrats. Now came the time to ask a favor. "This is a personal thing," he said. Solomont was teaching a course on the presidency at Tufts University, where he was an alumnus and trustee, and he hoped Emanuel would speak to his students. "You have my commitment after the election," Emanuel said. Solomont asked, "How is November sixteenth?" Emanuel was reluctant to promise a specific date. "Fuck, I don't even know what I'm doing tomorrow," he said.

Besides Solomont, Emanuel's money network included people such as Sheryl Sandberg, a former Clinton White House lawyer who was now vice president of Google, and Laurie David, wife of television actor, writer, and producer Larry David. Emanuel's brother Ari, a wealthy, well-connected Hollywood agent, also raised money for the Democrats. Rich people know other rich people, so donors would hold gatherings at their homes or restaurants and invite their wealthy friends. Sometimes Emanuel would appear, sometimes not. "It's like a Tupperware party," explained Leo Hindery, a New Yorker who'd made a fortune in telecommunications and held DCCC fund-raisers at the Regency Hotel and the Four Seasons. Mark Gorenberg, a California venture capitalist, assembled an elaborate network of Democratic donors in Silicon Valley. "We fundamentally believed we could win because of Rahm," Gorenberg said. "He has instilled discipline, recruited candidates, transformed them before our eyes, made us all believers." As Gorenberg suggested, the strands of the campaign overlapped in complex ways. If the DCCC recruited good candidates and forced them to run skilled campaigns, donors were more easily persuaded to give money. That money, in turn, could be poured back into the campaigns to make them better still. For better or worse, Emanuel took that dynamic—using money to enforce discipline on candidates, and using discipline to attract more money—to new heights.

At the Boston law firm on August 16, after he finished his fund-raising spiel, several of the assembled lawyers pulled out checkbooks on the spot, and the event raised $20,000. Someone asked Emanuel how he planned to spend the money he was raising nationally. His answer reflected why he could be so persuasive with certain donors and so disliked by others in the party. He would not distribute funds to candidates based on their personal qualities, Emanuel said. He would not support the most loyal Democrats, or those whose populism was purest. His only criterion, he said, was who could win. "I'm cutthroat about this," he said. "I don't give a crap where I pick up seats. I plan on winning. There is no emotional attachment."

Republicans, of course, were hardly sitting still for Emanuel's onslaught, and in fact their fears were becoming more urgent. The Note, the smartalecky political diary sponsored by ABC News, announced that GOP now stood for "Got Oversized Problems" and listed among the reasons, "Mr. Schumer and Mr. Emanuel: These cats are not fooling around." Then in August, all eyes turned to the Connecticut Democratic primary, where longtime senator Joseph Lieberman had been defeated by a scrappy antiwar activist. Just six years earlier, Lieberman had been the Democrats' vice presidential nominee, and he remained a senior statesman and one of the party's strongest voices supporting the Iraq war. Now the Republicans believed the unheralded Ned Lamont had handed them a gift by humiliating Lieberman. Abandoning their strategy of focusing on local matters, which was demonstrably failing, Republicans seized almost desperately on national security.

The day after the primary, Vice President Dick Cheney, who usually spoke only to conservative news organizations, suggested to wire service reporters that terrorists were happy with Lieberman's loss. "The al-Qaeda types, they clearly are betting on the proposition that ultimately they can break the will of the American people in terms of our ability to stay in the fight and complete the task," Cheney said. "And when we see the Democratic Party reject one of its own, a man they selected to be their vice presidential nominee just a few short years ago, it would seem to say a lot about the state the party is in today." The same day, Republican Party Chairman Ken Mehlman said, "Joe Lieberman believed in a strong national defense, and for that, he was purged from his party." Cheney also had used the word *purge,* a term redolent of Stalinism, to describe the results of a standard primary election.

Two days after Lieberman's loss, British authorities announced they'd broken up a plot to blow up ten airplanes on their way to the United States. The NRCC quickly instructed Republican candidates to take advantage of the news. "In the days to come, you should move to question your opponent's commitment to the defeat of terror, and in turn, create a definitive contrast on the issue," the NRCC said in an August 11 memo to its candidates. "You will certainly benefit from bringing into stark focus the cut-and-run, surrender message that Democrats coast to coast are currently—and foolishly—embracing."

A striking difference between 2006 and 1994, the year to which it was increasingly being compared, was that the Republicans were worried. Unlike Democrats twelve years earlier, they fully recognized that they could lose the House, and they were doing all they could to fight back. One increasingly popular GOP tactic was to try to scare apathetic Republicans by painting a vivid picture of what a Democratic Congress might do. We may not be perfect, the Republicans were saying, but don't forget how bad the Democrats are. Republicans began airing ads emphasizing that Nancy Pelosi, the San Francisco liberal, would become House Speaker if the Democrats captured the majority.

Democrat Heath Shuler, a religious social conservative in North Carolina, was among those targeted by these ads. "Looking for a change? Put liberals in charge," began one of these campaign commercials as the figures of Pelosi, Howard Dean, and Hillary Rodham Clinton popped up on the screen. "They've already said they'd raise our taxes, and they have a plan to do it. Heath Shuler and the liberals—they're the wrong kind of change." Another Taylor ad intoned, "They'll give us partial-birth abortion on demand. They'll approve gay marriage. They'll give amnesty to illegal immigrants." These were not Shuler's positions, but Taylor was warning that a vote for Shuler was a vote to empower liberal Democrats.

Similarly, Sheriff Brad Ellsworth was a popular Democrat running in a conservative Indiana district. As an anti-abortion, anti-gun-control, church-going law enforcement officer, he could hardly be painted as a liberal. So the Republicans ran ads pointing out that Ellsworth's election would boost Pelosi. "Control of Congress is at stake in the coming election. Will Brad Ellsworth vote for liberal Democrat Nancy Pelosi for Speaker of the House?" an announcer asked gravely. "Remember, a vote for Brad Ellsworth is a vote to open the floodgate of ideas that are bad for America and expensive for you." This line of attack was not a surprise. When Pelosi had run for Democratic whip in 2001, her opponents within the party argued that Democrats would be making a mistake to pick such a liberal as their public face. But Pelosi's other assets, her organization and her fund-raising, had prevailed over those concerns.

In a lighter vein, the Republican National Committee published an imaginary newspaper of the future called *America Weakly*, purportedly from one year after a Democratic takeover of Congress. Articles described the impeachment of President Bush, the junking of Bush's anti-terror measures, and Hollywood figures running rampant in Washington.

A Republican rally at a fire station in King of Prussia, Pennsylvania, on August 23 provided a further glimpse of the Republican tactics. Former New York mayor Rudolph Giuliani, a hero of the September 11 attacks, appeared on behalf of two struggling GOP congressmen, Jim Gerlach and Curt Weldon. The theme was Democratic weakness on security. Rows of Gerlach and Weldon signs lined the fire station entryway, and about 250 Republicans gathered in the 90-degree dusk. "The other party is damn soft on terrorism," said one of them, Paul Hallman, an eighty-year-old retired insurance agent from East Vincent Township, as he waited for the rally to start. "They oppose everything the administration does to fight it. They're soft on terrorism and the war in general." Jean Hoffman, a forty-one-year-old stay-at-home mom from nearby Downingtown, seconded Hallman's opinion. "The number one issue is security. I'm just not quite trusting the Democrats with that," she said. "They're on the wrong side of every issue relating to security. It's my only issue, because if you don't have that, there's nothing else."

Ten uniformed firefighters emerged onto the stage, and a retired admiral said the pledge of allegiance. Then the lawmakers spoke. With black hair, dark eyes, and jutting jaw, Gerlach looked very much like a congressman. His tone was reasonable as he extolled the virtues of firefighters. "At the end of the day, our families' safety, our communities' safety, indeed our nation's safety starts right here," Gerlach said. But Weldon—whose chubby face, puffy white hair, and spectacles had made him a recognizable figure on Capitol Hill—was less restrained. Democrats had done nothing to help firefighters, he said: "zero, nothing, nada." And because they had not funded these "first responders," Weldon added, Democrats were at fault that the country had not been better prepared for September 11. "Back in the nineties we were being told, 'Don't worry, be happy. Stand in a circle and sing Kumbaya, because everything will be okay,'" Weldon said. "We were taking away the preparation for this country to deal with the inevitable."

Giuliani was the evening's star. This was one of dozens of appearances he was making to build up favors for his anticipated presidential run. "I think there is a kind of a division in American politics right now," Giuliani told the crowd, mopping his bulbous forehead. "When you have to face ultimate evil and hatred, it's hard for some people to really recognize it.

They want to wish it away. They want to make believe it isn't so." Gerlach and Weldon, of course, were not such people. "You have two leaders in Pennsylvania who are very realistic," Giuliani said. "They understand what we're facing." The crowd chanted, "Rudy! Rudy! Rudy!" and as the three men waded through the crowd and climbed onto a fire truck to wave, many snapped photos with cell phones and cameras. After the rally, Gerlach acknowledged that for a time there had been a "sour climate" in his district, but now that people were focusing on the election, "I feel more and more upbeat." Giuliani was similarly optimistic, citing Democratic disunity on national security. "They've got serious divisions, and that's what they're presenting to the American people—division, no plan, lack of unity," Giuliani said. "And I think as the American people focus more and more on what's at stake . . . You know, off-year elections are tough, the sixth year of any presidency is tough, but I think they're going to win"—he indicated Gerlach and Weldon—"and I think the Republicans will win."

Suddenly the summer was over and it was Labor Day, the traditional launch of the campaign season. In fact, energetic campaigning had been under way for some time, but Labor Day nonetheless allowed analysts to engage in their ritual assessments of the political parties' relative strengths. Their general conclusion was that, two months before the election, the Democrats were holding their advantage and time was running out for Republicans. Strategists in both parties cautioned that a surprise event, such as the capture of Osama bin Laden, could alter the landscape, but newspapers vied to describe the Republican woes. The *New York Times* proclaimed, "G.O.P. Faces Peril of Losing House, Strategists Say." The conservative *Washington Times,* which almost always could find a way to spin things in Republicans' favor, admitted in a headline, "History Favors Democrats in Congress Races." The *National Journal* found that, for the first time, Republican "insiders" believed the Democrats would take over.

The situation was in truth more complicated. Republicans had an impressive get-out-the-vote operation that had proven itself capable of last-minute miracles, and a shift of just two points in the polls could make a big difference. Nonetheless, the feeling in early September was one of Democratic momentum and Republican malaise. Emanuel was contemptuous of such predictions. "The people frothing about us taking over the House—sixteen months ago they were saying we were the permanent minority," Emanuel said. "How right were they then? That's how right they are now." The press always had to have a story line, he felt. For the moment, it was that Democrats were poised for an historic upset, but that could change quickly. "I try to temper my mood," Emanuel said. "I still have a deep pit in my stomach that says, 'Maybe there ain't the [Democratic] wave we hope there is.'" Emanuel now believed, based on models by DCCC consultants, that the Democrats would win a minimum of eleven seats and a maximum of nineteen, exactly bracketing the magic number of fifteen they needed for a majority. His biggest concern remained that the Republicans and their wealthy supporters would flood key states with money. "I spend every waking hour thinking about it," he said.

Emanuel also continued to be angry at Democratic Party Chairman Howard Dean, who, he felt, was laying grandiose plans to make the Democrats the majority of the distant future while neglecting the opportunities in front of his face. "When you're Democratic chairman, you don't get to say, 'I'm only chairman for four presidential elections from now, and none of the elections before then,'" Emanuel said. "His management of money has left us at a historic disadvantage at a historic time. I don't know how else to say it." Then, a few days later, Emanuel and Dean finally struck a deal. Dean agreed to spend $12 million on a get-out-the-vote drive that would help candidates for Congress and other offices. That was far less than Emanuel wanted, but more than Dean had originally planned. Dean's staffers estimated that overall, they were spending about $30 million on the midterm elections, which they said was much more than previous DNC chairmen had spent. The two fiery Democrats were hardly reconciled, but the agreement allowed them to give up sniping at each other—actually, Emanuel had done most of the public sniping—and focus more intently on the election.

On September 13, Emanuel summoned the Democrats' top three dozen candidates to Washington to build momentum for the final push. In a daylong pep rally, the candidates met Democratic leaders, received last-minute briefings, and attended a fund-raiser at the Sewall-Belmont House, a museum of the women's movement. They also attended a two-hour boot camp on preparing for debates. Many were political novices, and they were about to face seasoned Republicans in one-on-one televised combat. A thoughtless comment or an ill-conceived phrase could destroy a candidacy that had been two years in the making. Political lore was full of infamous, sometimes fatal mistakes that candidates had made in debates. Al Gore never recovered from his loud, theatrical sighing at the responses of then-governor George Bush in 2000. When Vice President Dan Quayle in 1988 compared himself to President John F. Kennedy, he left himself open to the classic retort from Senator Lloyd Bentsen: "Senator, you're no Jack Kennedy."

Nancy Mathis, a former television reporter enlisted by the DCCC for the debate training, held court in a small classroom at Democratic headquarters, sounding like a cross between a schoolteacher and a motivational speaker. Mathis urged the candidates not to look down and mumble: "For goodness' sake, when the debate starts, don't talk to the little man who lives in the podium." Stressing the importance of a strong opening, she said, "A Broadway show doesn't start like this"—she made a mockingly small gesture—"it starts like this!" Here she threw her arms out dramatically. On a small television screen, Mathis showed footage of oratorical masters at work, such as Barack Obama parrying an interviewer's question on spending and former Texas governor Ann Richards, at the 1988 Democratic convention, saying the first President Bush "was born with a silver foot in his mouth." Mathis also showed failures, such as John Kerry stumbling when asked about being wishy-washy. She urged the candidates to be ready with one-liners apt to be quoted by reporters. "In your back pocket you should be loaded for bear, and when the opportunity presents itself I want you to deliver," Mathis said. But it was equally important to be ready for a rival's attacks. "If there are places you think your opponent is going to nail you, you bring it up," Mathis said. "I cannot tell you how much more power you have if you bring it up before they do." The candidates listened, scrawling tips like "use your hands" on white legal pads. One candidate had a question: Her opponent kept accusing her of running a "hate-filled" campaign, she said, and she wondered how to respond if he did it during a debate. Mathis urged her not to react defensively but to emphasize her positive ideas and proposals. Another candidate asked, "But what if they hold up a piece of negative mail we've sent and say, 'What about this?'" Mathis replied, "You say something like, 'Are there differences between us? You bet. If I didn't have criticisms of the job he was doing, I wouldn't be running.' And then you go into your positive proposals."

Emanuel showed up unannounced in the middle of Mathis' presentation. He wanted to impress on the candidates the importance of being ready—not just for debates, but for every minute of public campaigning from now on. "One bad statement can end a campaign," he told his charges. "That doesn't mean be scared. It does mean take this seriously." The candidates were entering the campaign's final pressure-filled weeks, Emanuel emphasized. "This is where the intensity gets hard," he said. "They'll be looking for a mistake. You'll find your consultants yelling at you, your kids will be upset because you're missing something that's important to them, that bastard Emanuel will be calling you on the phone." And the Republicans would spare no effort to bring them down. "They're on you. They know if they can stop you, they've taken a race off the field." The press was no better. "We all know reporters come up with questions they want to ask," Emanuel said, ticking off his points on his fingers. "They don't care—they don't give a rat's ass—what you want to say. [Iowa candidate] Bruce Braley told me he was asked seven times the other day his position on gay marriage. Seven times. You can give the right answer six times, but if you make a mistake on the seventh, that will be the one that matters. So don't give an inch. Repeat your answer until they give up.

"You are on at all times," he warned. "The moment you open that door, prep time is over. This is where mistakes happen. The intensity will get hard. Take a deep breath. If you don't think an answer will look good on the air, don't say it. Every day until Election Day is debate day. Any answer where you can't work in 'change' or 'new direction' or 'I will not be a rubber stamp'—don't give that answer."

Emanuel had cultivated each candidate in the room: Brad Ellsworth, the handsome sheriff from Indiana; Linda Stender, the diminutive state legislator from New Jersey; Lois Murphy, the lawyer running an intense campaign in the Philadelphia suburbs. For months, he'd been speaking to them every few days, living through their successes and setbacks. He knew many of their cell numbers by heart. "I'm really proud of everything you guys have done," he concluded. "But everything we did for the past one and a half years now comes to fruition. This is game day. You know yourselves. You know who's a hothead, who's going to mouth off, who needs to show they're the smartest person in the room. So just remember: Less is more."

The pace of the campaign was quickening. At a DCCC meeting a week later, staffer Brian Wolff told Emanuel that Congressman Jack Murtha had agreed to send an e-mail to his supporters asking them to contribute to the DCCC. "Jack Murtha has agreed to raise half a million dollars for us," Wolff said. "That's a big deal for Murtha to do, so if you could thank him . . ." That prompted Emanuel to wonder if the Democrats were using their stars as efficiently as possible. "Can we get Gore to go a couple more places?" he asked.

At the same meeting, communications director Bill Burton reported that journalists were beginning to say Bush had slowed the Democratic momentum with his renewed push on terrorism, and noted that a Gallup poll showed Bush's popularity climbing back up to 44 percent. He urged Emanuel to hold a press conference to assert that the Democrats still had the momentum. "The tide has turned a little," Burton said. "People see the Gallup poll, people think the terrorism thing is working." Emanuel did not want to do this, at least not by himself, and he proposed holding a joint press conference with Senator Chuck Schumer instead. But several staffers warned that Schumer would hog the limelight, distracting from

Emanuel's message about the House races. "Figure it out," Emanuel said wearily. "I'll do it with him, I'll do it alone." He concluded the meeting by saying, "You guys look as tired as I feel."

Emanuel did look exhausted. He had shed several pounds from his already slight frame, and his clothes hung from his body. He adopted a tough pose, but the endless criticism that came with running the campaign was getting to him. "I'm very tense," he said on September 21. "Nineteen months of hard work and I'm down to forty-eight days to go. And I've got a lot of pressure on me. And you have to constantly make decisions. By eight in the morning my wife has identified five things I've done wrong. By nine-thirty the blogs have told me about fifteen things on how stupid I am, and they haven't even gotten out of their underwear. By eleven o'clock, my colleagues have identified at least twenty-two failures on my part. By one o'clock my wife calls me and says, 'I left two off the list.' At three o'clock the blogs have identified another seventeen things about how stupid I am, and my colleagues would like to know if they can replace the [DCCC] chairman immediately instead of waiting for the end of the cycle. And that's my day."

He was especially tired of prodding other Democrats to do more. In addition to picking a public fight with Dean, Emanuel was frustrated that large liberal groups, such as America Coming Together, after spending millions in 2004, had been lethargic or inactive this time around. As he recounted the pressures he was under, Emanuel expressed the frustrated urgency that had energized his entire management of the campaign, his almost obsessive desire to grab his own party and shake it by the lapels.

"Our party has never been campaign battle-tested," Emanuel said. "You know what our party thinks? 'We're good people with good ideas. That's just enough, isn't it?' Being tough enough, mean enough, and vicious enough is just not what they want. Now, would they like to have someone around like that? They say yes. But the notion of doing what you've got to do and telling people, 'You know what? You're not putting enough money in the field here. You're not on the ground enough. Why did you go and advertise for a week and then leave?' Nobody wants to hear that. They just want to be patted on the back for the noble effort. No. We have not been successful for a reason."

Only a month and a half remained before the election. President Bush's approval had crept up, yet the Republican Congress was as unpopular as ever. It was hard for anyone to know what this portended. In a *New York Times*/CBS News poll published on September 21, only 25 percent of voters approved of Congress, its lowest rating since the Republican takeover in 1994. The *Times* nonetheless concluded that it was "highly unlikely" the Democrats would achieve a sweep similar to the 1994 Republican takeover because so many fewer seats were in play. Emanuel was an expert at reading polls, but he confessed to having no clue what it all meant. "I've seen all these polls coming in and the more data I get, the less I understand what's going on," he said. The country's mood was intense, volatile, and dark. But it was still unclear how that would play out.

Emanuel returned to Chicago at the end of September for Yom Kippur, the Jewish Day of Atonement, and his family observed the holy day with his brother Ezekiel. During the worship service, humanity's sins were enumerated, and the brothers began jokingly imputing them to each other. "This one—badmouthing people—that's your sin," Ezekiel said. Rahm pointed out another sin and answered, "This one's yours." Ezekiel Emanuel did not detect any excitement in his brother, just stress. The congressman was intensely aware that he had only a small window left. Rahm Emanuel told his brother he was concerned that Democratic candidates, feeling confident, would begin to ease up. In the early part of the campaign, the Democrats' problem had been that they did not believe they could win. Now their big danger was overconfidence. "You'd better not be like everyone else and count the chickens before they hatch," Rahm Emanuel told his brother. "I know you're a medical ethicist, but I am not interested in moral victories. I'm interested in victories."

That was the state of play on the morning of Thursday, September 28, when something happened that threatened to turn the political tide irreversibly against the Republicans. It was the kind of last-minute disaster that few campaigns can withstand. It began with a report on the ABC

News Web site at 3:06 P.M. that Congressman Mark Foley, a Florida Republican, had sent highly personal e-mails to a former congressional page. Using the e-mail address maf54@aol.com, Foley had asked about the page's hobbies, inquired what he wanted for his birthday, requested a photo, and referred to another page as being "in really great shape." The former page, upset by this unwanted attention, had forwarded the e-mails to a congressional staffer he knew, saying, "This freaked me out," and describing Foley's approaches as "sick, sick, sick, sick sick."

Foley's office reacted ferociously to the ABC News report, blaming it on an "ugly smear campaign." But that defiant attitude did not last long. The next day, September 29, ABC News obtained thirty-six pages of instant messages, or IMs, that Foley had exchanged with two other former pages, and posted them on its Web site. If the initial e-mails were oddly personal, the IMs were far worse, showing the congressman had engaged in graphic, sexually explicit conversations with an underage page who had worked on Capitol Hill. The IMs were filled with the usual typos and shorthand, but their meaning was unmistakable. The congressman and the former page, among other things, had engaged in a remarkably graphic discussion in which Foley prodded the young man for details on how he masturbated.

Top Republicans, including House Speaker Dennis Hastert and campaign director Tom Reynolds, hastily convened at the NRCC offices on Capitol Hill, where they agreed that Foley had to quit immediately. A one-sentence resignation letter was drafted. An aide was dispatched to Foley's house. The congressman signed the letter and left town to avoid an onslaught of reporters.

The impact on the elections was instantaneous and multilayered. Foley had been on course to certain reelection, and neither party had paid much attention to his race. Now the seat would automatically turn Democratic, because the Republicans did not have time to replace Foley's name on the ballot. But the broader impact was potentially much worse. When staffers called Emanuel to tell him Foley had quit, Emanuel said, "You know what to do." By now, everyone knew what that meant: "Don't say anything publicly. Let the story run its course." It was the same order Emanuel had given at other key moments, such as when Tom DeLay had been indicted. ABC was breaking the stories on the Foley scandal, so the ABC News broadcast became the day's central event at the DCCC offices, with staffers huddling around whichever television was closest. Emanuel, characteristically, was concerned about overconfidence and renewed predictions by some reporters that the Democrats surely were now guaranteed to retake the House. "I'm worried about everybody saying it's for sure," Emanuel said. "On Sunday, the Republicans were on a roll; by Friday, we couldn't lose. A lot can happen in a campaign." He added dryly, "I will say this, though. Our job is to keep our base energized and their base demoralized. I don't think this will energize their base."

The scandal obliterated Republican efforts to turn the national conversation back to terrorism. Five weeks before Election Day, three Republican seats were now all but guaranteed to flip to the Democrats. In Texas, an unexpected court decision had left the Republicans with only a write-in candidate in Tom DeLay's district. In Arizona, anti-immigration activist Randy Graf had unexpectedly won the Republican primary, and his radical views had prompted even the GOP to abandon him. And in Foley's seat, the Democrats' solid if unspectacular candidate, Tim Mahoney, was now a shoo-in. While Foley was not considered vulnerable before the scandal, his district had a healthy proportion of Democrats, and the DCCC had tried to field a decent candidate there just in case. Emanuel had started out having to win fifteen seats, and he was down to twelve before a single vote had been cast.

The Foley story quickly became a serious threat to the Republican regime. GOP leaders acknowledged they had known about Foley's e-mails since at least the previous year—and other inappropriate behavior on Foley's part for longer—but had done nothing other than occasionally confronting Foley. The pages were high school students who did errands for lawmakers, things like delivering packages, and they obviously had little power when approached by a lawmaker such as Foley. The Republican behavior played directly into the Democrats' message that the GOP,

in power too long, cared more about themselves than "people like you."
Even the conservative *Washington Times* called for Hastert's resignation.
"Either he was grossly negligent for not taking the red flags fully into
account and ordering a swift investigation," the *Times* said, "or he deliberately looked the other way in hopes that a brewing scandal would simply
blow away."

The timing and explosiveness of the story convinced some Republicans
that Emanuel must have been behind it. The scandal, they felt, was too perfect and too well timed to have erupted by chance. Emanuel was soon
pressed to say whether he had known of Foley's e-mails before they had
become public. In an October 8 appearance on ABC's *This Week*, host
George Stephanopoulos asked, "Did you or your staff know anything . . . ?"
Emanuel replied, "No. George, never saw them." Republican congressman
Adam Putnam, who was also on the show, tried to pin Emanuel down. "But
were you aware of them? You said you didn't see them," he asked. Emanuel
answered, "Never saw them." Stephanopoulos pressed, "So you were not
aware and no involvement?" Emanuel answered, "No, we never saw them.
No involvement." Putnam tried one more time, asking, "Was there any
awareness?" And again Emanuel responded, "No. Never saw them."

Emanuel was dancing because he had indeed been informed about the
e-mails (though not the more explicit IMs) a year earlier, in late 2005. A
Democratic Capitol Hill staffer had come across the e-mails and provided
them to Emanuel's communications director, Bill Burton, who in turn
had mentioned them to Emanuel. Emanuel, as he said to Stephanopoulos, had not actually seen them. There was no evidence that Emanuel had
provided the story to ABC News, and in fact he seemed to have done
nothing at all with the information. A bigger question, however, was
whether Emanuel, knowing about the e-mails, should have done more to
stop Foley. Emanuel's defenders said he did not know, as GOP leaders did,
that Foley had a long history of inappropriate behavior toward pages, and
that outside this context the e-mails seemed strange but not incriminat-
ing. As a member of the minority party, they added, there was little
Emanuel could have done.

Before the news erupted, Republicans had been fighting for weeks to reduce the number of GOP congressmen at risk—to "shrink the playing field"—while Democrats had been pushing to expand it. Foley's escapades instantly expanded the playing field, forcing Republicans to fight on a growing number of fronts. Reynolds, the House GOP's campaign leader, was one of those who had known about the e-mails early on, and that suddenly put him in danger of losing his own seat. Reynolds knew a vulnerable Republican when he saw one, even if it was himself, and he quickly switched to damage control. He aired an ad in which he apologized for not doing more to stop Foley and said, "Nobody is angrier and more disappointed than me that I didn't catch his lies." With only five weeks left in the race, the man in charge of running the Republican House campaigns would now be focused on his own survival instead of strategizing on how to defeat Democrats.

The ripples washed into other races as well. Democrat Patty Wetterling, a longtime children's advocate whose son had been abducted years earlier, surged in the polls after airing a harsh ad on the Republicans' handling of Foley. Allegations that Pennsylvania Republican congressman Don Sherwood had abused his mistress took on new life. Even Republicans who faced unrelated ethical questions, such as Congressman Richard Pombo of California, looked shakier. The DCCC, while keeping a low profile, encouraged Democratic candidates to tie their opponents to Foley, even if those connections were dubious. Democrat Mary Jo Kilroy, running against Congresswoman Deborah Pryce in Ohio, broadcast an ad asking, "What is going on in Washington? . . . Deborah Pryce's friend Mark Foley is caught using his position to take advantage of sixteen-year-old pages."

Republican candidates struggled mightily to show they took the matter seriously and to distance themselves from GOP leaders. Several canceled fund-raisers with Hastert. Gerlach, declaring himself "outraged" by Foley's conduct, donated a $1,000 contribution he had received from the disgraced congressman to a crime victims' center. Gerlach also ostentatiously canceled a fund-raiser with House majority leader John Boehner, saying he "felt it was inappropriate to move ahead with it as planned." On October 10, after a week and a half of nonstop Foley news coverage, a series of surveys predicted a disaster for the Republicans. A *USA Today* poll gave Democrats a twenty-three-point lead in the race for Congress. *Newsweek* found that 53 percent of Americans wanted the Democrats to retake Congress, compared to 35 percent who wanted the GOP to stay in power.

Republicans had already suffered two distinct jolts in the campaign, moments when their otherwise grinding decline in popularity had accelerated abruptly. The first had come in September 2005, when Hurricane Katrina struck a blow at Republican claims to competence. The second arrived in May 2006, when Bush's approval ratings hit their lowest point. The Foley scandal was a third. But while the first two blows were absorbed mostly by Bush, damaging House Republicans only indirectly, the third was a direct hit, engulfing House Republicans in a sex scandal five weeks before they were to face already disgusted voters.

There seemed to be no end to the Republicans' ability to cripple themselves. Until now GOP leaders had been hoping for, and Democrats had been fearing, a brilliant endgame or last-minute miracle. But now they were finally running out of time.

9

THE FINAL SPRINT

Democratic staffers in a shabby office across the street from the DCCC were scrutinizing two alternative mailings one day in late October, deciding which attack to launch next against Republican congressman Mike Ferguson of New Jersey. One mailing featured a striking image of a shattered U.S. Capitol, with a message about how Congress was broken and Ferguson was part of the problem. The second showed a baby in a diaper and included the slogan, "When something stinks, it's time for a change." "I like the dirty diaper," said one of the staffers. The other agreed. And just like that, a decision was made to spend thousands of Democratic dollars so voters in Ferguson's district could get mailings comparing Congress to a soiled diaper.

The room where that decision was made, along with hundreds of others like it, was affectionately called the "boiler room" by those who frequented it. Covered with election maps and political paraphernalia, it was home to the DCCC's Independent Expenditure operation. Campaign finance laws had required Emanuel to create this independent group to direct the vast majority of Democratic TV ads. Its independence was in truth limited, since it was run by John Lapp and Ali Wade, who'd been two of Emanuel's top DCCC aides before switching over. Still, Emanuel was forced to transfer half the money he was raising to this operation, with little control over the message. Emanuel could decide how many dollars flowed to which races, but he had no influence over the nature or content of the ads. This was a source of great frustration to a man who wanted to control every aspect of the campaign.

With the election now eighteen days away, Lapp and Wade were signing off on dozens of ads each day. They were making strategic decisions, literally by the minute, on how to spend money in a fast-changing political landscape. This was the back end of the money pipeline, the place where the millions raised by Emanuel and others were shaped into attacks on Republicans. Many more Republicans had become vulnerable since the Mark Foley scandal, so the Democrats were airing ads in a good number of new races, as reflected in a long list of congressional districts scrawled on a white board along one wall. In the last few days, Lapp had spent $200,000 targeting Congressman David Reichert, $316,000 attacking Congressman John Porter in Nevada, and $100,000 against Congresswoman Melissa Hart in Pennsylvania.

From morning until late night, staffers brought in ads crafted by media consultants for Lapp and Wade to approve or reject, which they usually did within seconds. On this day, October 20, a staffer handed over a script for a TV spot attacking Minnesota Republican Michele Bachmann for her stand on taxes. But Wade wanted to go after Bachmann's record on child care instead, to portray her as bad for American families. "Let's have a 'bad for family' script," she said. The aide took the script back to be reworked.

Almost all the DCCC ads, like those of the Republicans, were negative. As Lapp and Wade watched them unfurl on their computers, they all seemed to feature grainy footage, scornful phrases, and announcers who sounded like they could scarcely believe the sheer depravity of the Republican in question. Lapp insisted this negativity energized rather than depressed him. "This is combat—suit up," he said, adding that it was important to stay on the offensive. "I hate Ping-Pong," Lapp said. "If they're going to volley, I'd rather take a metal folding chair and smash it over their head."

Lapp and Wade also argued about an ad accusing Pennsylvania congressman Mike Fitzpatrick of wanting to "stay the course" on Iraq. The problem was, Fitzpatrick had actually said he was against staying the course in the war. But Lapp insisted Fitzpatrick's votes in Congress showed otherwise. "Fuck 'em," Lapp exploded. He believed Republicans would not hesitate to air a similar ad against a Democrat. "They would fuck us with this fucker," he said. "Why do we get all caught up in this?"

The scene in the boiler room was chaotic in these final weeks, with phones beeping and staffers running in and out. James Carville called at one point, prompting Wade to say with exasperation, "Can we change our phone number so he stops calling?" Adjustments were constant and the strategy was always shifting. If a Democratic candidate was doing better than expected, the Democrats would cancel a planned advertising blitz in his district and move the money elsewhere. If a Republican suddenly looked vulnerable, new attacks were ordered against him. When the Mark Foley story broke, Lapp and Wade had rolled out commercials tying Republicans to the scandal. This was a fast-moving, high-stakes game. A good choice, a good ad, could give a struggling campaign a shot at victory. But it also was easy to choose wrong, to pick a message that did not work.

With Election Day so close, the parties had cast aside any restraint and were now releasing torrents of commercials. The Democratic spots hammered Republicans for opposing an increase in the minimum wage and failing to protect Social Security. The GOP ads attacked Democrats as soft on immigration and national security. The sums involved were enormous, running into the tens of millions on each side. The Democrats' first big expenditure, over the summer, had been $400,000 in Kentucky and Indiana—an attempt to soften up two Republican-leaning battlegrounds—and it had escalated from there.

Outside groups also were pouring in money. The AFL-CIO had spent $40 million to motivate its members to vote, and a trial lawyers' association had bought ads to boost the Democrats in several districts. On the Republican side, the U.S. Chamber of Commerce announced it was spending $11 million, and a secretive group called the Economic Freedom Fund had also jumped in. The most effective and controversial ads, however, were crafted by MoveOn.org, a liberal group that targeted several Republicans with ads saying they'd been "caught red-handed." The spots unfolded in black-and-white, then the candidates' hands turned a bright, bloody red. "Congressman Chris Chocola—seniors relied on him," the narrator intoned in one ad, referring to an Indiana lawmaker. "Yet Congressman Chocola accepted $40,000 from big drug companies and got caught red-handed voting for a law that actually prevents Medicare from negotiating lower drug prices for our seniors." MoveOn produced successive waves of "red-handed" ads on different topics, from the Iraq war to energy policy. Republicans protested strenuously that the ads were misleading—the lawmakers had not done anything illegal, they had only been "caught" voting—and a number of television stations refused to run them.

As the campaign's volume increased, Emanuel was increasingly showing the strain. He'd been campaigning ferociously since his appointment almost two years earlier, believing his predecessors had waited too long to shift into high gear. As it started to seem that the Democrats had a chance to retake the House, the pressure had risen. When analysts began flatly predicting victory, the pressure had shot up even further. Emanuel's political future rested on the outcome. If the election was successful, he would probably be thrust into the House Democratic leadership at a relatively young age, putting him in line to be House Speaker someday. If the Democrats disappointed once again, Emanuel's career might never recover, and it would always be said he had muffed the party's best opportunity in a generation.

The personal toll was significant. Emanuel spoke frequently of missing his children, Zach, Ilana, and Leah. When he was on the road, he called his wife, Amy, several times a day for updates on the kids. Ilana, eight, at one point said she hoped he'd lose the next election so he wouldn't have to travel so much. "I hate this fucking job," Emanuel said after recounting that story. Zach, who was nine at the end of the campaign, stopped talking to him on the phone when he called from the road. At home,

Zach had to beg him to stop talking on his cell phone while they were tossing a football. After a fund-raiser in Boston around this time, Emanuel called Amy and told her, "I didn't get much sleep last night. Shit going on in the head . . . How are the kids?" After listening to her report, he added, "I'm so sorry I'm missing two little girls in the bathtub. Sounds peaceful." In a discussion with his old friend George Stephanopoulos, Emanuel wondered aloud how they'd been able to work so hard during the 1992 Clinton campaign. "Three things," Stephanopoulos replied. "We were younger, we didn't have wives, and we didn't have kids."

Emanuel also suffered physically. His hair had turned much whiter during the campaign and he had lost fourteen pounds, his clothes hanging on a scarecrow frame. As Election Day neared, he awoke every morning at three o'clock, agitating and strategizing. By day's end, his fingers would be trembling and his nose running from fatigue. He not infrequently felt sick; sometimes he had to put his head in his hands for several seconds to recover his equilibrium. One day Emanuel was in his office, wearing a blue-and-yellow striped tie and a white shirt whose fold lines were still evident. The Bruce Springsteen song "Hungry Heart" was playing on his iPod. Emanuel had been suffering various health problems, including a slipped disk and high cholesterol. He was due that day to get results of a blood test for yet another ailment. This was a man who had always kept in shape through ballet, running, and swimming. The chaos of his life was evident. At one point, buzzers were going off to signal a vote on the House floor; his brother Ari was on the cell phone; an assistant came in to report a sudden change to his schedule; and a reporter was sitting on the couch with a tape recorder. Emanuel seemed agitated. But he grinned and said, "Do I seem unflappable?"

The biggest source of stress, of course, was the progress of individual campaigns. Emanuel was keeping close track of about four dozen races. The number of competitive contests was expanding, which was good, because it meant more Democrats were putting up strong challenges, but it also created increasingly difficult choices. A Democrat somewhere would unexpectedly edge into contention—Harry Mitchell in Arizona, say, or Tessa Hafen in Nevada—and Emanuel would quickly need to familiarize himself with the details of the race so he could make an informed decision on whether to inject more money into it. Over and over, he had to sift through the cacophonous advice directed his way and decide which candidates were worth the investment.

Emanuel took his forty-seventh and penultimate trip around the country—to Hartford, Boston, and upstate New York—two weeks before the election. Every independent analyst by this point was predicting an electoral bloodbath. "The outline of this election couldn't be clearer: 2006 is a Democratic year," political scientist Larry Sabato wrote in his Crystal Ball newsletter. "Republicans are more despondent than they have been for decades." In addition to the broad sweep of issues such as Iraq and corruption, the Republicans were spooked, and they seemed curiously intent on self-destruction. In one of the stranger episodes, Congresswoman Barbara Cubin, a Wyoming Republican, was forced to apologize for threatening to hit a wheelchair-bound opponent.

Yet Emanuel was hardly upbeat. It was his nature to assume the worst. His own analysis led him to believe the Democrats were leading by big margins in twelve Republican-held districts, leading slightly in six more, dead even in another fourteen, and within striking distance in thirteen others. That math looked good, given that the Democrats needed just fifteen seats. But predictions of success only increased Emanuel's anxiety. He snapped at journalists and ridiculed Democrats who were predicting victory, even admonishing Democratic leader Nancy Pelosi to take nothing for granted.

He sounded more upbeat for public consumption, especially when he was addressing party activists. In such settings, Emanuel tried to fire up the troops by making them feel they could be part of history. The first stop on Emanuel's trip was a fund-raiser for Connecticut Democrat Joe Courtney at a supporter's large Tudor-style house in West Hartford. Courtney was running in the most Democratic-leaning district in the nation that was represented by a Republican. Democrats had been trying to knock off that Republican, Congressman Rob Simmons, since his election in 2000. When several dozen guests had settled in the living room with roast beef sandwiches, Emanuel lashed out at the GOP and the Iraq war. "Donald Rumsfeld is from Chicago, and when he gets home I'm going to meet him with a baseball bat," Emanuel said. "As my grandparents would say, it's a *shandeh* what he has done." *Shandeh* is a Yiddish word for "travesty" or "scandal." This was the year, Emanuel told Courtney's supporters, that they could finally beat Simmons. "You've never had an environment like this," he said. "You've never had a candidate who's well funded like this. Do not become woulda-coulda-shoulda Democrats. When you think you've knocked on the last door, knock on ten more doors."

Emanuel flew to Boston that night for the campaign's final big fundraising dinner, an event that turned out to be a surprisingly emotional moment in the campaign. When Emanuel arrived, Nancy Pelosi and other lawmakers were mingling with 150 wealthy Democratic donors. The prospect of finally retaking the House hung in the air, giving the evening a restless energy. Victory seemed at hand, but no one was quite prepared to believe it, creating an odd mix of euphoria and apprehension. Massachusetts senators Edward Kennedy and John Kerry were contributing $500,000 each, and the dinner raised $2.5 million, the most for any event in DCCC history. The setting was the enormous modern-style home of Alan Solomont, the prominent Democratic fund-raiser. The living room featured a wavy red wall, a sloping twenty-five-foot ceiling, and large windows looking onto a floodlit pool. Abstract wooden sculptures resembling wading birds stood against one wall, and black-clad servers circulated with trays of wine and sushi. In one corner, Pelosi, in black pants and a checkered jacket, chatted with a small group; in another, Congressman Barney Frank was holding court while renowned Harvard law professor Laurence Tribe looked on.

The dinner itself, consisting of almond-crusted chicken, orzo, and donkey-shaped cookies, was held in a large tent in Solomont's backyard. Massachusetts congressman Ed Markey rose to introduce Emanuel. "When people call him abrupt, I have to laugh—not compared to the nuns at Immaculate Conception grammar school," Markey said. "I have never seen Rahm hit anyone with a ruler. But he hits you with the potential pain of more years of Republican rule, and that is what really hurts." When Emanuel spoke, he hid his personal anxiety about the election's outcome. "This is an election of historic magnitude," he told the gathering. "Twenty months ago, all the, as my grandparents used to say, all the *chochems* in this business—if you don't get that, there will be a translation later—all the geniuses said that the Democratic Party was the minority party and we'd better get used to it. Now those same people are having very different predictions." The Democrats now had just three vulnerable incumbents, he said, while they were actively challenging forty-six Republicans. "In the last two weeks, we want to close this election on the Iraq war," Emanuel said. "This is a referendum on Iraq. We want to make sure people know we have a different direction, different goals, for this country. And if we do that we can have a very, very good result."

Pelosi then rose and promised that the Democrats would transform the country if they won. "We will make a tremendous difference, God willing, if we win in the next thirteen days," Pelosi said. Then she looked at Emanuel. "Is it okay if I say 'God willing'?" she joked. "Rahm always says to me, 'Don't raise expectations.'" Emanuel answered, "There's a Jewish tradition—never put the crib up until the baby is born." That prompted Frank to chime in, "You have to be ecumenical, Rahm. In the Catholic tradition, you never take the crib down."

As the laughter died down, a familiar silhouette appeared outside the tent, and Pelosi introduced "the forty-second president of the United States." Bill Clinton strode in, looking slim and fit, as he had since his heart surgery not long before, though the bags under his eyes were pronounced and his hair was a pure snowy white. When he spoke, without notes, Clinton showed why Democrats missed him so badly. "When Robert Kennedy was killed in 1968, when I was a boy, that was the last chance we had to bring this country together across racial and income lines and to build a unifying politics," Clinton said. "All the rest of us, all this long time, who've longed for it, who've fought for it, who've devoted our public lives to it, we never wanted to see the Republicans as enemies.

We always wanted campaigns to be arguments about what we should do and what the best ideas were. We were always willing to sit down and listen to someone who wanted to do something we didn't, and try to find a way to bring the country together and move the country forward. These candidates for the House and Senate are giving us a chance to replenish something I have been fighting for all my life."

By seven-forty-five the next morning Emanuel was at Logan International Airport, clutching a small Starbucks coffee and pacing around the waiting area as he talked on his cell phone with various Democratic candidates and waited for a small plane to Albany. When he reached a candidate, he asked brusquely, "What's goin' on?" If he got voice mail, he left a curt message: "It's Rahm. Call me." He could not keep still, at one point riding up an escalator and down another just to keep moving. Among those he reached was Pennsylvania candidate Lois Murphy. "No mistakes—take a deep breath," Emanuel urged the evidently nervous Democrat. Murphy worried that she had insufficient money for the campaign's final stretch. "Don't game out your head," Emanuel said, somewhat incoherently.

Emerging later into the Albany airport, Emanuel was hustled to a rally for candidate Kirsten Gillibrand, a former Clinton administration official. Emanuel's job was to introduce Clinton, who told the crowd, "Don't give up on anyone. Not independents who say they've never voted. Not Republicans who've never voted for a Democrat." Next Emanuel sped to a fund-raiser where he warned two hundred Gillibrand supporters the Republicans were not going to let up. "It's not like they're going to roll over in eleven days and let you scratch their bellies," Emanuel said. "They will not give up power easily." He focused on Gillibrand's opponent, Republican congressman John Sweeney. "We have built, for the last eighteen months, toward this moment," he said. "This is the moment of truth. We've got a gun. We've got it pointed at him. We can see the whites of his eyes. For the next eleven days, we're going to fire at him. He won't know what hit him."

Back in his car, hurtling toward Utica, Emanuel once again bemoaned the high expectations that surrounded the Democrats' campaign. The predictions of a landslide victory could lead to overconfidence; on the other hand, lowered expectations could result in apathy. The expectations game was tricky. "It's a lot of people in the bleachers predicting the outcome of the game," Emanuel said. "But what am I going to do about it? If I say we're not going to do well, it hurts our fund-raising and excitement. I don't have enough hours in the day to deal with it. It's not what I would want, but—and I'm not very good at accepting this—there are some things I can't control." With Election Day in his sights, Emanuel was still bitter at how Republicans, and even some in his own party, had initially belittled the candidates he'd recruited. "We got Joe Sestak in Pennsylvania, a three-star vice admiral," Emanuel said. "At first, when he was down twenty points, they said I was smoking crack. Well, we got him a campaign manager, a media consultant, a polling consultant, and he's a great fund-raiser. And he's now up fifty to forty-three [percent]. They laughed at Heath Shuler—'He's just a football player, and he wasn't very good.' All the candidates they dismissed, saying they're second-tier, B candidates . . ." He shook his head. "Let me tell you, they've got some C incumbents."

Arriving at a small senior citizens' center in Utica, Emanuel joined the local candidate, Mike Arcuri, in chatting with three dozen elderly men and women. Arcuri was a handsome, likeable Italian American district attorney, and Emanuel considered him a natural politician like Clinton, the highest compliment he could pay. The seniors seemed to enjoy the attention from the two men. Emanuel, bantering in a casual way that few of his colleagues ever saw, joined a Scrabble game and helped one elderly woman spell a high-value word—*zit*—to her great pleasure. "Mike, I got her thirteen points," Emanuel told Arcuri. "What have you done for her?" Arcuri, for his part, clearly wanted to impress Emanuel. "One of the important things about being able to campaign with Rahm is that he gets an idea of my message and how it's resonating," Arcuri said. "When I talk to him on the phone, I say, 'Here's what I'm dealing with.' But when he comes here, he can see it." Emanuel began flirting with Arcuri's mother, who had just walked in. "We have a lot in common, our traditions do," she said. Emanuel answered, "Yes, our mothers drive us both crazy."

Back in the car, Emanuel called Congressman Alan Mollohan of West Virginia, whose prospects had improved tremendously. Earlier, Emanuel and the DCCC staff had worried that Mollohan was not mounting a sufficiently vigorous campaign, but he'd picked up his pace and his Republican challenger had faded. Emanuel now urged him not to get distracted in the final days. "Alan, you are a hundred percent focused on Alan Mollohan," Emanuel said. "Alan, finish your campaign, please. I love you."

As Emanuel raced round the country, individual campaigns were entering their endgames. Every misstep on either side was magnified, because voters were paying attention now and there was little time to recover. The inexperience of some Democratic candidates was beginning to show, especially when it came to debates. Patsy Madrid, the New Mexico attorney general, performed poorly in a televised debate with Republican Heather Wilson, appearing nervous and making several gaffes. At one point she said, "You have to be careful about taking large sums of money from lobbyists, but even if you do, it is only to give them access." Wilson pounced, saying, "I can't believe what I just heard. . . . No one buys access in my office." When Madrid was asked whether she would prevent a tax increase, she stood uncomfortable and silent for several seconds before answering the question. Madrid had been leading in the polls, but the performance threw her lead into question.

In Illinois, Tammy Duckworth's race against Republican Peter Roskam had become ugly. Each party had sunk about $3 million into the campaign, making it one of the most expensive in the country. Duckworth portrayed Roskam as both a right-wing extremist and a typical politician. "Rubber Stamp Roskam—Just another go-along, spend-a-lot, bust-the-budget politician," said one of her mailings. One of the more vivid Republican mailings attacked Duckworth for being insufficiently hardline on taxes. "Taxes or diapers?" asked the mailing, apparently on the theory that if people paid more taxes they'd be broke when the time came to buy diapers. Duckworth and Roskam also faced off in a last-minute debate. "Over and over, he has made it clear he supports the status quo," Duckworth said of Roskam. Roskam replied by suggesting Duckworth was a tool of Emanuel and the Democratic machine. "My opponent, in her name-calling, has called me a rubber stamp," he said. "But I challenge my opponent to come up with one issue on which she differs from Congressman Rahm Emanuel." Roskam was smooth while Duckworth was edgy.

Five hundred miles away in North Carolina, Democrat Heath Shuler, another of Emanuel's star candidates, was having better luck. As the election approached, the *Wall Street Journal* published a page-one story describing how Shuler's opponent, Congressman Charles Taylor, often benefited from the federal money he steered to his district. This confirmed for many voters that Taylor was a shady character. Then Shuler and Taylor had their own debate fiasco. They had agreed to a radio debate, but Taylor did not show up at the agreed-upon time, appearing instead at a different radio station and proposing to take part remotely. Shuler angrily charged that the congressman was afraid to confront him in person; Taylor said he did not see what difference it made whether they were in the same studio. After a brief opening statement, Shuler ripped off his headset and stormed off the set. Taylor told the *Asheville Citizen-Times* that Shuler was being immature, while Shuler said bitterly, "We've got to do this face-to-face. He's got to look at me when he lies about me." Neither candidate looked particularly statesmanlike.

On November 2—after twenty months of campaigning, six hundred polls, more than four hundred cheesecakes sent out, seventy House districts visited, and countless hours with candidates—Emanuel set off for his final trip, to a district outside Las Vegas. The destination epitomized how the political field had shifted in the Democrats' favor: The Democratic candidate there, Tessa Hafen, had not even been on Emanuel's radar a few weeks earlier, but she was rapidly gaining ground on Congressman Jon Porter. Emanuel's mood careened between a dark, almost overwhelming anxiety and a giddiness that the ordeal was nearly over. In classic Las Vegas style, Hafen's fund-raiser was held at The Gin Mill, a bar and casino with twenty-four-hour video poker. Patrons watched college football on an assortment of televisions around the bar. James Carville and Paul Begala had flown in to lend their celebrity to the event, and when they showed up, Carville, wearing jeans and a long-sleeved black T-shirt, immediately headed for the beer. Asked how the campaign for the House was going, he hesitated uncharacteristically. "I don't know," Carville said. "You'd think someone sixty-two years old, who's been doing this so long, would have some idea. But I'm nervous. I try to convince myself something bad is going to happen, and I can't. In my brain, I think we'll do fine." In his heart, however, he was less sure.

Hafen, a former press secretary to Senator Harry Reid, was smilingly at ease—"It's time to end the scandal-ridden Republican Congress," she told her supporters as they gnawed on Buffalo wings—but Emanuel took a more somber tone. "We're all having a good time, but you know one thing in the back of your mind: This race will be decided by a thousand votes either way," he warned. "My mother, who introduced me to politics, taught me, when she was taking us to civil rights marches, 'You never give in and you never give up.' We're not giving in and we're not giving up." When it was Carville's turn, he gesticulated jerkily as he ripped into Congressman Porter for being a lackey of House Republican leaders. "I always thought he had an appropriate last name—Porter—because he carries their baggage very well," Carville said scornfully. "If you look at him, he just is what he is—he is a porter for power. He kind of schleps it. He can carry five bags at a time."

The next morning, Emanuel's mood was expansive. This was his last day of school; in an hour he would be attending his final candidate event of the 2006 campaign, a press conference with Hafen. He had been desperately anticipating an end to the countless plane trips, the cramped seats and cheap food and unpredictable delays. Gulping down two cups of black coffee in the lobby of Las Vegas' Mandalay Bay hotel and casino, Emanuel chattered nonstop. "We have a seat in New Hampshire we are going to fucking steal," he said, referring to Republican congressman Charlie Bass, whose polls had plummeted unexpectedly. "Our party is always, 'Oh, we can't do it,'" Emanuel added, mimicking a whiny child. "Half of winning is thinking you can win." Then proximity to the Hooters casino in Las Vegas prompted him to reminisce about how President

Clinton had gotten visibly angry when his own Justice Department had sued Hooters for sex discrimination. That misunderstood the whole point of Hooters, Clinton felt. Emanuel, who was then Clinton's senior advisor, remembered telling the president sarcastically, "I'm sure Hooters would be happy if you'd file a brief on their behalf, Mr. President." He laughed uproariously at his own story.

On the way to the press conference, Emanuel called Arizona Democrat Harry Mitchell. Like many Democrats these days, Mitchell, after months of trailing, suddenly seemed to have a shot at knocking off a longtime incumbent. Emanuel ordered Mitchell to wrap up his campaign by stressing his support for stem cell research. "I want you to close on stem cell," Emanuel said. He told Mitchell what his message should be: "'It's not a Democratic issue, a Republican issue, or an independent issue. It's about moving forward versus moving back. Arizona needs to send a wake-up call to Washington.'" Then, forgoing his usual sign-off of "Fuck you, I love you," Emanuel told Mitchell, "Harry, I'm proud of you. You're going to win." In a rare fit of exuberance, Emanuel called his assistant, Katie Johnson, and ordered her to send cheesecakes to all the major Democratic challengers. "I just think everyone should get one last cheesecake," he said. Seventy more cheesecakes went out, to be received on Election Day.

At the Hafen press conference, on the sunny driveway of her adobe-style campaign headquarters, Emanuel told reporters, "This is my last stop of twenty months traveling around the country. I've been to more than seventy districts, and I cannot think of a better place to talk about the winds of change."

That was November 3. Two days later, November 5, the Sunday before the election, Emanuel appeared on NBC's *Meet the Press* with his Republican counterpart, Tom Reynolds, and the heads of the Senate campaigns, Democrat Charles Schumer and Republican Elizabeth Dole. Reynolds was still reeling from the Foley scandal and appeared dispirited, while Dole was harshly aggressive, talking over the other participants. All the lawmakers except Schumer seemed on edge, and tempers simmered.

When moderator Tim Russert asked about the Iraq war, Dole said, "You know, it's almost as if the Democrats, it's like they are content with losing, because to pull out, to withdraw, from this war is losing—no question about it." Emanuel, enraged at the message that Democrats were happy to lose a war, tried to interject. Russert wanted to let him respond, but Dole kept talking. "Senator, you've said something that's wrong," Emanuel put in. Dole said, "Rahm, I want to finish what—" The two lawmakers continued to talk over each other. Emanuel said, "I will not sit idly by with an accusation that Democrats are content with losing. We want to win, and we want a new direction to Iraq, because after three years—" Dole kept talking, and Russert said, "Time out, time out." Emanuel said angrily, "You should take that back, Senator."

Other developments that day made the Democrats wonder one last time if their worst fears were coming true, if somehow, despite two years of unrelenting bad news for the Republicans, the GOP would pull out a victory. Shortly before the *Meet the Press* show, the Iraqi high tribunal had found former Iraqi leader Saddam Hussein guilty of crimes against humanity and sentenced him to die. This was just the kind of dramatic last-minute news that politicians dread. President Bush and many Republican candidates seized eagerly on the announcement in an attempt to shift the momentum in the campaign's final hours. At the same time, several polls were suggesting that the Democrats' lead had significantly narrowed. Most dramatically, a Pew Research Center survey found that Democrats were favored by 47 percent to 43 percent among likely voters—significantly less than the eleven-point lead they had enjoyed two weeks earlier and dangerously close to the margin of error. Emanuel called his brother Ari and told him he did not know how to react to these last-minute polls. Democrats still seemed to be doing well in their individual races, he said, but that was a hard case to make.

Republicans played on these doubts, trying to deflate the enthusiasm among Democratic activists and build up excitement on their own side. Republicans insisted their vaunted "seventy-two-hour program," a last-minute mobilization designed to bring GOP voters to the polls, would

wipe out Democratic leads in many places. Karl Rove, a master of psychological warfare, made a point of appearing buoyant in public, suggesting
he knew something outsiders did not. President Bush took off on a ten-
state campaign swing, predicting a Republican victory everywhere he
went. "You might remember in 2004, some of the folks in Washington listened to the prognosticators and they started picking out their offices in
the West Wing," Bush said in Springfield, Missouri. "And then it turned
out the people went to the polls, and the movers weren't needed."

The day before the election, Democrats hammered doggedly for a
final time on the failures of the Iraq war, trying to ensure the war was on
voters' minds as they went to the polls. Vice President Dick Cheney
played into their hands by declaring that the administration would continue "full steam ahead" in Iraq no matter what the election's outcome.
Not for the first time, Cheney sounded suspiciously as though he had
contempt for the views of the electorate. At noon, Emanuel held a conference call with reporters to reinforce the Democratic criticism of the
war. "We've had a policy that is long on slogans and short on strategy," he
said. "We've heard 'Mission accomplished,' 'The terrorists are in their last
throes,' 'We have turned the corner,' 'When they stand up we'll stand
down.' None of those are a strategy."

Election Day dawned pleasant and autumnal in Washington, with temperatures rising to 59 degrees. It was 61 degrees in Illinois, where Tammy
Duckworth was battling for a seat outside Chicago. It was rainy in western North Carolina, where Heath Shuler was trying to oust longtime
incumbent Charles Taylor. "Polls Give GOP a Lift on Election Eve," proclaimed the *Washington Times*, always happy to make things look as bad as
possible for Democrats. As the morning progressed, Emanuel called
Democratic Party chairmen in five key states, checking on voter turnout,
absentee ballots, and early voting. But little meaningful information
would be available until night fell and the polls closed. Thousands of
lawyers for both parties had been stationed at voting places around the
country, standard procedure since the 2000 presidential race, but there
were no significant reports of voter intimidation or fraud. Throughout

the day, Emanuel alternated between confidence and caution. "Obviously, everyone who's ever done politics is very nervous on Election Day," he said. But finally, a moment had arrived when there was nothing more he could do. "We're on top of every piece of information," Emanuel said. "Let it be noted: I'm trying to be calm just once in my life."

10

ELECTION NIGHT

Members of Congress, top strategists, and other Democrats drifted toward DCCC headquarters at dusk on November 7 to await the election results. It had been a wild two years since the last congressional election, when Democrats lost three seats in the House. In the interim, a newly reelected president had seen his popularity utterly disintegrate. The public had turned in frustration against a war originally supported by a large, enthusiastic majority. And a Republican Party that had seemed positioned to rule for decades had been undermined by scandal, war, and misjudgment. Analysts who had originally forecast minimal Democratic gains had dramatically recalibrated their predictions by Election Night and were now saying the Democrats would swamp the opposition. The question now, as the polls began to close across the country, was whether the longtime Republican advantages in money and organization would limit the Democrats' gains, perhaps even holding them under the fifteen seats they needed to retake the House majority.

As night fell, Emanuel's family members arrived from Chicago and joined him in his office to wait. His wife, Amy, was there, along with their three children. The kids were aware this was a big night, but they were too young to truly comprehend its significance. For the moment, they were more concerned with eating cookies and playing on the office computer. Emanuel's brother Ezekiel also showed up, and the two hugged. Other old friends materialized, such as David Axelrod, who had first worked with Emanuel on Mayor Richard Daley's 1989 campaign in Chicago and had since become one of his most trusted advisors. Nancy Pelosi, who hoped to end the night as the presumptive Speaker of the House, was ensconced in an office a few feet away, with her own family and friends.

Outside Emanuel's office, the DCCC staffers who had worked on the campaign for nearly two years were gathering in clusters around various desks and televisions. A somewhat scruffy group of young men and women, many still in their twenties, they had dressed up moderately for the evening, exchanging jeans and T-shirts for slacks and dress shirts. In the closing weeks of the campaign, the male staffers had held a "moustaches for the majority" contest, to see who could grow the best moustache by Election Day. During the contest, one staffer had e-mailed around each morning a "moustache of the day," a photo of the moustache of a member of Congress, to see if the other staffers could guess whose it was. But many staffers had difficulty generating much facial hair, leaving them with a somewhat untidy look, and they had been ordered to shave by Election Day.

The DCCC was hardly an elegant location for an Election Night party. The room was filled with cubicles, and small offices for Emanuel and his senior staffers lined the walls. A metal vat, filled with bottles of Heineken and Amstel Light on ice, was tucked under one desk. Catered food was spread out in a small kitchen, including sad-looking roast beef sandwiches and the inevitable cookies shaped like American flags. Staffers had ordered boxes of pizza, that staple of campaign life. The small press office shared by Bill Burton and Sarah Feinberg always had copies of the day's front pages taped to its door, and today those pages reflected the importance of the moment. A headline in the *Arizona Republic* read, "Arizona Casts Its Vote." The *Hartford Courant* asked, "Is the Mood Blue?" The *Palm Beach Post* announced, "The Final Push." Televisions scattered around the DCCC offices were tuned to news networks, mostly CNN.

The center of attention for the evening was a large, white dry-erase board that had been attached to one wall and was divided into some eighty squares for various contested House races. Each square had the name of a district written at the top in blue or green ink—"KY-04" for the Fourth District of Kentucky, for example. One square said "IL-05 (Rahmie)"; that referred to the Fifth District of Illinois, represented by Emanuel. The outcome of that race was not actually in doubt.

It was not until 8 P.M. that the first partial results from around the country trickled in, and interns dashed up to the board to record the percentages in Magic Marker, eliciting cheers or groans from the assembled staffers. As newer figures came in, old ones were erased.

The big surprise early in the evening came from Kentucky, where, based on preliminary results, Democrat John Yarmuth seemed to have defeated longtime GOP congresswoman Anne Northrup, whom the Democrats had been trying to knock off for years. Yarmuth, who had never held elected office, was founder and editor of an alternative weekly called the *Louisville Eccentric Observer*. Yarmuth had not been given much of a chance to win, and the DCCC had invested little money in his campaign. The fact that he had apparently won anyway seemed a promising sign.

The first candidate to be officially declared a winner was Sheriff Brad Ellsworth in Indiana, one of Emanuel's star candidates and a macho figure in a conservative district. When CNN anchor Wolf Blitzer intoned, "Brad Ellsworth will be elected the next congressman from Indiana's Eighth District," the staffers applauded and whooped. When a race was definitively called like this, the interns drew a big red square around it. As the night proceeded, more and more red squares would fill up the board. It was hardly a high-tech display, but it had the effect of laying out the results starkly.

The numbers looked good in Indiana's Second District as well, when an intern at 8:30 wrote "D-59.2, R-40.9" in that box. The polls in Indiana and Kentucky had closed before those in other parts of the country, and they were being watched as early indicators of where the night might lead.

As the results rolled in, Emanuel was in his office talking to his family and friends, but he popped out frequently to confer with staffers and check the board. He would rap on individual squares with his finger and render his assessment. "Hey, our guy may make it," he would say, or "That's not going so well." Zach, a brown-haired, dark-eyed boy of nine, was running messages between Emanuel and various staffers. At one point Zach dashed over to Emanuel and informed him excitedly, "Menendez won!" This was a reference to New Jersey senator Bob Menendez. "Oh, really?" said Emanuel as Zach exuberantly jumped into his arms. "Now run get me some more numbers." At another point Zach breathlessly told Katie Johnson, Emanuel's assistant, "I'm supposed to tell my dad that Tim Mahoney is in a tight race." He clearly had little idea what he was saying, but just as clearly he was enjoying himself immensely.

Everyone in the room was watching the Senate races as well, of course, if a little less emotionally. The Democrats needed six seats to take that chamber, and that seemed all but impossible. Still, when Democrat Bob Casey was declared the winner in Pennsylvania, defeating Republican Rick Santorum, a staffer proclaimed, "The devil goes down."

If Yarmuth's surprise victory buoyed Emanuel at this early stage, he was beginning to worry about two incumbent Democratic congressmen from Georgia, Jim Marshall and John Barrow, who seemed to be in trouble. They had always faced stiff challenges in their conservative Southern districts, and this year was proving no different. "Marshall's behind and Barrow's behind," Emanuel said. "I'd like to know what's going on with the incumbents." He dispatched a staffer to call those campaigns for a fuller report.

When Yarmuth was officially declared the victor in Kentucky, confirming the preliminary numbers, excited cheers erupted. "Yarmuth—at a bargain, three hundred grand," yelled John Lapp. That was how much the DCCC had spent in his district. Northrup had been defeated after outmaneuvering the Democrats for five consecutive elections. "I can't believe we got rid of her," Ali Wade said. Feinberg, the DCCC secretary, added, "That's awesome. That is fucking huge."

With significant results now filtering in, Emanuel began calling the Democratic candidates who seemed headed for victory. His assistant, Katie Johnson, would get someone on a cell phone, and when Emanuel finished that conversation she would hand him a second phone with someone else on the line. When Emanuel called candidate Joe Donnelly in Indiana, he reached Donnelly's young son instead. "Joe Junior—your dad, you should be proud of him," Emanuel said. "Did you like the cheesecake?" Emanuel was exuding nervous energy and restrained jubilation. His eyes were bloodshot—he had not been sleeping much—and he periodically rubbed his face with fatigue. Happiness and exhaustion were warring.

More results came in, and they continued to look good. In North Carolina's Eleventh District, Heath Shuler was ahead with 20 percent of the precincts reporting. An intern scrawled "D-55, R-45" in the square reading "NC-11." Lapp turned to Emanuel and told him, "You're going to be a leader." Emanuel brushed it off. "Nah, I'm too small," he said absently.

By 9:30 the Democrats still had only three official pickups. The results looked promising, but they were coming in more slowly than expected, and the Democrats' impatience was building. At 9:35 someone yelled, "Rahm Emanuel won!" prompting joking applause. Emanuel had been reelected with 79 percent of the vote, roughly what was expected in his heavily Democratic district. Zach ran in to hug Emanuel again as though this were a signal triumph.

The prospects of the two endangered Georgia Democrats now began to look a little better. That was significant, because the Democrats could not afford to lose many seats if they were to win the House. "We pulled up in Georgia? All right," Emanuel said with relief. He tapped his finger on the "FL-22" box on the white board, which showed Democrat Ron Klein taking a big lead in Florida's Twenty-second District over Congressman E. Clay Shaw, who had been one of Emanuel's biggest Republican targets. Shaw had never forgiven Emanuel for attacking him so aggressively. "This has to hold," Emanuel said. "This is huge."

As the number of red squares began to grow, they all showed Democratic gains. Not a single Democratic incumbent was losing. Even more impressive, not a single open seat being vacated by a Democrat was switching to Republican control.

That did not mean the Democrats were winning every close race. Emanuel had badly wanted to knock off Republican congressman Ron Lewis in Kentucky, but at 9:45 that box read, "R-53, D-47." "This looks bad," Emanuel said. He asked Lapp, "Where are we in the Senate?" "I didn't know there was a Senate," Lapp joked.

Tapping on another square, the one for Shuler's race, which now read "D-53.1, R-46.9," Emanuel said, "Buncombe County isn't even in yet. That means Shuler is going to smoke him." Buncombe County was home to Asheville, a heavily Democratic area. If Shuler was winning the more conservative outlying counties by such a healthy margin, he seemed certain to defeat Republican Charles Taylor.

At 9:50 former congressman Vic Fazio wandered in. Fazio had headed the DCCC in 1994, when the Democrats lost control of the House for the first time in forty years. He had left Congress in 1998 and, at age sixty-four, now worked for a Washington law firm. "How are you doing?" Emanuel asked Fazio gently. "I'm very relieved, twelve years later," Fazio said. He had been haunted since 1994 by his role in leading the Democrats into the wilderness. Fazio seemed almost wistful as he surveyed the whiteboard, which was now beginning to provide an inkling of the magnitude of the Democrats' gains. "I wasn't even able to be here when we lost—I had to be in my district," he confided to Emanuel. "This is a huge monkey off my back." Emanuel chuckled. "Glad we were able to do that for you."

At 10:01, a third heated Indiana race was declared for the Democrats. Now all three of the contested Indiana seats had switched from Republican to Democratic.

Emanuel walked downstairs to another room in Democratic headquarters to sit for prearranged interviews with several television networks. He tried to strike a note of measured optimism. On MSNBC, he said, "The message on the new direction is really coming through in all these districts. It's a long night, but I'd rather be us than them." Host Chris Matthews was bolder. "Even though Rahm is playing it low-key, it looks to me like he's getting significant penetration in Republican areas," Matthews told his audience. "He's winning some of the hard races."

At 10:05, Republican congresswoman Nancy Johnson of Connecticut went down to defeat. At the beginning of the campaign, Emanuel had tried to attack Johnson so harshly that she would retire rather than seek reelection. That had failed, but Johnson had been weakened, and an energetic young challenger had now managed to knock her off. Johnson's loss brought the number of official GOP defeats to five, one-third of the way to victory. Cheers erupted as an intern drew a glaring red square around Johnson's race.

At 10:10, another cheer sounded—they were coming faster now—as Democrat Zack Space officially defeated Republican Joy Padgett in Ohio. This race had been the subject of a heated debate among the Democrats over how to attack Padgett. Some had wanted to stress the Republicans' broad responsibility for job losses in Ohio, while others wanted to attack Padgett, who had filed for bankruptcy, on her personal financial failings. The latter plan had won out, and the DCCC had spent $2.7 million attacking Padgett.

A minute later, Republican congressman Charlie Bass conceded in New Hampshire, bringing the number of Democratic pickups to seven, almost halfway to the magic number of fifteen.

Now Emanuel was live on CNN. "The evening is early, but we're halfway around the bend already," he said. At 10:35, two GOP seats in the Pennsylvania suburbs fell to the Democrats. At 10:41, Democrat Mike Arcuri was declared the victor in upstate New York. At 10:47, Shuler's race was officially called for the Democrat. "*Yaaaa!* Come on!" Lapp screamed as staffers exchanged high fives. The Democrats now had eleven of the fifteen seats they needed.

Emanuel returned to the DCCC office from his television interviews and continued making calls to Democratic candidates, congratulating winners and talking strategy with those who were almost there. In Florida, the networks had declared Ron Klein the winner over Clay Shaw, but Shaw was refusing to concede. Emanuel called Klein. "Congratulations—ABC just called it for you," he said. Then he urged Klein to try to prod Shaw into admitting defeat. "Have your campaign manager call his campaign manager and say, 'He wants to go down [and declare victory], but he wants to give you due respect,'" Emanuel said. He wanted to close the door on that race.

Then he called Connecticut Democrat Joe Courtney, who was locked in a close race with his Republican opponent. Emanuel urged him to simply declare victory. *"Act like a winner!"* Emanuel shouted into the phone, pumping his fist into the air, although Courtney of course could not see him. "You're up!" It was true, Courtney was up—but only by four hundred votes, with six hundred absentee ballots yet to be counted.

Noting that Clay Shaw and Nancy Johnson—both of whom served with him on the House Ways and Means Committee—had lost, Emanuel joked, "We killed my two people on Ways and Means. Now I can pass an amendment." With the vulnerable Georgia Democrats seemingly back in control of their races, Emanuel said, "You know what that means? If we win those, we've lost no incumbents. That hasn't happened since 1934." When Kirstin Gillibrand was declared the winner in Albany, Emanuel chortled, "I'm going to call her fucking husband, who told her not to fucking run."

The whiteboard was more than a scoreboard for Emanuel. It reflected the fruits of two years of relentless recruiting, fund-raising, traveling, and strategizing. Each square represented an individual with whom he had become personally close. When a candidate won, Emanuel knew exactly how he would react and what he had done to accomplish the victory. And when a candidate lost, he often felt personally pained.

Among the worst losses of the night was the defeat of Tammy Duckworth, the wounded Iraq veteran who had become a nationally known figure. On the campaign trail, Duckworth's inexperience had sometimes showed, while Roskam, a trial lawyer and longtime politician, was articulate and smooth. And as the board now reflected, the district outside Chicago was to remain in Republican hands, as Roskam narrowly defeated Duckworth 51 percent to 49 percent.

At 11, an aide told Emanuel the networks were estimating that the Democrats would ultimately pick up twenty-nine seats. "No," Emanuel said flatly. "It's going to be twenty-two."

At 11:08 CNN's Wolf Blitzer intoned, "We can now project that the Democrats will be in the majority in the House of Representatives." This was it—official confirmation.

Emanuel seemed momentarily, and uncharacteristically, dazed, hugging his brother Ezekiel and kissing his wife, Amy. Six minutes later, Nancy Pelosi, wearing a lavender pantsuit and looking jittery and happy, walked from the office where she'd been watching the returns into Emanuel's office. When Emanuel saw her he roared, "Fellas—Madam Speaker!" Pelosi and Emanuel hugged, rocking gently together for a few seconds, locked in their embrace. Brian Wolff, a staffer who worked for both Emanuel and Pelosi, called out, "Mission accomplished!"

At that moment Senator Barack Obama, who had campaigned for numerous Democratic House candidates, called to offer his congratulations. Pelosi took a cell phone from an aide. "Barack," she said. "Thank you, thank you, thank you for all that you did." She then walked back to her office muttering, "I've got to call my brother." As Pelosi made her way through the DCCC staffers, some began applauding, then more joined in, then the entire staff rose in a standing ovation and began whooping. "This is so much better than losing," a staffer said to no one in particular.

Emanuel walked out of his office into the throng of his staff. It had been ten minutes since CNN had called the election for the Democrats. "Where's my favorite table?" he said. For the past twenty-two months, Emanuel had periodically stood on a table to address his staff. Now he hopped on the desk of Adrienne Elrod, an assistant DCCC press secretary. His comments reflected how nervous he had been about Republican claims that their last-minute voter turnout program would overcome the Democratic lead in the polls. "I'll tell you this," Emanuel shouted. "The Republicans may have the seventy-two-hour program, but they have not seen the twenty-two-month program. Since my kids are gone, I can say it: They can go fuck themselves!"

Emanuel's face was red, tired, euphoric. But it would not have been Emanuel if he had been completely relaxed. "We still have one or two recounts—nobody gives up," Emanuel told his staff. "You have done a phenomenal job. And the beauty is, you are part of history. Nobody can ever take that away from you."

The night had seen its share of disappointments. In Pennsylvania, Republican congressman Jim Gerlach had held on to defeat Lois Murphy, one of Emanuel's favorite candidates. Patsy Madrid in New Mexico lost by fewer than nine hundred votes. Tessa Hafen, the very last candidate Emanuel had campaigned for, had not quite caught up to her opponent, Congressman Jon Porter.

There were also some unexpected wins. Emanuel had been frustrated at his difficulty in lining up a candidate to challenge Congressman Richard Pombo in California, but Pombo had lost anyway, to a candidate supported by the bloggers. Congressman Jim Leach—a respected moderate Republican from Iowa who opposed the Iraq war—had gone down in one of the night's big surprises. Democratic congressman Alan Mollohan, whom Emanuel had urged for months to take his race more seriously, had in the end dispatched his challenger with ease.

In Louisiana, the source of so much concern after Hurricane Katrina, no seats changed hands.

Tom Reynolds, Emanuel's GOP counterpart, managed to hang on to his seat despite being caught up in the Mark Foley scandal. That may have been small comfort for him, given that he had presided over a historic loss as NRCC chairman. Reynolds' frequent proclamations in the campaign that House races were about local issues and that voters' views of President Bush and Tom DeLay were irrelevant had been emphatically disproved, at least for this year. The 2006 midterm elections, it turned out, were all about Iraq and corruption.

After his speech on the desk, Emanuel jumped into a motorcade and sped to the Hyatt Regency Washington, where a raucous victory party was under way. Democrats had not enjoyed a win this cathartic, this emotional, since 1992, when Bill Clinton had recaptured the White House after twelve years—the same period of exile that had just ended in the House. Emanuel was ushered into a private room at the Hyatt with other top Democrats. Senator Charles Schumer, who headed the Democratic Senate campaign, was gently teasing Pelosi's husband, Paul. "The First Man of the House!" he pronounced in mock solemnity. "The First Gentleman!" Paul Pelosi had his arm around his wife, lightly caressing her back. When Schumer saw Emanuel he asked, "How many seats you think you'll pick up?" "Twenty-four," Emanuel guessed, adding, "It looks like we'll take Wyoming." "Really?" said Schumer, in the tone of one political virtuoso impressed by another. In the Senate, the Democrats had taken three of the six seats they needed, but the races in Missouri, Montana, and Virginia were still undecided.

The Democratic leaders were waiting to go onstage and greet the wild crowd waiting for them. Pelosi asked Emanuel, "How'd our Georgians do?" Like Emanuel, she had been concerned about the fate of the two vulnerable Democratic incumbents from Georgia. "Okay," Emanuel told her. They seemed to be holding on.

As the exultant Democrats waited, an aide called to Emanuel, "It's fifty-three to forty-seven Mitchell!" Democrat Harry Mitchell had improbably knocked off Arizona Republican congressman J. D. Hayworth. This was a symbolic win; Hayworth had been swept into office with the 1994 Republican revolution, and now he was being swept out by a Democratic one. "Kicked his fucking ass!" shouted Emanuel, exchanging a high five with Pelosi.

In a corner of the room, DCCC communications director Bill Burton was incredulously trying out the new titles of victorious Democrats no one at the Committee had believed had a chance of winning. "Congresswoman Shea-Porter," Burton enunciated slowly, referring to Carol Shea-Porter, who had just won a seat in New Hampshire. "Congressman [Jason] Altmire. What the fuck?"

In the final tally, the Democrats would capture thirty seats, exactly double what they needed, and win a 233–202 majority in the House. That was slightly bigger than the 232–203 advantage the Republicans had enjoyed before the election.

Even in the midst of the celebration, Emanuel knew he had to wake up at five the next morning to appear on several morning talk shows. He had a press conference scheduled for 11 A.M. He had to peruse a report on the recounts and legal challenges that still complicated five House races. And he would have to decide within days whether to seek a high-level leadership position in the House. "You have to be chipper tomorrow morning," warned his press secretary, Sarah Feinberg. Emanuel replied, "I'll be chipper."

But for now, it was show time. Emanuel and Schumer—two scrappy politicians who had won by hitting back as hard as the Republicans hit them—emerged into a delirious crowd at the Hyatt. The Rolling Stones' "Start Me Up," a perennial campaign rally favorite, rocked through the loudspeakers. In contrast to his invitation a moment ago to the Republicans to "go fuck themselves," Emanuel spoke loftily of bipartisanship for the consumption of the television audience. Like Pelosi, Emanuel had been thinking for months that if the Democrats wanted to retain whatever majority they won, they would have to show voters a more civil face than the Republicans had. "We accept your votes not as a victory for our party, but as an opportunity for our country," Emanuel told the crowd. When he mentioned Pelosi's name, calling her "a tireless campaigner, a heroic fund-raiser," the crowd broke into chants of "Nancy! Nancy!" then switched to "Speaker! Speaker!" Waiting in the wings, Pelosi looked both gleeful and edgy. It was she who had chosen Emanuel to lead the battle, she who had raised a startling $60 million to help retake the House, and she who would now become the first woman Speaker of the House.

After Emanuel and Schumer spoke, Pelosi and Senate Democratic leader Harry Reid emerged onto the stage to join them in a circular group hug. Pelosi and Reid also stressed their desire to work with Republicans. "Today we have made history," Pelosi told the audience. "Now let us make progress."

After the speeches, as Emanuel headed out of the hotel, supporters grabbed him to shake his hand. "Thanks for your hard work," said one. "No problem," Emanuel responded.

Then he added, after a pause, "I can't say I enjoyed it."

AFTERWORD

On January 4, 2007, Congresswoman Nancy Pelosi, leader of the newly victorious House Democrats, sat in the House chamber surrounded by her six grandchildren. Rahm Emanuel, seated on her right, stood to nominate her as Speaker of the House, then leaned over and gave her a high five. The House proceeded to vote. The process was slow, but to no one's surprise, Pelosi prevailed over House Republican leader John Boehner by a 233–202 margin, exactly mirroring the size of the new Democratic majority. Pelosi walked to the podium and at 2:08 P.M. received the heavy wooden Speaker's gavel from Boehner, who was gracious as he spoke of Pelosi's role as the first woman Speaker. "Today marks an occasion I think the Founding Fathers would view favorably," he said. Pelosi replied in kind: "I accept this gavel in the spirit of partnership, not partisanship." Dennis Hastert, who had been Speaker for eight years, stood grimly in the back of the House chamber, now just another congressman. He had been the longest-serving Republican Speaker in history, but his ultimate fate was to serve as a bridge between two more dynamic, historic figures, Newt Gingrich and Pelosi. Many lawmakers had brought their children for the event. Heath Shuler, the new congressman from North Carolina, was pleased that his daughter, Island, two, was sitting in his lap. She was too young to understand the significance of Pelosi's ascent, he knew, but later she might take pleasure from knowing she had been there. Across the Capitol, Democrat Harry Reid of Nevada had just become the new Senate majority leader.

Two weeks later, Democratic leaders announced that they had completed their "Six for '06" agenda, passing their top half-dozen priority items within the first one hundred hours of taking over the House. Republicans protested that they had been shut out of the process, unable to offer amendments or alternatives. It had taken only days for the longtime roles to be reversed; for twelve years it had been Republicans who pushed bills through, using extraordinary parliamentary tactics if necessary, and the Democrats who complained of being excluded. While it was unclear how many of the Democratic bills would survive the Senate or a White House veto, the Democrats were able to brag that they'd fulfilled their campaign promise, and what's more, sizable numbers of Republicans had joined them in voting for the measures. Despite an early embarrassment for Pelosi when her fellow Democrats chose Steny Hoyer as majority leader despite her support for John Murtha, the Democrats had gotten off to a solid start.

The midterm elections of 2006 were a pivotal political event. For the first time since 1922, a party did not lose a single congressional seat, as every Democrat running for reelection won, and every retiring Democrat was replaced by another. In taking thirty seats from the Republicans, the Democrats emphatically ended a Republican onslaught that had begun in 1994, when Gingrich and the GOP swept to power in the House. President Bush, who had been accustomed to a pliant Congress, now faced an emboldened, even hostile one. In most congressional elections, local issues are paramount, and a moderately interested public, its choices limited by heavily gerrymandered districts, makes modest changes in the status quo. The 2006 election joined the short list of exceptions, landmark votes that reflected a sweeping public disgust.

Under a parliamentary system, the Republican government would have fallen. The 2006 election was the American equivalent.

The day after the election, Emanuel, who had slept from 3 to 5 A.M., held one last press conference at DCCC headquarters. "Democrats haven't been this happy since 2000, when CNN declared Florida for Al Gore, and that only lasted about an hour," Emanuel said. "Not a single Democratic seat was lost—not a single seat—whether incumbent or open." Emanuel attributed the size of the victory to the DCCC's strong recruitment, its willingness to challenge a wide array of Republicans, and its focus on corruption. In addition, the DCCC had raised close to $140 million, surpassing its previous record by about $40 million. The Republicans had raised $175 million, but given their historic fund-raising advantage, that almost amounted to parity.

Still, despite some Republicans' obsession with him, Emanuel was not responsible for the major factors behind the Republican rout. He had not affected the course of the Iraq war, persuaded the Republicans to botch the Hurricane Katrina recovery, or created the GOP corruption scandals.

Emanuel's job had been to position the Democrats so that if a political tidal wave did emerge, the party would reap the benefit. That is what he did. "When nobody thought they could do it, Rahm went out and said, 'We don't know what is going to happen. We will put together a team and raise the most money we can, so if something happens, we can take advantage of it,'" said Dee Dee Myers, Emanuel's old friend from the Clinton White House. "And suddenly, as you looked around, you saw Democratic challengers were raising more money. There were more credible candidates. And what happens? Here comes this tidal wave, and Rahm has them all in sturdy little boats ready to row to shore."

As the magnitude of the Democratic victory became clear, groups on all sides rushed to claim credit. Some chafed at the praise Emanuel was receiving. And the victory on November 7 was not tidy. Many kinds of Democrats won—liberals and conservatives, anti-war activists and anti-abortion stalwarts. Liberals eagerly pointed to victories by progressive candidates in places such as Kentucky and New Hampshire to claim a resurgent liberalism. Those on the right, with equal certainty, focused on the victories of moderates like Shuler and Brad Ellsworth as proof that the real winners were conservatives.

Ultimately, the voters were simply fed up with the GOP in general, and they took it out on Republicans of all stripes. They were frustrated with the war, with corruption, perhaps with the idea of one-party government. Only a handful of vulnerable Republicans—notably Jim Gerlach, Heather Wilson, and Chris Shays—marshaled enough resources to fight off the Democratic attack.

Tom Reynolds, the GOP House campaign chief, also held a post-election press conference, and he downplayed the loss, portraying the results as almost inevitable. "The election really was a matter of history repeating itself," Reynolds said. "Second-term midterm elections are the toughest for the president's party, and one like last night is absolutely no different." He also blamed Republican ethical problems and House members "who were caught unprepared."

President Bush, too, spoke to reporters, inviting them to the White House East Room. Bush acknowledged that voters had sent a message about Iraq, and he quickly announced that Secretary of Defense Donald Rumsfeld was departing, something many Republicans wished he had done before the election.

Bush also promised to work with the incoming Democratic majority. "This is a close election. If you look at it race by race, it was close," the president said. "The cumulative effect, however, was not too close. It was a thumpin'."

The nastiest battle to take credit for this "thumpin'" was between Emanuel's supporters and the liberal faction led by Howard Dean and the progressive bloggers.

Barely had the polls closed when liberals began asserting that Emanuel had little to do with the victory, that he had even prevented the Democrats from winning more seats. Emanuel had picked the wrong type of candidates, they said, focusing on inoffensive centrists rather than forthright anti-war populists who had more grassroots support.

The critics pointed to Tammy Duckworth's race in Illinois, where Emanuel had steamrolled a liberal candidate and put $3 million behind Duckworth, only to see her lose to her Republican opponent. In other races, Emanuel's preferred candidates had lost primary fights to Democratic progressives, who had gone on to knock off Republicans. To many liberals, these incidents proved that Emanuel's strategy was flawed, and that especially in a year distinguished by an anti-war populism, he should have supported more liberal candidates.

"Many of the Democrats who prevailed on November 7 did so despite the Illinois congressman's efforts, not because of them," John Nichols insisted on *The Nation*'s Web site. "Could Democrats have won additional seats in 2006 with a different DCCC chair—one who not only knew how to raise money and had a good strategic sense, but who was willing to support candidates who tapped into the anti-war and anti-free-trade sentiments that ran so strong this year? Of course."

A related argument was that Howard Dean deserved much of the credit for the win. Dean's "fifty-state strategy" of hiring Democratic organizers around the country had produced results in just a few months, this argument went. "Howard Dean, Vindicated," declared a piece by Joe Conason, a journalist for the online publication Salon. Conason cited Indiana, where Dean had placed three Democratic staffers a year before the election.

Indiana was perhaps the biggest Democratic success story on Election Night, since the Democrats captured three seats there from the Republicans. The DCCC had expended tremendous effort and money in the state, recruiting three strong candidates and spending $6.4 million on ads supporting them. Dean's field organizers may have helped, but it took a strained reading of events to conclude that Dean was largely responsible for those victories.

Dean's focus on rebuilding the party was undoubtedly admirable, and few Democrats disagreed with the goal. And Dean's DNC had contributed to the victory. But at times during the campaign, Dean had seemed curiously indifferent to the opportunities before him, saying it would take years to see results of his fifty-state strategy. So his more zealous supporters' quick claim to credit after the election did not ring true.

The idea of denying credit for the victory to Emanuel, meanwhile, was a curious one. In January 2005 Emanuel had been told he would be in charge of fund-raising, recruiting, strategizing, troubleshooting, and all other aspects of the House effort. Almost two years later, the effort resulted in a dramatic win. To claim now that Emanuel had somehow been an obstacle to the victory better served an ideological predisposition than a dispassionate analysis.

And indeed, that claim had more to do with concerns about the future of the Democratic Party than the results of the election. Emanuel had aggressively recruited candidates who "fit" their districts, and he was openly contemptuous of the party's purists. Those purists, in turn, were quick to reject the notion that the win was attributable to a willingness to stray from liberal principles.

Of the thirty Democratic candidates who took seats from the Republicans, about twenty had been nurtured, funded, advised, and yelled at by Emanuel for months. Perhaps a half dozen had been supported by grassroots activists with little help from the DCCC. But the deeper reality was that it was impossible to divide the Democratic victors cleanly into "DCCC candidates" and "grassroots candidates." Many Democrats had the support of both camps. In some cases, Emanuel had recognized late in the campaign that a candidate was doing better than expected, and he provided a shot of cash to put them over the top.

In the end, the Republicans were clearly most responsible for their own collapse. But the Democrats also mounted a strong campaign, and various Democratic factions played important roles. Emanuel ran the campaign, but Dean helped lay the groundwork in many states, and grassroots activists injected an enormous amount of energy, including in places the DCCC had written off.

After the election, the factions of the Democratic Party seemed to be edging toward a rough consensus on the notion that the party should be flexible on social issues—abortion, gay marriage, gun control—while drawing a sharp contrast with Republicans on populist economic issues. Deeply felt differences remained within the party, especially on issues such as free trade. But even there the party had been moving in a more worker-friendly direction since the days when Emanuel helped President Clinton push NAFTA through Congress.

Given the success of Emanuel in the House campaign and Charles Schumer in the Senate, the 2008 presidential aspirants, who started formally campaigning immediately after the new Democratic Congress took office, are likely to take a lesson from the 2006 campaign. Emanuel and Schumer had worked to expand the Democratic playing field and, with the help of others, had forced the Republicans to defend usually safe turf. This was a departure from John Kerry's intense focus on a few swing states in 2004.

As he had hoped to do from the outset, Emanuel used the campaign to catapult himself into a position of greater power. His colleagues chose him to serve as chairman of the House Democratic Caucus, the party's fourth-ranking post. From there Emanuel would continue to help orchestrate the party's message and strategy. The perch put Emanuel in line to become House Speaker someday, especially since the three Democrats ranking above him—Pelosi, Hoyer, and Jim Clyburn—were all about twenty years older than he.

As the 2008 presidential campaign began, the Illinois congressman also had the ear of the Democrats' two biggest stars and leading candidates. A longtime part of the Clinton circle, Emanuel was an ally of Senator Hillary Rodham Clinton. At the same time, he had worked closely with Senator Barack Obama, who like Emanuel had risen through Chicago politics, and the two were personal friends. This put Emanuel in a difficult spot, and he was torn between the two presidential hopefuls. The Washington Post spoke of a "Rahm primary" as Democratic heavyweights vied for the support of power brokers such as Emanuel.

After Emanuel's all-out blitz during the 2006 campaign, it would be hard for congressional campaigns to be run in the old way again. The parties' choices to lead their campaigns for the next House election, in 2008, reflected this. The Republicans chose Congressman Tom Cole of Oklahoma partly on the strength of his promise to be a Republican Rahm Emanuel. On the Democratic side, Pelosi selected Maryland congressman Chris Van Hollen, Emanuel's top lieutenant, to succeed him. Debbie Wasserman Schultz, another key member of Emanuel's team, was chosen for another crucial role, organizing the defense of vulnerable Democratic incumbents.

The biggest question for House leaders after the 2006 election was whether the Democrats could hold on to their majority in 2008 and beyond. Many of the newly elected Democrats probably would have lost in a year without a strong Democratic tide. It was difficult to know how the ongoing war in Iraq and the upcoming presidential election would affect the next race for Congress.

But that was no longer Rahm Emanuel's problem.

AUTHOR'S NOTE

I first met Rahm Emanuel in the mid-1990s, when I was working for *Legal Times* and Emanuel was a top strategist at the Clinton White House. At the time, Justice Department officials were upset that Emanuel, in his usual hard-hitting way, was steering Clinton's crime-fighting policy toward a less liberal approach. The complaints about Emanuel were essentially the same as they would be during the 2006 campaign: He screamed at people, compromised principles, and did whatever it took to win. The positive points were the same also—Emanuel exuded passion, was driven, and knew how to get things done.

In the following years, I moved to the *Chicago Tribune* and Emanuel was elected to Congress from the Fifth District of Illinois. When he took over the Democratic Congressional Campaign Committee in early 2005, I asked for special access to its workings to write a long article for the *Tribune*. The idea was to provide a look at the way campaigns are really run—the compromises, the strategizing, the brutality, the scarring personal toll. It never occurred to me—nor, I'm certain, to Emanuel—that the Democrats would actually retake the House. Emanuel feared that with a single ill-chosen word he or his staff might inadvertently capsize one of his campaigns. So Emanuel and the *Tribune* agreed that I would get the access, but nothing would be published until after Election Day.

I spent the 2006 campaign attending DCCC strategy sessions, traveling with Emanuel, and listening to his phone calls. I watched him exhort and berate candidates, beg contributors for money, and yell at his staff. The great majority of the conversations, meetings, and scenes recorded in this book were witnessed firsthand. The 2006 election, of course, turned out to be historic. The article on Emanuel and the midterm campaign appeared in the *Chicago Tribune* shortly after Election Day, and while it was a lengthy piece by newspaper standards, any such article by necessity omits a great deal. Given the election's outcome and what it showed about the American political system, it seemed worthy of a book that would incorporate elements that had been left on the cutting room floor and tease out broader themes.

I owe many debts for the help I received during the project's two-year duration. My editors and colleagues at the *Tribune* could not have been more supportive. At a time when many newspapers are cutting back, the *Tribune* has remained dedicated to in-depth, substantial journalism. Jim O'Shea, the *Tribune*'s former managing editor, was an early and enthusiastic backer of the project. Other editors, including Ann Marie Lipinski, George de Lama, Joycelyn Winnecke, and Jim Warren, were unfailingly supportive. Easily the greatest sacrifice was made by Mike Tackett, the *Tribune*'s Washington bureau chief, who had to shoulder the workload of two people for months at a time while I was completing the article and book. He was an advisor, editor, and friend, and I deeply appreciate his support.

Others at the *Tribune* were equally selfless. My colleagues Jill Zuckman and Jeff Zeleny, two first-rate reporters, could have taken this project as an intrusion into their territory. Instead, they eagerly allowed me to bounce ideas off them, and they regularly helped out by contributing details they had picked up on the reporting trail. Flynn McRoberts and George Papajohn edited the original article, providing guidance and careful reading despite an incredibly tight deadline. Rick Clough proved to be a skilled, meticulous researcher, unearthing obscure facts and transcripts, sometimes within minutes.

The staffers of the DCCC, once they got used to the idea of a reporter scrutinizing their actions so closely, were nothing but professional. Bill Burton, Sarah Feinberg, John Lapp, Karin Johanson, Ali Wade, Brian Wolff, Christina Reynolds, Sean Sweeney, Adrienne Elrod, and others shared with me whatever information they could. Kathleen Connery in Emanuel's congressional office also was enormously helpful. These staffers recognized they would have no control over the content, and they never sought any.

My friend Mitchell Zuckoff, an accomplished journalist and author, was overly generous with his time and advice. He was quick to offer strategies for reporting and writing, and he carefully read large parts of the manuscript. More important, he seemed almost as enthusiastic about the book as I was.

Rafe Sagalyn, my agent, was instrumental in moving the project along quickly, which was crucial given the fast pace of events. Kris Puopolo at Doubleday was a thoughtful, patient editor who undoubtedly made the work much better. Bill Thomas at Doubleday also was a great supporter. It goes without saying that any errors of fact or judgment are my responsibility.

I would be remiss not to mention my friends Joseph Sokal and Chuck Rombro, not so much because of any contributions they made but because they wanted to be in the acknowledgments so badly. Steve "Razz" Rappaport was the source of many hours of political discussion that helped inform this narrative. I also feel compelled to thank Bill Press and Stuart Frank simply for being themselves.

Most important, I'm lucky to have a strong, supportive family. My parents, Leah and Avrom Bendavid-Val, were endlessly encouraging. Leah Bendavid-Val is an accomplished book editor and author, and her insights were uniquely helpful. My siblings, Ronnit and Oren Bendavid-Val, have also been remarkably supportive and the sources of lively conversations on politics and this project.

Finally, I could not have done any of this without my wife, Dara. Despite great professional responsibilities of her own, she never failed to share in the excitement of the project, make astute suggestions on the manuscript, provide encouragement during difficult times, and shoulder a disproportionate share of the family duties. My children, Geffen and Lily, are too young to know this yet, but all this would be meaningless without them.

NOTES

Note: Unattributed scenes and conversations witnessed directly by the author.

INTRODUCTION

page

2   their wives joked: Interview with Rahm Emanuel, Sept. 7, 2005.

2   they were frequently fighting: Interview with James Carville, Nov. 2, 2006.

2   "He's driving me crazy": Interview with James Carville, Nov. 2, 2006.

2   "James—*No, James, you listen*": Author witnessed Emanuel's side of this conversation, and the substance was later confirmed with Carville.

4   his right middle finger had been severed: Interview with Marsha and Benjamin Emanuel, Oct. 12, 2006.

5   "You need someone whose favorite word": Interview with Larry Sabato, Aug. 17, 2005.

5   "It's the hardest job in politics": Interview with James Carville, Nov. 2, 2006.

6   "I'll tell you this": Interview with Rahm Emanuel, Sept. 7, 2005.

7   "It's exhausting": Interview with Bill Paxon, Dec. 2005.

1: AN IMMOVABLE OBJECT

9   "It was fantastic": Interview with Shaun Marie Levine, Nov. 2006.

9   his White House office featured two pictures of Abraham Lincoln: Interview with Karl Rove, April 2001.

9   The first book Rove had ever read: Interview with Karl Rove, April 2001.

10   "It was natural for Republicans": Interview with Howard Lim, Nov. 2006.

10   "Election Night was tough to take": Interview with Michael Long, Nov. 2006.

11 "I don't want to abolish government": Grover Norquist confirmed he said this in an e-mail exchange on Nov. 29, 2006.

12 "morality of the Holocaust": NPR's *Fresh Air*, Oct. 2, 2003.

12 "Republicans have the House": PBS' *Frontline*, Feb. 1, 2005.

12 She ran the House Democrats: "How Nancy Pelosi Took Control," *American Prospect*, June 7, 2004.

12 In that race: "The Nancy I Knew," Realclearpolitics.com, Nov. 29, 2006.

13 "She looked around": Interview with George Miller, Jan. 11, 2006.

13 One candidate was California congressman Mike Thompson: *Roll Call*, Dec. 13, 2004.

13 Leaders of the labor movement: Interview with a Democratic aide, Dec. 22, 2006.

13 he had walked the streets: Interview with Marsha and Benjamin Emanuel, Oct. 12, 2006.

13 it was crucial: Interview with senior Democratic leadership aide, June 23, 2006.

14 "There were many people who wanted to be considered for it": Interview with Nancy Pelosi by Jill Zuckman, Oct. 2006.

14 "She is about matching": Interview with George Miller, Jan. 11, 2006.

14 Pelosi called Emanuel in December 2004: Interview with Rahm Emanuel, Nov. 29, 2006.

14 "Nancy, the truth is": Interview with Rahm Emanuel, Nov. 29, 2006.

14 "Given my background in politics": Interview with Rahm Emanuel, Sept. 7, 2005.

15 "If I make gains": Interview with Rahm Emanuel, Sept. 7, 2005.

15 "He wants that lean and hungry look": Interview with Larry Sabato, Aug. 17, 2005.

16 Van Hollen supporters groaned in unison: Interview with a debate audience member, Nov. 30, 2006.

16 "There is no question": Interview with Debbie Wasserman Schultz, June 16, 2006.

17 of the 400 incumbents: "Dubious Democracy," FairVote Web site, www.fairvote.org.

17 average victory margin of 40 percent: "Ten Stories About Election '06," FairVote Web site, www.fairvote.org.

17 packed into urban areas: Interview with Rob Richie, FairVote, Dec. 18, 2006; interview with Seth Masket, University of Denver, Dec. 18, 2006; interview with Gary Jacobson, University of California, San Diego, Sept. 14, 2005.

17 Democrats had received 51 percent: "Ten Stories About Election '06," FairVote Web site, www.fairvote.org.

18 analyst Charlie Cook: "Hill Majorities Unlikely to Be Erased in 2006," *National Journal*, Feb. 19, 2005.

18 "Basically it was strategizing": Interview with Debbie Wasserman Schultz, June 16, 2006.

18 "This is not a theoretical exercise": Interview with Chris Van Hollen, Nov. 3, 2005.

19 Emanuel started calling Madrid: Interview with Patsy Madrid, Nov. 10, 2005.

19 He knew she was a die-hard Democrat: Interview with Patsy Madrid, Nov. 10, 2005.

19 her fondness for basketball: Interview with Patsy Madrid, Nov. 10, 2005.

19 He enlisted: Interview with Patsy Madrid, Nov. 10, 2005.

19 "I got a call": Interview with Patsy Madrid, Nov. 10, 2005.

19 Madrid was worried: Interview with Patsy Madrid, Nov. 10, 2005.

19　He arranged for husbands and wives: Interview with Patsy Madrid, Nov. 10, 2005.

19　DCCC members even introduced: Interview with Chris Van Hollen, Nov. 3, 2005.

20　"It's a good recruit": Interview with Carl Forti, Oct. 24, 2005.

20　"We worked it hard": Interview with Rahm Emanuel, Nov. 2, 2005.

20　"Are you tired of being fucking mayor yet?": Interview with John Callahan, Jan. 26, 2007.

21　"He is on me every five minutes": Interview with Steny Hoyer, June 23, 2006.

21　"Sometimes I feel like a personal valet": Interview with Rahm Emanuel, Nov. 2, 2005.

21　"Right now we have forty good races": Interview with Rahm Emanuel, Sept. 5, 2005.

21　Etheridge mentioned a businessman: Interview with Bob Etheridge, Jan. 17, 2007; interview with Rahm Emanuel, Jan. 11, 2007.

21　"He is a football hero": Interview with Bob Etheridge, Jan. 17, 2007.

21　from Barack Obama to John Edwards: Interview with Heath Shuler, Jan. 17, 2007.

21　Roughly fifty Democratic House members: Interview with Heath Shuler, Jan. 17, 2007.

21　Shuler was driving through Jackson County: Account of Clinton's call from interview with Heath Shuler, Jan. 17, 2007.

22　Emanuel asked Congressman Ron Kind: Interview with Rahm Emanuel, Jan. 11, 2007.

22　Kind called Shuler: Interview with Ron Kind, Jan. 9, 2007.

22　"I would be home": Interview with Ron Kind, Jan. 9, 2007.

22　"Almost every congressman I spoke with": Interview with Heath Shuler by Jill Zuckman, Nov. 2005.

22　Emanuel began calling Shuler: Interview with Heath Shuler by Jill Zuckman, Nov. 2005.

22　"It was halftime": Interview with Rahm Emanuel, Nov. 2, 2005.

22　"I was recruited": Interview with Heath Shuler by Jill Zuckman, Nov. 2005.

22　President Bush . . . asked to meet: Interview with Heath Shuler, Jan. 17, 2007.

23　"That's the stuff I love": Interview with John Lapp, Sept. 23, 2005.

23　"I don't know if he's going to win": Interview with Rahm Emanuel, Sept. 5, 2005.

24　"There's so much in politics": Interview with John Lapp, Sept. 23, 2005.

25　"Here's what's missing": Interview with Rahm Emanuel, Sept. 28, 2005.

25　"Beat the shit out of them": Interview with Rahm Emanuel, Sept. 28, 2005.

2: AN UNSTOPPABLE FORCE

28　Secrest accused Emanuel: Interview with Joe Sinsheimer, Dec. 4, 2006; interview with Alan Secrest, Dec. 13, 2006.

28　argued repeatedly over strategy: Interview with Alan Secrest, Dec. 13, 2006.

28　The DCCC was slow: Interview with Joe Sinsheimer, Dec. 4, 2006; interview with Alan Secrest, Dec. 13, 2006.

28　"It drove myself": Interview with Joe Sinsheimer, Dec. 4, 2006.

28　the final blow: Interview with Rahm Emanuel, Dec. 1, 2006.

29　Secrest dismissed that account: Interview with Alan Secrest, Dec. 13, 2006.

29　"Our data processor": Interview with Alan Secrest, Dec. 13, 2006.

29　Sinsheimer read: Interview with Joe Sinsheimer, Dec. 4, 2006.

29　"Let's send a fish": Interview with Joe Sinsheimer, Dec. 4, 2006.

29   Secrest wrote a long letter: Interview with Rahm Emanuel, Dec. 1, 2006; interview with Alan Secrest, Dec. 13, 2006.

29   "I'm not interested": *Campaigns & Elections,* June/July 1990.

29   "I thought it was silly": Interview with Richard Bates, Dec. 6, 2006.

29   Emanuel claimed that he realized: Interview with Rahm Emanuel, Dec. 1, 2006.

29   *The West Wing:* Interview with Joe Sinsheimer, Dec. 4, 2006.

30   Born in Chicago: Rahm Emanuel's official congressional biography.

30   lethargic: Interview with Rahm Emanuel, Dec. 1, 2006.

30   slow to talk: Interview with Ezekiel Emanuel, Oct. 9, 2006.

30   he was a peacemaker: Interview with Marsha Emanuel, Oct. 12, 2006.

30   "Of the three, he was the calmest": Interview with Ezekiel Emanuel, Oct. 9, 2006.

30   Ari got the top bunk: Interview with Ari Emanuel, Nov. 8, 2006.

30   "I was physically stronger": Interview with Ari Emanuel, Nov. 8, 2006.

30   "Ari would be wrestling": Interview with Marsha Emanuel, Oct. 12, 2006.

30   President Bush once told Emanuel: Interview with Rahm Emanuel, Aug. 16, 2006.

30   "Every article I see": Interview with Marsha Emanuel, Oct. 12, 2006.

30   "He was a little spitfire": Interview with Gerald Noskin, Nov. 2006.

31   "Intense would be a word": Interview with Kerry Hubata, Oct. 2006.

31   "He wasn't one": Interview with Larry Grote, Oct. 2006.

31   He was a gregarious: Interview with Larry Grote, Oct. 2006.

31   B-plus average: Interview with Marsha Emanuel, Oct. 12, 2006.

31   reaching the bone: Interview with Benjamin Emanuel, Oct. 12, 2006.

31   infected with water-borne bacteria: Interview with Benjamin Emanuel, Oct. 12, 2006.

31   his fever reached 106 degrees: Interview with Marsha Emanuel, Oct. 12, 2006.

31   a hand surgeon was brought in: Interview with Benjamin Emanuel, Oct. 12, 2006.

31   "Ben . . . was busy": Interview with Marsha Emanuel, Oct. 12, 2006.

32   "That was a big turning point": Interview with Marsha Emanuel, Oct. 12, 2006.

32   pulled the IV tube: Interview with Benjamin Emanuel, Oct. 12, 2006.

32   "Afterwards I was worried": Interview with Marsha Emanuel, Oct. 12, 2006.

32   The oldest, Ezekiel, is a leading: Information on Ezekiel Emanuel from his official NIH biography.

33   Shoshana's mother: Information on Shoshana Emanuel from interview with Benjamin and Marsha Emanuel, Oct. 12, 2006.

33   Benjamin Emanuel was born in Jerusalem: Interview with Benjamin Emanuel, Oct. 12, 2006.

34   "He was notorious": Interview with Ezekiel Emanuel, Oct. 9, 2006.

34   She took her young children: Interview with Marsha Emanuel, Oct. 12, 2006.

34   they were pelted: Interview with Marsha Emanuel, Oct. 12, 2006.

34   "I remember some women": Interview with Marsha Emanuel, Oct. 12, 2006.

34   the brothers wanted to build an igloo: Interview with Marsha Emanuel, Oct. 12, 2006.

34   the boys wanted to create a computer: Interview with Ezekiel Emanuel, Oct. 9, 2006.

34   Ezekiel . . . had a fascination with dissection: Interview with Ezekiel Emanuel, Oct. 9, 2006.

34   "I told everybody RA stood for": Interview with Meryl Rosen, Nov. 2006.

35   he encouraged Rosen: Interview with Meryl Rosen, Nov. 2006.

35   "He was like": Interview with Meryl Rosen, Nov. 2006.

35   The few male students: Interview with Meryl Rosen, Nov. 2006.

35   "Rahm marched to his own drummer": Interview with Meryl Rosen, Nov. 2006.

35   "He was challenging": Interview with H. H. Kleinman, Oct. 2006.

35   "A lot of Democrats": Interview with Jefferson Adams, Oct. 2006.

35   Emanuel was starting: Interview with Jefferson Adams, Oct. 2006.

35   "I didn't recognize him": Interview with Jefferson Adams, Oct. 2006.

35   His grandfather was a union organizer: Interview with Marsha Emanuel, Oct. 12, 2006.

36   His mother was active: Interview with Marsha Emanuel, Oct. 12, 2006.

36   As early as high school: Interview with Marsha Emanuel, Oct. 12, 2006.

36   Emanuel worked unsuccessfully: Interview with Benjamin and Marsha Emanuel, Oct. 12, 2006.

36   Trying to persuade: Interview with David Axelrod, Oct. 2006.

36   "The first word that comes": Interview with David Axelrod, Oct. 2006.

36   "if your early ventures fail": "How to Beat a Republican," *Campaign & Elections,* August/September 1988.

36   On one trip to Raleigh: Interview with Joe Sinsheimer, Dec. 4, 2006.

37   "I forget the topic": Interview with Joe Sinsheimer, Dec. 4, 2006.

37   he referred to Washington: Interview with Rahm Emanuel, Sept. 5, 2005.

37   "Let's not nominate fucking idiots": Interview with Rahm Emanuel, Nov. 2, 2005.

37   "My fault": Interview with Marsha Emanuel, Oct. 12, 2006.

38   He told contributors: Interview with William Daley, Dec. 6, 2006.

38   Emanuel told one donor: Interview with William Daley, Dec. 6, 2006.

38   the Daley campaign raised: Interview with William Daley, Dec. 6, 2006.

38   Wilhelm . . . called Emanuel every night: Interview with David Wilhelm, Oct. 2006.

38   his father questioned: Interview with Benjamin Emanuel, Oct. 12, 2006.

38   "We never thought": Interview with Benjamin Emanuel, Oct. 12, 2006.

38   "He was then a little more brash": Response by President Bill Clinton to written questions submitted by the author.

39   He fought with others: Interview with Richard Mintz, Oct. 2006.

39   "I was on the [campaign] plane": Interview with Richard Mintz, Oct. 2006.

39   Emanuel's initial goal: Interview with Richard Mintz, Oct. 2006.

39   Emanuel jumped on a table: Interview with Richard Mintz, Oct. 2006.

39   telling donors who contributed: Interview with Richard Mintz, Oct. 2006.

39   "I remember him yelling": Interview with Richard Mintz, Oct. 2006.

39   Such tactics led: "Clinton Leader in Funding Requests," *Washington Post,* Jan. 3, 1992.

39   Emanuel organized: Interview with Paul Begala, Dec. 6, 2006.

39   with his funds: Interview with Paul Begala, Dec. 6, 2006.

40   When he yelled: Interview with Dee Dee Myers, Oct. 2006.

40   highly organized . . . sense of loyalty: Interview with David Wilhelm, Oct. 2006.

40   "You aren't as successful": Interview with Dee Dee Myers, Oct. 2006.

40   The night after the election: Interview with Paul Begala, Dec. 6, 2006.

40   Emanuel himself blamed: Interview with Rahm Emanuel, Dec. 1, 2006.

41   Thomases said: Interview with Susan Thomases, Dec. 6, 2006.

41   Adding to the humiliation: Interview with Rahm Emanuel, Dec. 1, 2006.

41   Emanuel handled the embarassment: Interview with Rahm Emanuel, Dec. 1, 2006.

41   "I could have had": Interview with Rahm Emanuel, Dec. 1, 2006.

41   "It was a huge experience": Interview with Marsha Emanuel, Oct. 12, 2006.

41   a total of five: Interview with William Daley, Dec. 6, 2006.

41   Illinois congressman Dan Rostenkowski: Interview with William Daley, Dec. 6, 2006.

41   a war room in the Old Executive Office Building: Interview with William Daley, Dec. 6, 2006.

41   Emanuel felt Congressman Robert Torricelli: Interview with Rahm Emanuel, Dec. 1, 2006. Torricelli, through a spokesman, discounted this anecdote on Dec. 20, 2006.

42   something for everyone to hate: Interview with Andrew Fois, Dec. 6, 2006.

42   About twenty staffers: Interview with John Podesta, July 26, 2006.

42   "That was Rahm's great moment": Interview with Jose Cerda, Dec. 5, 2006.

43   "Rahm could be": Interview with John Podesta, July 26, 2006.

43   "He doesn't give a shit": Interview with Ezekiel Emanuel, Oct. 10, 2006.

44   "Rahm really understands": Interview with John Podesta, July 26, 2006.

44   "He has taken all that fury": Interview with Paul Begala, Dec. 6, 2006.

44   a blind date: Interview with Rahm Emanuel, Nov. 8, 2006.

44   he attended virtually all: Interview with Jack Moline, Dec. 5, 2006.

44   Rule came from: Interview with Marsha Emanuel, Oct. 12, 2006.

45   a brief, lucrative stint: Information about Emanuel's investment banking career comes from "Rahm Emanuel: From Clinton Aide to Money Maker," *Chicago Tribune,* Nov. 9, 2003.

45   Emanuel's aides infiltrated: "Emanuel Hits, Kaszak Defends House Record," *Chicago Tribune,* Jan. 31, 2002.

45   Edward Moskal . . . claimed: "Ethnic Comments Rattle Race for Congress," *New York Times,* March 6, 2002.

46   "Rich was a big supporter": Interview with William Daley, Dec. 6, 2006.

46   Emanuel was trying: Interview with Democratic staffer.

46   "He was extremely rude": Interview with Patsy Madrid, Nov. 10, 2005.

47   "He is the ultimate alpha male": Interview with Dee Dee Myers, Oct. 2006.

47   Anna Greenberg: Interview with Anna Greenberg, Oct. 2006.

47   "You can't swear": Interview with Anna Greenberg, Oct. 2006.

47   Emanuel took the job seriously: Interview with Anna Greenberg, Oct. 2006.

47   "Jews do not": E-mail from Anna Greenberg, Oct. 2006.

47   Emanuel made a few: Interview with Anna Greenberg, Oct. 2006.

47   His family had often spent: Interview with Benjamin and Marsha Emanuel, Oct. 12, 2006.

47   he asked Moline: Interview with Jack Moline, Dec. 5, 2006.

47   They managed to get in: Interview with Jack Moline, Dec. 5, 2006.

47   Clinton himself showed up: Interview with Jack Moline, Dec. 5, 2006.

47   "It scared the shit": Interview with Jack Moline, Dec. 5, 2006.

48   Moline and Emanuel discussed: Interview with Jack Moline, Dec. 5, 2006.

48   One year, during the Jewish High Holidays: This anecdote is from interview with
      Jack Moline, Dec. 5, 2006.

3: CRACKS IN THE EDIFICE

51   "not the apocalyptic storm": "Super Soaker," *Chicago Tribune,* Aug. 30, 2005.

51   80 percent: "New Orleans Ravaged," *Chicago Tribune,* Aug. 31, 2005.

51   "Thousands Feared Dead": *Chicago Tribune,* Sept. 1, 2005.

52   A *Newsweek* poll: *Newsweek* Web site, Sept. 10, 2005.

52   sought to ensure good stagecraft: "Bush: U.S. to Fund Massive Rebuilding," *Chicago
      Tribune,* Sept. 16, 2005.

53   "I think Katrina": Interview with Rahm Emanuel, Sept. 7, 2005.

54   "There is a modest Democratic tide": Interview with Gary Jacobson, Sept. 14, 2006.

54   "not that great": Interview with Kimball Brace, Sept. 21, 2005.

55   Burton . . . was in his office: Interview with Bill Burton, Oct. 2005.

55   Burton called Emanuel: Interview with Bill Burton, Oct. 2005.

55   He broke the rule: Interview with Bill Burton, Oct. 2005.

55   Burton sent an e-mail: Interview with Bill Burton, Oct. 2005.

55   On the House floor: Interview with Bill Burton, Oct. 2005.

55   "When someone is digging": Interview with Sarah Feinberg, Oct. 2005.

56   Feinberg dismissed: Interview with Sarah Feinberg, Oct. 2005.

57   *The Hill,* a congressional newspaper: *The Hill,* Sept. 29, 2005.

58   "They [voters] may just say": Interview with Rahm Emanuel, Sept. 7, 2005.

61   Republican spokesman Carl Forti: Interview with Carl Forti, Oct. 24, 2005.

61   "Ethics is a losing issue": Interview with Ed Patru, Dec. 1, 2005.

63   three minutes long: Interview with John Lapp, Dec. 12, 2006.

63   Emanuel's longtime friend David Axelrod: Interview with John Lapp, Dec. 12, 2006.

63   unnerving to staffers: Interview with John Lapp and Bill Burton, Sept. 23, 2005.

64   "There is only one way": Interview with John Lapp, Dec. 12, 2006.

64   "You look for the old": Interview with John Lapp, Sept. 23, 2005.

64   "You've got to step": Interview with John Lapp, Sept. 23, 2005.

64   forty-five seconds: Interview with Bill Burton, Dec. 12, 2006.

64   considered himself black: Interview with Bill Burton.

64   found herself explaining: Interview with Sarah Feinberg.

64   giving her time off: Numerous interviews with DCCC staff.

64   send in Feinberg: Numerous interviews with DCCC staff.

65   "I consider myself": Interview with Christina Reynolds, May 16, 2006.

65   frustrated by their determination: Interview with Christina Reynolds, May 16, 2006.

65   Emanuel lured her: Interview with Christina Reynolds, May 16, 2006.

65   as many as fifteen phone calls: Interview with Karin Johanson, April 21, 2006.

65   Emanuel also would call Burton: Interview with Bill Burton, Sept. 23, 2005.

65   "It's been a long time": Interview with Karin Johanson, April 21, 2006.

65   the staff started compiling: Interview with Bill Burton.

66   "It's not for the faint of heart": Interview with John Lapp, Sept. 23, 2005.

4: FEAR AND LOATHING

69   "a lot of angst": Interview with Tom Cole, Dec. 2005.

69   One accused: Interview with Dennis Hastert staffer.

70   Other Republicans . . . became Rahm experts: Interview with Mark Kirk by Jill Zuckman.

70   "Now they're finally serious": Interview with Rahm Emanuel.

70   Cole . . . promised his colleagues: Interview with Tom Cole, Dec. 2005.

70   "He won't give us quarter": Interview with Tom Cole, Dec. 2005.

70   "in a lead-pipe-cinch": Interview with Tom Cole, Dec. 2005.

70   Congressman Chris Shays: Interview with Rahm Emanuel.

71   "Don't underestimate what happens": Interview with Rahm Emanuel, July 20, 2006.

71   "I don't scare them enough": Interview with Rahm Emanuel, Sept. 7, 2005.

72   "Rahm has brought": Interview with Carl Forti, Oct. 24, 2005.

72   "It's just two jackasses": Interview with Rahm Emanuel, Sept. 28, 2005.

73   "I respect his hard work": Interview with Tom Reynolds, Jan. 27, 2006.

73   "If this was a tennis game": Tom Reynolds, roundtable discussion with reporters.

74   "a big radio buy": Interview with Chris Van Hollen, Nov. 3, 2005.

74   "That personalizes things": Interview with Tom Cole, Dec. 2005.

74   "Apparently a campaign decision": Tom Reynolds, roundtable discussion with reporters.

74   "One of the reasons": Interview with Rahm Emanuel, Nov. 29, 2005.

74   neither party thought: Interview with Karin Johanson, Dec. 14, 2006.

75   The DCCC spent: Interview with Karin Johanson, Dec. 14, 2006.

75   "It's different from any other model": Interview with Karin Johanson, April 21, 2006.

77   Alcee Hastings . . . was quoted: *South Florida Sun-Sentinel,* Jan. 28, 2006.

77   in a closed meeting: Interview with Rahm Emanuel, Feb. 8, 2006.

77   "He's great on lectures": Interview with Rahm Emanuel, Feb. 8, 2006.

78   "Rahm Emanuel is a brilliant strategist": Interview with Alcee Hastings, May 17, 2006.

78   "How in the hell": Interview with Alcee Hastings, May 17, 2006.

78   "Ron Klein is my friend": Interview with Alcee Hastings, May 17, 2006.

78   "I've got hundreds of those": Interview with Rahm Emanuel, Feb. 8, 2006.

79   Congressman Adam Schiff: Interview with a Democratic staffer.

79   "I thought Rahm": Interview with a Democratic staffer.

79   "He is universally admired": Interview with a senior Democratic leadership aide, June 23, 2006.

81   "I don't like the idea": Interview with Danny Davis.

81   shouting matches: Interview with Danny Davis.

81   "I hate to say it": Interview with Al Wynn.

81   "If a person says": Interview with Danny Davis.

81   "I don't think": Interview with Mel Watt.

82   "every [DCCC] chairman has faced": Interview with Rahm Emanuel, July 20, 2006.

82   "I think the Republicans": Interview with Howard Dean by Jeff Zeleny, June 2006.

83   Ken Mehlman . . . called: Interview with Rahm Emanuel, May 17, 2006.

83   "To find out if the 50-state strategy": "Democrats Fear Rifts Risk Election Victory,"
     Chicago Tribune, July 5, 2006.

84   "If you are trying to build": Interview with Rahm Emanuel, Feb. 8, 2006.

85   At the meeting, Schumer told Dean: Account of the Emanuel-Schumer-Dean meet-
     ing is from an interview with Rahm Emanuel, May 17, 2006. Dean on numerous
     occasions during the campaign and afterward declined to speak to the author.

85   "Chuck was as hard as me": Interview with Rahm Emanuel, May 17, 2006.

86   "That was a meeting": Interview with Howard Dean by Jeff Zeleny, June 2006.

86   "I don't believe": Interview with Howard Dean by Jeff Zeleny, June 2006.

86   "I'm not going to": Interview with Howard Dean by Jeff Zeleny, June 2006.

87   "parties are important": Interview with Dave Johnson, Oct. 31, 2005.

88   "Part of the appeal": Interview with John Lapp.

88   "If they can get more money": Interview with John Lapp.

90   "For many, many years": Interview with David Sirota, Jan. 16, 2006.

90   invited him out for a beer: Interview with Bill Burton.

90   "Bob Brigham is such a pussy": E-mail from Bill Burton, Oct. 26, 2005.

91   "The DCCC can focus": Interview with Markos Moulitsas Zúniga, Nov. 1, 2005.

5: FRIENDLY FIRE

93   *Washington Post:* "After War Injury, an Iraq Vet Takes on Politics," *Washington Post,*
     Feb. 19, 2006.

93   *USA Today:* "War Veterans Ready for New Battle: Illinois Amputee Among 10 Post-
     9/11 Veterans Making Runs for Congress," *USA Today,* Jan. 23, 2006.

93   *Chicago Tribune* and *Chicago Sun-Times:* "For Democrats: Duckworth," *Chicago Tri-
     bune,* Feb. 27, 2006; "Our Endorsements in Congressional Races," *Chicago Sun-Times,*
     Mar. 7, 2006.

94   "I will not support": Interview with Connie Baker, Jan. 24, 2006.

94   On the same night: Interview with Christine Cegelis, Jan. 25, 2006.

95   an avid Democrat: Interview with Christine Cegelis, Jan. 25, 2006.

95   "I was helping": Interview with Christine Cegelis, Jan. 25, 2006.

95   She held fund-raisers: Interview with Christine Cegelis, Jan. 25, 2006.

95   Greg Sweigert . . . was attracted: Interview with Greg Sweigert, Jan. 24, 2006.

95   "She talked about a lot": Interview with Greg Sweigert, Jan. 24, 2006.

96   "She cared so much": Interview with Connie Baker, Jan. 24, 2006.

96   Tammy Duckworth . . . was co-piloting: Account of Duckworth's accident from an
     interview with Tammy Duckworth.

97   Senator Durbin asked his staff: Interview with Dick Durbin.

97   "There she was": Interview with Dick Durbin.

97   a reporter from the *Chicago Sun-Times:* Interview with Dick Durbin.

97   He fully expected: Interview with Dick Durbin.

97   Durbin immediately called Emanuel: Interview with Dick Durbin.

97   Durbin called Obama: Interview with Dick Durbin.

98   Durbin wasn't even sure: Interview with Dick Durbin.

98   "Four months in a hospital bed": Interview with Tammy Duckworth.

98   the Illinois AFL-CIO announced its support: "Duckworth Wins AFL-CIO Nod for Congress," *Chicago Tribune*, Jan. 12, 2006.

99   saying he'd worked harder: Interview with Dick Durbin.

99   "Being Asian American": Interview with Mike Honda.

101   "We Democrats have a surge": Interview with Jeff Latas, April 3, 2006.

102   "It's not that an Iraqi veteran": Interview with Stuart Rothenberg, April 2006.

102   an embarrassing television appearance: MSNBC's *Hardball with Chris Matthews*, Aug. 17, 2005.

102   "I'm a Democrat": Interview with Christine Cegelis, Jan. 25, 2006.

103   "she doesn't live in the district": Interview with Christine Cegelis, Jan. 25, 2006.

103   "Rahm Emanuel has done a great service": Interview with Greg Sweigert, Jan. 24, 2006.

103   "It's like Vietnam": Interview with Greg Sweigert, Jan. 24, 2006.

103   "the difficult, painful part": Interview with Dick Durbin.

103   "If she would only work": Interview with Rahm Emanuel, Jan. 31, 2006.

104   "Am I supposed to take": Interview with Rahm Emanuel, Jan. 31, 2006.

104   "You think Obama": Interview with Rahm Emanuel, Jan. 31, 2006.

104   Shuler had grown up: Details of Shuler's life from his official campaign biography.

105   spent Friday nights at high school football games: Interview with Jerry Meek, chairman, North Carolina Democratic Party, Jan. 9, 2007.

105   He refused to campaign on Sundays: Interview with Heath Shuler, Jan. 17, 2007.

105   "She said, 'Heath'": Interview with Heath Shuler, Jan. 17, 2007.

106   "I am the person": Interview with Tammy Duckworth.

106   "We took on the communists": Interview with Rahm Emanuel, March 22, 2006.

106   She refused to endorse: "State by State," *The Hill*, April 4, 2006.

107   he'd raised $1.1 million: "Gearing Up for Next Battle, Duckworth Sets Sights on Roskam," *Chicago Tribune*, March 23, 2006.

107   Duckworth had raised: "Gearing Up for Next Battle, Duckworth Sets Sights on Roskam," *Chicago Tribune*, March 23, 2006.

6: SIGNS OF SPRING

108   He admitted he'd tried to influence: "Abramoff pleads guilty to three counts," *Washington Post*, Jan. 4, 2006.

108   hurried phone conversation: Interview with Sarah Feinberg, Jan. 5, 2006.

109   Emanuel convened a strategy meeting: Interview with Sarah Feinberg, Jan. 5, 2006.

109   quietly furnish reporters: Interview with Sarah Feinberg, Jan. 5, 2006.

110   "Guns have little or nothing to do": "Get Rid of the Damned Things," *Time*, Aug. 9, 1999.

110   "the blame-America-first hate speech": "The Evolution of Tom DeLay," *National Journal*, Nov. 15, 2003.

110   Jay Leno's *Tonight Show* monologues: Quoted in the *New York Times*.

112   "people that were eager": Interview with Charlie Wilson, May 5, 2006.

113   Wilson and his supporters: Interview with Charlie Wilson, May 5, 2006.

114 "We moved forward": Interview with Charlie Wilson, May 5, 2006.

114 "I don't like the son-of-a-bitch": "Democratic Candidates Tout Iraq War Experience," *USA Today*, July 28, 2005.

114 "I said it": "The Ohio Insurgency," *Mother Jones*, Nov./Dec. 2005.

115 "that rarest of modern political animals": "The Ohio Insurgency," *Mother Jones*, Nov./Dec. 2005.

115 he called Emanuel: The account for Hackett's interaction with Emanuel and the DCCC from DCCC staffers. Hackett refused to return numerous phone calls.

116 "There has hardly been": Interview with Rob Richie, March 3, 2006.

116 "It depends who comes back": Interview with Andrew Koneschusky, Mar. 6, 2006.

118 Bush quickly halted: "Fact Sheet: President Bush's Four-Part Plan to Confront High Gasoline Prices," The White House, April 25, 2006.

120 Emanuel's daughter Ilana: This story recounted by Rahm Emanuel at a gathering of candidates, Sept. 13, 2006.

120 "Batman and Robin": Interview with Sean Sweeney, Dec. 21, 2006.

123 "the reason I decided to [run]": Interview with Chris Murphy, Jan. 13, 2006.

123 he had grown up on a local farm: Official biography, John Laesch campaign Web site.

123 Emanuel did not talk: Interview with John Laesch, July 10, 2006.

123 "Rahm Emanuel's job": Interview with John Laesch, July 10, 2006.

124 Seals . . . had become frustrated: Interview with Dan Seals, June 21, 2006.

124 "I had some late-night conversations": Interview with Dan Seals, June 21, 2006.

124 Kirk talked like a moderate: Interview with Dan Seals, June 21, 2006.

124 DCCC staffers were helpful: Interview with Dan Seals, June 21, 2006.

124 Emanuel told Seals bluntly: Interview with Dan Seals, June 21, 2006.

124 "Rahm helps those": Interview with Dan Seals, June 21, 2006.

125 "A lot of times guys": Interview with Ali Wade, April 2006.

126 Mollohan had directed: "Appropriations, Local Ties, and Now a Probe of a Legislator," *Wall Street Journal*, April 7, 2006.

126 Sarah Feinberg . . . called reporters: Interview with Sarah Feinberg, April 2006.

126 He began raising money: Interview with Sarah Feinberg, April 2006.

127 his Treo rang: Interview with John Lapp, April 2006.

127 they could not reach him: Interview with John Lapp, April 2006.

127 watching college basketball: Interview with Rahm Emanuel, April 2006.

127 decided to remain incommunicado: Interview with Rahm Emanuel, April 2006.

128 a "pen-and-pad" briefing: Account of this event based on notes from Jill Zuckman.

128 "it really neuters": "DeLay's Exit a Relief for GOP," *Chicago Tribune*, April 5, 2006.

129 Democrats were benefiting: "Poll Gives Bush His Worst Marks Yet," *New York Times*, May 10, 2006.

129 A Harris Interactive poll: "Bush Dips into the 20s," *Wall Street Journal*, May 11, 2006.

129 President Richard Nixon's approval rating: Roper Center for Public Opinion research Web site.

129 the Republicans' popularity had sunk: The *Cook Political Report* from this period showed that while Democrats had ten seats at risk, the Republicans had thirty-six by the end of May.

130   Emanuel decided to summon: Account of this meeting provided by several House
      members and staffers. PowerPoint presentation and video viewed by author.

7: A FAMILIAR FEAR

133   Republicans outnumbered Democrats: Interview with Bill Burton.

133   many military families: Interview with Bill Burton.

133   President Bush had defeated John Kerry: *Almanac of American Politics*, 2006 edition.

133   each spent $1.2 million: Interview with Bill Burton.

133   the national parties' contributions: Interview with John Lapp.

133   had worked for a group: official biography, Congressman Brian Bilbray Web site.

133   he adopted . . . his campaign slogan: Bilbray for Congress Web site.

133   the *San Diego Union-Tribune* endorsed: "Bilbray for Congress," *San Diego Union-
      Tribune,* May 17, 2006.

133   McCain . . . canceled a campaign appearance: "McCain Won't Appear at Bilbray
      Fundraiser," *San Diego Union-Tribune,* May 31, 2006.

133   She often called her opponent: Busby for Congress Web site.

134   Cheney . . . Hastert . . . Pelosi: "Bilbray and Busby to Get Boosts from Party Lead-
      ers," *San Diego Union-Tribune,* May 26, 2006.

134   An NRCC ad for Bilbray: "Congressional GOP Assails Busby," *San Diego Union-
      Tribune,* April 22, 2006.

134   campaign spots in . . . radio traffic reports: Text of radio ad received from DCCC.

135   "It's a special election": Interview with Tucker Bounds, June 6, 2006.

135   a last-minute gaffe: "Candidate on Defense, Says She Misspoke at Event," *San Diego
      Union-Tribune,* June 3, 2006.

135   John Lapp . . . answered: Interview with John Lapp.

135   Republicans . . . launched a final radio ad: *The Hotline,* June 5, 2006.

137   Emanuel was furious: Interview with Rahm Emanuel, Nov. 14, 2006.

137   "If anybody fucking steals": Interview with Bill Burton, Nov. 2006.

140   "Democrats Vow": *The Onion,* Feb. 27, 2006.

141   "You have to clear the bar": Interview with Rahm Emanuel, Jan. 31, 2006.

141   "It threatened to come apart": Interview with George Miller, Jan. 11, 2007.

141   Consultants told the Democrats: Interview with George Miller, Jan. 11, 2007.

141   Emanuel came up: Interview with George Miller, Jan. 11, 2007.

143   "I get along great with Nancy": Interview with Rahm Emanuel, Feb. 8, 2006.

143   "A lot of people are very comfortable": Interview with Rahm Emanuel, Feb. 8, 2006.

143   "they're thinking about it": Interview with Rahm Emanuel, Feb. 8, 2006.

143   Harry Reid . . . once told him: Interview with Rahm Emanuel, Feb. 8, 2006.

144   "It's a problem": Interview with Rahm Emanuel, Feb. 8, 2006.

144   "I love people who are operational": Interview with Nancy Pelosi by Jill Zuckman,
      Oct. 2006.

144   "The temptation is": Interview with Nancy Pelosi by Jill Zuckman, Oct. 2006.

144   She had laid the groundwork: Interview with Brian Wolff, DCCC staffer, Dec. 2006.

145   Pelosi also was unafraid: Multiple conversations with Democratic staffers.

145 Pelosi and her staff were jealous: Multiple conversations with Democratic staffers.

145 In late June they unveiled: "House GOP to Focus on Abortion, Guns, Other Controversies in Pre-election Votes," Associated Press, June 26, 2006.

146 the Republicans initiated furious debates: "Congress Erupts in Partisan Fight over War in Iraq," *New York Times*, June 16, 2006; "Party Lines Clear in Debate on War," *Chicago Tribune*, June 1, 2006.

148 "I haven't read it": Interview with Rahm Emanuel.

148 "The most important thing": Interview with Rahm Emanuel.

149 "I don't know": Interview with Carl Forti, July 6, 2006.

149 also declined to talk: Call to Texas Republican Party, July 6, 2006.

151 "If I can alter these races": Interview with Rahm Emanuel, Aug. 8, 2006.

152 a headline in *Roll Call*: "Mollohan Foe Battles Resume Charges," *Roll Call*, Aug. 2, 2006.

152 "Part of our goal was": Interview with Christina Reynolds.

153 "The thing that is scaring": Interview with Rahm Emanuel, Aug. 8, 2006.

153 commercials had to be changed: "Pro-Reichert Ad Changed After Democrats Call Foul," *Seattle Post-Intelligencer*, Aug. 4, 2006.

153 "Vote for Business Bandwagon": Statement from U.S. Chamber of Commerce, Aug. 1, 2006.

8: IMPLOSION

155 and its clients included: Web site of Prince, Lobel, Glovsky & Tye.

157 "The first third of your campaign": Emanuel discussion with Capitol Hill press secretaries, July 11, 2006.

157 "He'll scream at them": Interview with John Lapp, Oct. 6, 2005.

157 "You wouldn't think": Interview with Dan Seals, June 21, 2006.

158 By the middle of 2006: Fund-raising figures from statements of the DCCC and NRCC.

158 An astounding $27 million: "Bush Raises $27 Million for GOP," *Washington Post*, June 20, 2006.

159 Emanuel had initially set a goal: Interview with Brian Wolff, April 2006.

160 "It's like a Tupperware party": Interview with Leo Hindery, May 2006.

161 "We fundamentally believed": Interview with Mark Gorenberg, May 2006.

161 "Got Oversized Problems": ABC's "The Note," July 24, 2000.

162 "The al Qaeda types": Vice president interview with wire service reporters, Aug. 9, 2006, official transcript.

162 "Joe Lieberman believed": Ken Mehlman address to the City Club of Cleveland, Aug. 9, 2006, official RNC transcript.

165 The *New York Times* proclaimed: "GOP Faces Peril of Losing House, Strategists Say," *New York Times*, Sept. 4, 2006.

165 The conservative *Washington Times*: "History Favors Democrats in Congress Races," *Washington Times*, Sept. 5, 2006.

165 The *National Journal* found: "Insiders Poll," *National Journal*, Sept. 2006.

166 "The people frothing": Interview with Rahm Emanuel, Sept. 2006.

166 "I try to temper my mood": Interview with Rahm Emanuel, Sept. 2006.

166 "I spend every waking hour": Interview with Rahm Emanuel, Sept. 2006.

166 "When you're Democratic chairman": Interview with Rahm Emanuel, Sept. 2006.

166 Dean agreed to spend: Interviews with DCCC staffers, Sept. 2006.

170 "I'm very tense": Interview with Rahm Emanuel, Sept. 21, 2006.

170 "Our party has never been campaign battle-tested": Interview with Rahm Emanuel, Sept. 21, 2006.

171 In a *New York Times*/CBS News poll: "Only 25 Percent in Poll Approve of the Congress," *New York Times*, Sept. 21, 2006.

171 Emanuel returned to Chicago: Interview with Ezekiel Emanuel, Oct. 10, 2006.

172 a report on the ABC News Web site: "Sixteen-Year-Old Who Worked as Capitol Hill Page Concerned About E-mail Exchange with Congressman," ABC News Web site, Sept. 28, 2006.

172 ABC News obtained: "Investigation of Allegations Related to Improper Conduct Involving Members and Current or Former Pages," House Committee on Standards of Official Conduct, p. 62.

172 The IMs were filled: "Foley's Exchange with Underage Page," ABC News Web site, Sept. 29, 2006.

172 Top Republicans . . . hastily convened: "Investigation of Allegations Related to Improper Conduct Involving Members and Current or Former Pages," House Committee on Standards of Official Conduct, p. 64.

174 the conservative *Washington Times*: "Resign, Mr. Speaker," *Washington Times*, Oct. 3, 2006.

174 an October 8 appearance: Transcript, ABC *This Week*, Oct. 8, 2006.

174 he had indeed been informed: Interviews on background.

174 A Democratic Capitol Hill staffer: Interviews on background.

176 A *USA Today* poll: "Voters Shift Toward House Democrats," *USA Today*, Oct. 10, 2006.

176 *Newsweek* found: "A Political Limbo; How Low Can the Republicans Go?" *Newsweek* Web site, Oct. 7, 2006.

9: THE FINAL SPRINT

179 Democrats' first big expenditure: Interview with John Lapp, Oct. 20, 2006.

179 The AFL-CIO had spent: AFL-CIO press briefing, Aug. 30, 2006.

179 Chamber of Commerce: Chamber of Commerce Web site.

180 MoveOn.org: MoveOn.org Web site.

181 his old friend George Stephanopoulos: Interview with Rahm Emanuel, Jan. 31, 2006.

188 a page-one story: "Seat in Congress Helps Mr. Taylor Help His Business," *Wall Street Journal*, Oct. 11, 2006.

188 their own debate fiasco: "Taylor-Shuler Radio Debate Falls Apart," *Asheville Citizen-Times*, Nov. 4, 2006.

190 Emanuel appeared: *Meet the Press*, Nov. 5, 2006, official transcript.

191 a Pew Research Center survey: "Bush Trumpets Verdict in Iraq as Some Polls Lift GOP Spirit," *New York Times*, Nov. 6, 2006.

191 Emanuel called his brother: Interview with Ari Emanuel, Nov. 8, 2006.

192 Karl Rove . . . made a point: "The Red-State Review, Starring G. W. Bush," *Washington Post,* Nov. 4, 2006.

192 "You might remember": "The Red-State Review, Starring G. W. Bush," *Washington Post,* Nov. 4, 2006.

192 "full steam ahead": "Cheney Says Vote Will Not Deflect U.S. in Iraq," *Financial Times,* Nov. 5, 2006.

192 temperatures rising: All temperatures from *Chicago Tribune* weather page, Nov. 7, 2006.

192 Emanuel called Democratic Party chairmen: Rahm Emanuel press conference, Nov. 7, 2006.

AFTERWORD

206 Congresswoman Nancy Pelosi: "Democrats Flex Muscle," *Chicago Tribune,* Jan. 5, 2007; "Jubilant Democrats Assume Control on Capitol Hill," *New York Times,* Jan. 5, 2007.

208 "When nobody thought they could do it": Interview with Dee Dee Myers, Oct. 2006.

209 "The election really": Tom Reynolds press conference, official transcript, Nov. 8, 2006.

209 "This is a close election": President Bush press conference, official transcript, Nov. 8, 2006.

210 "Many of the Democrats": From "The Online Beat," by John Nichols, a political blog on *The Nation's* Web site, posted Dec. 27, 2006.

210 a piece by Joe Conason: "Howard Dean, Vindicated," Salon.com, Nov. 10, 2006.

210 $6.4 million on ads: Interview with John Lapp, Jan. 2007.

212 "Rahm primary": "For Democratic Advisers, a Season of Tough Choices," *Washington Post,* Jan. 21, 2007.

2006 HOUSE RACES
BY STATE AND DISTRICT

R: Republican; D: Democrat; I: Independent; O: Other

ALABAMA

District	Candidate	Votes	Percentage
1	R: Bonner (Incumbent)	112,841	68
	D: Beckerle	52,723	32
2	R: Everett (Incumbent)	124,212	70
	D: James	54,398	30
3	R: Rogers (Incumbent)	97,742	60
	D: Pierce	62,891	38
4	R: Aderholt (Incumbent)	128,412	70
	D: Bobo	54,338	30
5	D: Cramer (Incumbent)	Unopposed	
6	R: Bachus (Incumbent)	Unopposed	
7	D: Davis (Incumbent)	Unopposed	

ALASKA

District	Candidate	Votes	Percentage
1	R: Young (Incumbent)	115,062	57
	D: Benson	81,408	40

ARIZONA

District	Candidate	Votes	Percentage
1	R: Renzi (Incumbent)	88,760	51
	D: Simon	75,257	44
2	R: Franks (Incumbent)	97,100	58
	D: Thrasher	65,490	39
3	R: Shadegg (Incumbent)	76,739	58
	D: Paine	51,021	39
4	D: Pastor (Incumbent)	38,786	72
	R: Karg	12,994	24
5	D: Mitchell	73,762	51
	R: Hayworth (Incumbent)	67,830	46
6	R: Flake (Incumbent)	109,288	74
	L: Blair	38,230	26
7	D: Grijalva (Incumbent)	62,679	60
	R: Drake	36,954	36
8	D: Giffords	114,263	54
	R: Graf	89,104	42

ARKANSAS

District	Candidate	Votes	Percentage
1	D: Berry (Incumbent)	122,741	69
	R: Stumbaugh	54,758	31
2	D: Snyder (Incumbent)	124,698	61
	R: Mayberry	81,278	39
3	R: Boozman (Incumbent)	121,210	62
	D: Anderson	74,015	38
4	D: Ross (Incumbent)	128,114	75
	R: Ross	43,287	25

CALIFORNIA

District	Candidate	Votes	Percentage
1	D: Thompson (Incumbent)	111,650	66
	R: Jones	49,663	29
2	R: Herger (Incumbent)	108,002	64
	D: Sekhon	54,829	33
3	R: Lungren (Incumbent)	95,682	59
	D: Durston	61,579	38
4	R: Doolittle (Incumbent)	104,746	49
	D: Brown	97,217	46
5	D: Matsui (Incumbent)	76,013	71
	R: Yan	25,028	23
6	D: Woolsey (Incumbent)	127,777	69
	R: Hooper	50,061	27
7	D: Miller (Incumbent)	105,101	84
	L: McConnell	20,400	16
8	D: Pelosi (Incumbent)	110,989	80
	R: DeNunzio	14,596	11
9	D: Lee (Incumbent)	117,571	86
	R: den Dulk	15,724	11
10	D: Tauscher (Incumbent)	110,281	66
	R: Linn	56,200	34
11	D: McNerney	88,835	53
	R: Pombo (Incumbent)	78,223	47
12	D: Lantos (Incumbent)	107,586	76
	R: Moloney	34,655	24
13	D: Stark (Incumbent)	83,909	74
	R: Bruno	29,193	26
14	D: Eshoo (Incumbent)	118,509	71
	R: Smith	41,144	25
15	D: Honda (Incumbent)	106,742	72
	R: Chukwu	41,162	28
16	D: Lofgren (Incumbent)	90,724	73
	R: Winston	34,159	27
17	D: Farr (Incumbent)	86,617	77
	R: De Maio	26,013	23
18	D: Cardoza (Incumbent)	59,577	66
	R: Kanno	30,987	34
19	R: Radanovich (Incumbent)	91,863	60
	D: Cox	60,459	40
20	D: Costa (Incumbent)	Unopposed	
21	R: Nunes (Incumbent)	82,258	67
	D: Haze	37,374	30
22	R: McCarthy	114,540	71
	D: Beery	47,592	29
23	D: Capps (Incumbent)	86,712	65
	R: Tognazzini	46,964	35
24	R: Gallegly (Incumbent)	91,660	62
	D: Martinez	57,363	38

25	R: McKeon (Incumbent)	84,188	60
	D: Rodriguez	49,695	36
26	R: Dreier (Incumbent)	89,013	57
	D: Matthews	59,920	38
27	D: Sherman (Incumbent)	85,170	69
	R: Hankwitz	38,610	31
28	D: Berman (Incumbent)	72,904	74
	R: Kesselman	18,800	19
29	D: Schiff (Incumbent)	83,409	64
	R: Bodell	36,107	27
30	D: Waxman (Incumbent)	136,176	71
	R: Jones	50,849	27
31	D: Becerra (Incumbent)	Unopposed	
32	D: Solis (Incumbent)	70,637	83
	L: Faegre	14,598	17
33	D: Watson (Incumbent)	Unopposed	
34	D: Roybal-Allard (Incumbent)	52,516	77
	R: Miller	16,013	23
35	D: Waters (Incumbent)	74,431	83
	O: Mego	7,662	9
36	D: Harman (Incumbent)	96,332	63
	R: Gibson	48,677	32
37	D: Millender-McDonald (Incumbent)	72,726	82
	L: Peters	15,550	18
38	D: Napolitano (Incumbent)	68,917	75
	R: Street	22,591	25
39	D: Sanchez (Incumbent)	67,179	66
	R: Andion	34,872	34
40	R: Royce (Incumbent)	90,925	67
	D: Hoffman	41,552	31
41	R: Lewis (Incumbent)	82,011	67
	D: Contreras	40,777	33
42	R: Miller (Incumbent)	Unopposed	
43	D: Baca (Incumbent)	43,571	65
	R: Folkens	23,432	35
44	R: Calvert (Incumbent)	67,942	59
	D: Vandenberg	42,950	38
45	R: Bono (Incumbent)	62,007	59
	D: Roth	42,384	41
46	R: Rohrabacher (Incumbent)	105,232	59
	D: Brandt	65,192	37
47	D: Sanchez (Incumbent)	38,220	62
	R: Nguyen	23,893	38
48	R: Campbell (Incumbent)	108,666	60
	D: Young	67,835	37
49	R: Issa (Incumbent)	77,804	63
	D: Criscenzo	41,500	34
50	R: Bilbray (Incumbent)	101,967	54
	D: Busby	82,175	43
51	D: Filner (Incumbent)	62,412	67
	R: Miles	28,609	31
52	R: Hunter (Incumbent)	106,363	65
	D: Rinaldi	51,702	32
53	D: Davis (Incumbent)	80,305	67
	R: Woodrum	36,831	31

COLORADO

District	Candidate	Votes	Percentage
1	D: DeGette (Incumbent)	96,324	79
	G: Kelly	25,096	21

2	D: Udall (Incumbent)	133,456	67
	R: Mancuso	60,158	30
3	D: Salazar (Incumbent)	129,833	61
	R: Tipton	78,318	37
4	R: Musgrave (Incumbent)	104,876	46
	D: Paccione	97,670	43
5	R: Lamborn	101,603	59
	D: Fawcett	69,677	41
6	R: Tancredo (Incumbent)	149,919	59
	D: Winter	101,130	40
7	D: Perlmutter	99,824	55
	R: O'Donnell	76,825	42

CONNECTICUT

District	Candidate	Votes	Percentage
1	D: Larson (Incumbent)	154,539	74
	R: MacLean	53,010	26
2	D: Courtney	121,248	50
	R: Simmons (Incumbent)	121,157	50
3	D: DeLauro (Incumbent)	153,353	76
	R: Vollano	44,390	22
4	R: Shays (Incumbent)	106,558	51
	D: Farrell	99,913	48
5	D: Murphy	122,907	56
	R: Johnson (Incumbent)	95,891	44

DELAWARE

District	Candidate	Votes	Percentage
1	R: Castle (Incumbent)	143,892	57
	D: Spivack	97,555	39

FLORIDA

District	Candidate	Votes	Percentage
1	R: Miller (Incumbent)	134,928	69
	D: Roberts	61,851	31
2	D: Boyd (Incumbent)	Unopposed	
3	D: Brown (Incumbent)	Unopposed	
4	R: Crenshaw (Incumbent)	140,731	70
	D: Harms	60,987	30
5	R: Brown-Waite (Incumbent)	162,239	60
	D: Russell	108,832	40
6	R: Stearns (Incumbent)	136,281	60
	D: Bruderly	91,310	40
7	R: Mica (Incumbent)	149,248	63
	D: Chagnon	87,340	37
8	R: Keller (Incumbent)	94,867	53
	D: Stuart	82,261	46
9	R: Bilirakis	122,003	56
	D: Busansky	96,279	44
10	R: Young (Incumbent)	131,301	66
	D: Simpson	67,825	34
11	D: Castor	96,287	70
	R: Adams	41,816	30
12	R: Putnam (Incumbent)	122,871	69
	I: Viscusi	34,523	19
13	R: Buchanan	119,102	50
	D: Jennings	118,729	50
14	R: Mack (Incumbent)	150,145	64
	D: Neeld	83,458	36
15	R: Weldon (Incumbent)	120,070	56
	D: Bowman	93,662	44

16	D: Mahoney	115,506	49
	R: Foley	111,102	48
17	D: Meek (Incumbent)	Unopposed	
18	R: Ros-Lehtinen (Incumbent)	77,962	62
	D: Patlak	47,734	38
19	D: Wexler (Incumbent)	Unopposed	
20	D: Wasserman Schultz (Incumbent)	Unopposed	
21	R: Diaz-Balart (Incumbent)	65,368	59
	D: Gonzalez	44,972	41
22	D: Klein	107,357	51
	R: Shaw (Incumbent)	99,255	47
23	D: Hastings (Incumbent)	Unopposed	
24	R: Feeney (Incumbent)	123,557	58
	D: Curtis	89,672	42
25	R: Diaz-Balart (Incumbent)	59,507	58
	D: Calderin	42,624	42

GEORGIA

District	Candidate	Votes	Percentage
1	R: Kingston (Incumbent)	94,386	68
	D: Nelson	43,435	32
2	D: Bishop (Incumbent)	87,841	68
	R: Hughes	41,289	32
3	R: Westmoreland (Incumbent)	128,672	68
	D: McGraw	61,843	32
4	D: Johnson	102,595	76
	R: Davis	32,272	24
5	D: Lewis (Incumbent)	Unopposed	
6	R: Price (Incumbent)	138,515	72
	D: Sinton	53,351	28
7	R: Linder (Incumbent)	130,496	71
	D: Burns	53,501	29
8	D: Marshall (Incumbent)	80,614	51
	R: Collins	78,881	49
9	R: Deal (Incumbent)	126,374	77
	D: Bradbury	38,328	23
10	R: Norwood (Incumbent)	117,671	67
	D: Holley	57,013	33
11	R: Gingrey (Incumbent)	115,155	71
	D: Pillion	47,229	29
12	D: Barrow (Incumbent)	71,651	50
	R: Burns	70,787	50
13	D: Scott (Incumbent)	102,202	69
	R: Honeycutt	45,494	31

HAWAII

District	Candidate	Votes	Percentage
1	D: Abercrombie (Incumbent)	112,772	69
	R: Hough	49,857	31
2	D: Hirono	106,816	61
	R: Hogue	68,218	39

IDAHO

District	Candidate	Votes	Percentage
1	R: Sali	115,844	50
	D: Grant	103,914	45
2	R: Simpson (Incumbent)	131,393	62
	D: Hansen	72,843	34

ILLINOIS

District	Candidate	Votes	Percentage
1	D: Rush (Incumbent)	141,618	84
	R: Tabour	26,224	16
2	D: Jackson (Incumbent)	138,792	85
	R: Belin	19,113	12
3	D: Lipinski (Incumbent)	123,540	77
	R: Wardingley	36,523	23
4	D: Gutierrez (Incumbent)	68,666	86
	R: Melichar	11,144	14
5	D: Emanuel (Incumbent)	110,975	78
	R: White	31,361	22
6	R: Roskam	90,208	51
	D: Duckworth	85,398	49
7	D: Davis (Incumbent)	138,475	87
	R: Hutchinson	21,017	13
8	D: Bean (Incumbent)	84,795	51
	R: McSweeney	72,398	44
9	D: Schakowsky (Incumbent)	116,947	75
	R: Shannon	39,916	25
10	R: Kirk (Incumbent)	97,249	53
	D: Seals	84,625	47
11	R: Weller (Incumbent)	108,375	55
	D: Pavich	88,179	45
12	D: Costello (Incumbent)	Unopposed	
13	R: Biggert (Incumbent)	119,236	58
	D: Shannon	85,083	42
14	R: Hastert (Incumbent)	114,385	60
	D: Laesch	77,065	40
15	R: Johnson (Incumbent)	115,502	58
	D: Gill	85,343	42
16	R: Manzullo (Incumbent)	121,331	67
	D: Auman	61,105	33
17	D: Hare	114,638	57
	R: Zinga	85,734	43
18	R: LaHood (Incumbent)	147,108	67
	D: Waterworth	71,106	33
19	R: Shimkus (Incumbent)	142,603	61
	D: Stover	92,503	39

INDIANA

District	Candidate	Votes	Percentage
1	D: Visclosky (Incumbent)	103,704	70
	R: Leyva	40,030	27
2	D: Donnelly	104,016	54
	R: Chocola (Incumbent)	88,871	46
3	R: Souder (Incumbent)	94,929	54
	D: Hayhurst	79,683	46
4	R: Buyer (Incumbent)	111,987	62
	D: Sanders	67,322	38
5	R: Burton (Incumbent)	126,072	65
	D: Carr	61,378	31
6	R: Pence (Incumbent)	113,003	60
	D: Welsh	74,715	40
7	D: Carson (Incumbent)	72,983	54
	R: Dickerson	62,903	46
8	D: Ellsworth	128,765	61
	R: Hostettler (Incumbent)	82,271	39
9	D: Hill	110,185	50
	R: Sodrel (Incumbent)	100,503	46

IOWA

District	Candidate	Votes	Percentage
1	D: Braley	113,724	55
	R: Whalen	89,471	43
2	D: Loebsack	107,097	51
	R: Leach (Incumbent)	101,386	49
3	D: Boswell (Incumbent)	114,689	52
	R: Lamberti	103,182	46
4	R: Latham (Incumbent)	120,512	57
	D: Spencer	89,994	43
5	R: King (Incumbent)	105,245	58
	D: Schulte	64,004	36

KANSAS

District	Candidate	Votes	Percentage
1	R: Moran (Incumbent)	153,298	79
	D: Doll	38,820	20
2	D: Boyda	111,759	51
	R: Ryun (Incumbent)	104,128	47
3	D: Moore (Incumbent)	149,480	64
	R: Ahner	78,446	34
4	R: Tiahrt (Incumbent)	113,676	64
	D: McGinn	60,297	34

KENTUCKY

District	Candidate	Votes	Percentage
1	R: Whitfield (Incumbent)	123,676	60
	D: Barlow	82,948	40
2	R: Lewis (Incumbent)	117,424	55
	D: Weaver	94,191	45
3	D: Yarmuth	122,425	51
	R: Northrup (Incumbent)	116,535	48
4	R: Davis (Incumbent)	103,710	51
	D: Lucas	87,701	44
5	R: Rogers (Incumbent)	147,426	74
	D: Stepp	52,399	26
6	D: Chandler (Incumbent)	156,738	85
	L: Ard	26,656	15

LOUISIANA

District	Candidate	Votes	Percentage
1	R: Jindal (Incumbent)	130,277	88
	D: Gereighty	10,888	7
2	D: Jefferson (Incumbent)	27,706	30
	D: Carter		
	(Runoff: Jefferson 57%; Carter 43%)	19,972	22
3	D: Melancon (Incumbent)	74,869	55
	R: Romero	54,868	40
4	R: McCrery (Incumbent)	76,976	58
	D: Cash	22,702	17
5	R: Alexander (Incumbent)	78,835	68
	D: Hearn	33,466	29
6	R: Baker (Incumbent)	94,640	83
	L: Fontanesi	19,644	17
7	R: Boustany (Incumbent)	113,486	71
	D: Stagg	47,007	29

MAINE

District	Candidate	Votes	Percentage
1	D: Allen (Incumbent)	169,085	61
	R: Curley	87,860	31

2	D: Michaud (Incumbent)	176,211	70
	R: D'Amboise	73,773	30

MARYLAND

District	Candidate	Votes	Percentage
1	R: Gilchrest (Incumbent)	176,572	69
	D: Corwin	80,644	31
2	D: Ruppersberger (Incumbent)	126,330	70
	R: Mathis	53,422	30
3	D: Sarbanes	138,120	65
	R: White	68,987	33
4	D: Wynn (Incumbent)	130,764	82
	R: Starkman	28,384	18
5	D: Hoyer (Incumbent)	158,780	84
	G: Warner	31,273	16
6	R: Bartlett (Incumbent)	136,622	59
	D: Duck	89,501	39
7	D: Cummings (Incumbent)	Unopposed	
8	D: Van Hollen (Incumbent)	148,582	77
	R: Stein	40,678	21

MASSACHUSETTS

District	Candidate	Votes	Percentage
1	D: Olver (Incumbent)	158,035	76
	O: Szych	49,123	24
2	D: Neal (Incumbent)	Unopposed	
3	D: McGovern (Incumbent)	Unopposed	
4	D: Frank (Incumbent)	Unopposed	
5	D: Meehan (Incumbent)	Unopposed	
6	D: Tierney (Incumbent)	168,771	70
	R: Barton	72,405	30
7	D: Markey (Incumbent)	Unopposed	
8	D: Capuano (Incumbent)	125,167	91
	O: Garza	12,390	9
9	D: Lynch (Incumbent)	169,034	78
	R: Robinson	46,982	22
10	D: Delahunt (Incumbent)	171,612	65
	R: Beatty	78,335	29

MICHIGAN

District	Candidate	Votes	Percentage
1	D: Stupak (Incumbent)	180,388	69
	R: Hooper	72,709	28
2	R: Hoekstra (Incumbent)	182,879	66
	D: Kotos	86,803	32
3	R: Ehlers (Incumbent)	171,182	63
	D: Rinck	93,850	35
4	R: Camp (Incumbent)	160,767	60
	D: Huckleberry	100,679	38
5	D: Kildee (Incumbent)	176,144	73
	R: Klammer	60,957	25
6	R: Upton (Incumbent)	142,015	61
	D: Clark	88,976	38
7	R: Walberg	122,640	51
	D: Renier	112,623	46
8	R: Rogers (Incumbent)	156,414	55
	D: Marcinkowski	121,576	43
9	R: Knollenberg (Incumbent)	142,279	52
	D: Skinner	127,651	46
10	R: Miller (Incumbent)	178,843	66
	D: Denison	84,574	31

11	R: McCotter (Incumbent)	145,292	54
	D: Trupiano	115,106	43
12	D: Levin (Incumbent)	168,501	70
	R: Shafer	62,688	26
13	D: Cheeks Kilpatrick (Incumbent)	Unopposed	
14	D: Conyers (Incumbent)	156,928	85
	R: Miles	27,794	15
15	D: Dingell (Incumbent)	179,401	88
	G: Smith	9,379	5

MINNESOTA

District	Candidate	Votes	Percentage
1	D: Walz	141,622	53
	R: Gutknecht (Incumbent)	126,487	47
2	R: Kline (Incumbent)	163,292	56
	D: Rowley	116,360	40
3	R: Ramstad (Incumbent)	184,353	65
	D: Wilde	99,599	35
4	D: McCollum (Incumbent)	172,100	70
	R: Sium	74,797	30
5	D: Ellison	136,061	56
	R: Fine	52,263	21
6	R: Bachmann	151,962	50
	D: Wetterling	128,053	42
7	D: Peterson (Incumbent)	179,163	70
	R: Barrett	74,680	29
8	D: Oberstar (Incumbent)	180,666	64
	R: Grams	97,666	34

MISSISSIPPI

District	Candidate	Votes	Percentage
1	R: Wicker (Incumbent)	92,671	66
	D: Hurt	47,752	34
2	D: Thompson (Incumbent)	96,749	64
	R: Brown	54,158	36
3	R: Pickering (Incumbent)	122,253	78
	I: Giles	25,360	16
4	D: Taylor (Incumbent)	106,914	80
	R: McDonnell	26,886	20

MISSOURI

District	Candidate	Votes	Percentage
1	D: Clay (Incumbent)	139,561	73
	R: Byrne	47,352	25
2	R: Akin (Incumbent)	175,592	61
	D: Weber	104,646	37
3	D: Carnahan (Incumbent)	143,670	65
	R: Bertelsen	69,584	32
4	D: Skelton (Incumbent)	158,482	68
	R: Noland	68,869	29
5	D: Cleaver (Incumbent)	134,469	64
	R: Turk	67,424	32
6	R: Graves (Incumbent)	148,746	61
	D: Shettles	86,282	36
7	R: Blunt (Incumbent)	160,911	67
	D: Truman	72,573	30
8	R: Emerson (Incumbent)	156,139	72
	D: Hambacker	57,544	26
9	R: Hulshof (Incumbent)	149,066	61
	D: Burghard	87,109	36

MONTANA

District	Candidate	Votes	Percentage
1	R: Rehberg (Incumbent)	238,031	59
	D: Lindeen	157,499	39

NEBRASKA

District	Candidate	Votes	Percentage
1	R: Fortenberry (Incumbent)	117,890	59
	D: Moul	82,785	41
2	R: Terry (Incumbent)	96,945	55
	D: Esch	79,658	45
3	R: Smith	114,168	55
	D: Kleeb	94,771	45

NEVADA

District	Candidate	Votes	Percentage
1	D: Berkley (Incumbent)	84,979	65
	R: Wegner	40,901	31
2	R: Heller	116,160	51
	D: Derby	103,572	45
3	R: Porter (Incumbent)	102,176	48
	D: Hafen	98,210	47

NEW HAMPSHIRE

District	Candidate	Votes	Percentage
1	D: Shea-Porter	100,899	52
	R: Bradley (Incumbent)	94,869	48
2	D: Hodes	108,525	53
	R: Bass (Incumbent)	93,905	45

NEW JERSEY

District	Candidate	Votes	Percentage
1	D: Andrews (Incumbent)	Unopposed	
2	R: LoBiondo (Incumbent)	109,040	62
	D: Thomas-Hughes	62,364	35
3	R: Saxton (Incumbent)	120,061	58
	D: Sexton	84,310	41
4	R: Smith (Incumbent)	123,482	66
	D: Gay	62,389	33
5	R: Garrett (Incumbent)	109,133	55
	D: Aronsohn	86,426	44
6	D: Pallone (Incumbent)	96,443	69
	R: Bellew	42,814	30
7	R: Ferguson (Incumbent)	95,830	49
	D: Stender	92,591	48
8	D: Pascrell (Incumbent)	94,682	71
	R: Sandoval	38,114	28
9	D: Rothman (Incumbent)	100,301	71
	R: Micco	39,157	28
10	D: Payne (Incumbent)	Unopposed	
11	R: Frelinghuysen (Incumbent)	124,716	62
	D: Wyka	73,493	37
12	D: Holt (Incumbent)	122,810	66
	R: Sinagra	64,455	34
13	D: Sires	72,931	78
	R: Guarini	18,205	19

NEW MEXICO

District	Candidate	Votes	Percentage
1	R: Wilson (Incumbent)	105,916	50
	D: Madrid	105,037	50

2	R: Pearce (Incumbent)	90,169	60
	D: Kissling	60,496	40
3	D: Udall (Incumbent)	142,993	75
	R: Dolin	48,742	25

NEW YORK

District	Candidate	Votes	Percentage
1	D: Bishop (Incumbent)	96,921	61
	R: Zanzi	61,271	39
2	D: Israel (Incumbent)	99,847	70
	R: Bugler	42,617	30
3	R: King (Incumbent)	97,279	56
	D: Mejias	76,943	44
4	D: McCarthy (Incumbent)	98,011	65
	R: Blessinger	53,277	35
5	D: Ackerman (Incumbent)	Unopposed	
6	D: Meeks (Incumbent)	Unopposed	
7	D: Crowley (Incumbent)	58,713	84
	R: Brawley	11,533	16
8	D: Nadler (Incumbent)	97,186	83
	R: Friedman	17,173	15
9	D: Weiner (Incumbent)	Unopposed	
10	D: Towns (Incumbent)	67,964	92
	R: Anderson	4,469	6
11	D: Clarke	83,128	89
	R: Finger	7,277	8
12	D: Velazquez (Incumbent)	55,558	89
	R: Romaguera	6,582	11
13	R: Fossella (Incumbent)	55,981	57
	D: Harrison	42,739	43
14	D: Maloney (Incumbent)	105,342	84
	R: Maio	19,724	16
15	D: Rangel (Incumbent)	96,042	94
	R: Daniels	6,326	6
16	D: Serrano (Incumbent)	51,095	96
	R: Mohamed	2,383	4
17	D: Engel (Incumbent)	86,583	76
	R: Faulkner	27,573	24
18	D: Lowey (Incumbent)	113,282	70
	R: Hoffman	47,898	30
19	D: Hall	94,524	51
	R: Kelly (Incumbent)	90,269	49
20	D: Gillibrand	117,799	53
	R: Sweeney (Incumbent)	104,157	47
21	D: McNulty (Incumbent)	158,175	78
	R: Redlich	45,045	22
22	D: Hinchey (Incumbent)	Unopposed	
23	R: McHugh (Incumbent)	99,931	63
	D: Johnson	58,300	37
24	D: Arcuri	103,062	54
	R: Meier	86,593	45
25	R: Walsh (Incumbent)	105,235	51
	D: Maffei	101,322	49
26	R: Reynolds (Incumbent)	102,846	52
	D: Davis	95,449	48
27	D: Higgins (Incumbent)	127,808	79
	R: McHale	33,525	21
28	D: Slaughter (Incumbent)	105,259	73
	R: Donnelly	39,518	27
29	R: Kuhl (Incumbent)	99,926	52
	D: Massa	93,974	48

NORTH CAROLINA

District	Candidate	Votes	Percentage
1	D: Butterfield (Incumbent)	Unopposed	
2	D: Etheridge (Incumbent)	85,128	66
	R: Mansell	43,000	34
3	R: Jones (Incumbent)	98,688	69
	D: Weber	44,397	31
4	D: Price (Incumbent)	125,172	65
	R: Acuff	67,610	35
5	R: Foxx (Incumbent)	95,560	57
	D: Sharpe	71,584	43
6	R: Coble (Incumbent)	107,280	71
	D: Blake	44,172	29
7	D: McIntyre (Incumbent)	102,940	73
	R: Davis	38,878	27
8	R: Hayes (Incumbent)	60,926	50
	D: Kissell	60,597	50
9	R: Myrick (Incumbent)	105,621	67
	D: Glass	53,080	33
10	R: McHenry (Incumbent)	93,141	62
	D: Carsner	57,287	38
11	D: Shuler	123,986	54
	R: Taylor (Incumbent)	106,651	46
12	D: Watt (Incumbent)	70,796	67
	R: Fisher	34,978	33
13	D: Miller (Incumbent)	96,892	64
	R: Robinson	55,324	36

NORTH DAKOTA

District	Candidate	Votes	Percentage
1	D: Pomeroy (Incumbent)	142,121	66
	R: Mechtel	74,364	34

OHIO

District	Candidate	Votes	Percentage
1	R: Chabot (Incumbent)	101,838	53
	D: Cranley	90,963	47
2	R: Schmidt (Incumbent)	120,112	51
	D: Wulsin	117,595	49
3	R: Turner (Incumbent)	121,885	59
	D: Chema	86,389	41
4	R: Jordan	126,542	60
	D: Siferd	83,929	40
5	R: Gilmor (Incumbent)	126,898	57
	D: Weirauch	95,955	43
6	D: Wilson	131,322	62
	R: Blasdel	80,705	38
7	R: Hobson (Incumbent)	132,430	61
	D: Conner	84,747	39
8	R: Boehner (Incumbent)	132,743	64
	D: Meier	74,641	36
9	D: Kaptur (Incumbent)	149,886	74
	R: Leavitt	53,803	26
10	D: Kucinich (Incumbent)	127,294	66
	R: Dovilla	64,676	34
11	D: Tubbs Jones (Incumbent)	132,585	83
	R: String	26,582	17
12	R: Tiberi (Incumbent)	137,909	58
	D: Shamansky	99,287	42
13	D: Sutton	129,290	61
	R: Foltin	81,997	39

14	R: LaTourette (Incumbent)	136,375	58
	D: Katz	92,600	39
15	R: Pryce (Incumbent)	110,712	50
	D: Kilroy	109,657	50
16	R: Regula (Incumbent)	124,886	59
	D: Shaw	88,089	41
17	D: Ryan (Incumbent)	166,279	80
	R: Manning	41,004	20
18	D: Space	125,810	62
	R: Padgett	77,267	38

OKLAHOMA

District	Candidate	Votes	Percentage
1	R: Sullivan (Incumbent)	116,914	64
	D: Gentges	56,721	31
2	D: Boren (Incumbent)	122,320	73
	R: Miller	45,853	27
3	R: Lucas (Incumbent)	128,021	67
	D: Barton	61,740	33
4	R: Cole (Incumbent)	118,246	65
	D: Spake	64,766	35
5	R: Fallin	108,914	61
	D: Hunter	67,275	37

OREGON

District	Candidate	Votes	Percentage
1	D: Wu (Incumbent)	147,986	63
	R: Kitts	78,211	34
2	R: Walden (Incumbent)	175,352	67
	D: Voisin	79,666	30
3	D: Blumenauer (Incumbent)	178,071	74
	R: Broussard	56,804	23
4	D: DeFazio (Incumbent)	169,331	62
	R: Feldkamp	103,194	38
5	D: Hooley (Incumbent)	138,387	54
	R: Erickson	109,285	43

PENNSYLVANIA

District	Candidate	Votes	Percentage
1	D: Brady (Incumbent)	Unopposed	
2	D: Fattah (Incumbent)	161,832	89
	R: Gessner	16,823	9
3	R: English (Incumbent)	104,820	54
	D: Porter	82,317	42
4	D: Altmire	130,480	52
	R: Hart (Incumbent)	120,822	48
5	R: Peterson (Incumbent)	114,603	60
	D: Hilliard	76,188	40
6	R: Gerlach (Incumbent)	118,807	51
	D: Murphy	115,806	49
7	D: Sestak	147,347	56
	R: Weldon (Incumbent)	114,056	44
8	D: Murphy	125,667	50
	R: Fitzpatrick (Incumbent)	124,146	50
9	R: Shuster (Incumbent)	120,012	60
	D: Barr	78,952	40
10	D: Carney	108,832	53
	R: Sherwood (Incumbent)	96,463	47
11	D: Kanjorski (Incumbent)	132,481	72
	R: Leonardi	50,539	28

12	D: Murtha (Incumbent)	120,567	61
	R: Irey	78,041	39
13	D: Schwartz (Incumbent)	143,539	66
	R: Bhakta	73,591	34
14	D: Doyle (Incumbent)	159,107	90
	G: North	17,505	10
15	R: Dent (Incumbent)	101,086	53
	D: Dertinger	84,424	44
16	R: Pitts (Incumbent)	112,300	57
	D: Herr	78,342	39
17	D: Holden (Incumbent)	136,836	65
	R: Wertz	75,019	35
18	R: Murphy (Incumbent)	143,942	58
	D: Kluko	104,695	42
19	R: Platts (Incumbent)	140,365	64
	D: Avillo	73,557	33

RHODE ISLAND

District	Candidate	Votes	Percentage
1	D: Kennedy (Incumbent)	124,258	53
	R: Scott	41,753	23
2	D: Langevin (Incumbent)	139,843	73
	I: Driver	52,574	27

SOUTH CAROLINA

District	Candidate	Votes	Percentage
1	R: Brown (Incumbent)	114,993	60
	D: Maatta	72,342	38
2	R: Wilson (Incumbent)	124,839	63
	D: Ellisor	74,284	37
3	R: Barrett (Incumbent)	111,007	63
	D: Ballenger	65,426	37
4	R: Inglis (Incumbent)	115,162	64
	D: Griffith	57,308	32
5	D: Spratt (Incumbent)	97,442	57
	R: Norman	73,313	43
6	D: Clyburn (Incumbent)	99,671	64
	R: McLeod	53,325	34

SOUTH DAKOTA

District	Candidate	Votes	Percentage
1	D: Herseth (Incumbent)	230,473	69
	R: Whalen	97,868	29

TENNESSEE

District	Candidate	Votes	Percentage
1	R: Davis	108,228	61
	D: Trent	65,458	37
2	R: Duncan (Incumbent)	156,996	78
	D: Greene	45,007	22
3	R: Wamp (Incumbent)	130,770	66
	D: Benedict	68,305	34
4	D: Davis (Incumbent)	123,418	66
	R: Martin	62,386	34
5	D: Cooper (Incumbent)	121,892	69
	R: Kovach	49,366	28
6	D: Gordon (Incumbent)	130,268	67
	R: Davis	60,856	31
7	R: Blackburn (Incumbent)	152,291	66
	D: Morrison	73,380	32
8	D: Tanner (Incumbent)	129,597	73
	R: Farmer	47,482	27

9	D: Cohen	103,267	60
	I: Ford	38,221	22

TEXAS

District	Candidate	Votes	Percentage
1	R: Gohmert (Incumbent)	104,080	68
	D: Owen	46,290	30
2	R: Poe (Incumbent)	90,332	65
	D: Blinderim	45,027	33
3	R: Johnson (Incumbent)	88,634	62
	D: Dodd	49,488	35
4	R: Hall (Incumbent)	106,268	65
	D: Melancon	54,892	33
5	R: Hensarling (Incumbent)	85,081	62
	D: Thompson	49,253	36
6	R: Barton (Incumbent)	91,888	61
	D: Harris	56,342	37
7	R: Culberson (Incumbent)	98,761	59
	D: Henley	64,170	39
8	R: Brady (Incumbent)	106,943	67
	D: Wright	52,275	33
9	D: Green (Incumbent)	Unopposed	
10	R: McCaul (Incumbent)	97,618	55
	D: Ankrum	71,232	41
11	R: Conaway (Incumbent)	Unopposed	
12	R: Granger (Incumbent)	98,332	67
	D: Morris	45,653	31
13	R: Thornberry (Incumbent)	109,131	74
	D: Waun	33,975	23
14	R: Paul (Incumbent)	94,375	60
	D: Sklar	62,421	40
15	D: Hinojosa (Incumbent)	35,346	61
	R: Haring	13,920	24
16	D: Reyes (Incumbent)	61,074	79
	L: Strickland	16,559	21
17	D: Edwards (Incumbent)	93,198	58
	R: Taylor	64,617	40
18	D: Jackson Lee (Incumbent)	65,827	77
	R: Hassan	16,418	19
19	R: Neugebauer (Incumbent)	92,811	68
	D: Ricketts	40,853	30
20	D: Gonzalez (Incumbent)	68,284	87
	L: Idrogo	9,886	13
21	R: Smith (Incumbent)	122,206	60
	D: Courage	49,781	24
22	D: Lampson	76,782	52
	R: Sekula Gibbs	61,949	42
23	D: Rodriguez	24,593	20
	R: Bonilla (Incumbent)	60,147	48
	(Runoff: Rodriguez 57%; Bonilla 43%)		
24	R: Marchant (Incumbent)	83,620	60
	D: Page	51,833	37
25	D: Doggett (Incumbent)	109,839	67
	R: Rostig	42,956	27
26	R: Burgess (Incumbent)	92,734	60
	D: Barnwell	57,638	37
27	D: Ortiz (Incumbent)	62,063	57
	R: Vaden	42,562	39
28	D: Cuellar (Incumbent)	52,339	68
	D: Enriquez	15,531	20

29	D: Green (Incumbent)	37,118	74
	R: Story	12,329	24
30	D: Johnson (Incumbent)	81,212	80
	R: Aurbach	17,820	18
31	R: Carter (Incumbent)	94,242	58
	D: Harrell	62,761	39
32	R: Sessions (Incumbent)	71,406	57
	D: Pryor	52,233	41

UTAH

District	Candidate	Votes	Percentage
1	R: Bishop (Incumbent)	109,504	63
	D: Olsen	55,748	32
2	D: Matheson (Incumbent)	126,880	59
	R: Christensen	80,429	37
3	R: Cannon (Incumbent)	92,621	58
	D: Burridge	51,396	32

VERMONT

District	Candidate	Votes	Percentage
1	D: Welch	139,585	53
	R: Rainville	117,221	45

VIRGINIA

District	Candidate	Votes	Percentage
1	R: Davis (Incumbent)	143,681	63
	D: O'Donnell	80,715	35
2	R: Drake (Incumbent)	88,364	51
	D: Kellam	83,476	49
3	D: Scott (Incumbent)	Unopposed	
4	R: Forbes (Incumbent)	149,692	76
	O: Burckard	46,344	24
5	R: Goode (Incumbent)	123,944	59
	D: Weed	84,206	40
6	R: Goodlatte (Incumbent)	152,856	75
	I: Pryor	25,351	13
7	R: Cantor (Incumbent)	162,764	64
	D: Nachman	87,272	34
8	D: Moran (Incumbent)	144,471	66
	R: O'Donoghue	68,994	31
9	D: Boucher (Incumbent)	129,181	68
	R: Carrico	61,615	32
10	R: Wolf (Incumbent)	137,956	57
	D: Feder	98,710	41
11	R: Davis (Incumbent)	130,207	55
	D: Hurst	102,334	44

WASHINGTON

District	Candidate	Votes	Percentage
1	D: Inslee (Incumbent)	162,928	68
	R: Ishmael	77,698	32
2	D: Larsen (Incumbent)	156,717	64
	R: Roulstone	87,531	36
3	D: Baird (Incumbent)	146,693	63
	R: Messmore	85,697	37
4	R: Hastings (Incumbent)	114,994	60
	D: Wright	76,838	40
5	R: McMorris (Incumbent)	134,568	56
	D: Goldmark	104,071	44
6	D: Dicks (Incumbent)	158,007	71
	R: Cloud	65,765	29

7	D: McDermott (Incumbent)	193,064	79
	R: Beren	38,334	16
8	R: Reichert (Incumbent)	61,921	51
	D: Burner	59,268	49
9	D: Smith (Incumbent)	118,576	66
	R: Cofchin	61,837	34

WEST VIRGINIA

District	Candidate	Votes	Percentage
1	D: Mollohan (Incumbent)	98,759	64
	R: Wakim	54,524	36
2	R: Capito (Incumbent)	93,356	57
	D: Callaghan	69,867	43
3	D: Rahall (Incumbent)	89,812	69
	R: Wolfe	40,015	31

WISCONSIN

District	Candidate	Votes	Percentage
1	R: Ryan (Incumbent)	160,033	63
	D: Thomas	95,303	37
2	D: Baldwin (Incumbent)	191,361	63
	R: Magnum	112,976	37
3	D: Kind (Incumbent)	161,999	65
	R: Nelson	87,886	35
4	D: Moore (Incumbent)	136,722	72
	R: Rivera	54,468	28
5	R: Sensenbrenner (Incumbent)	194,480	62
	D: Kennedy	112,517	36
6	R: Petri (Incumbent)	Unopposed	
7	D: Obey (Incumbent)	161,754	62
	R: Reid	91,221	35
8	D: Kagen	141,598	51
	R: Gard	134,990	49

WYOMING

District	Candidate	Votes	Percentage
1	R: Cubin (Incumbent)	93,336	48
	D: Trauner	92,324	48

INDEX

ABOUT THE AUTHOR

Naftali Bendavid is deputy Washington bureau chief for the *Chicago Tribune*. Since coming to the *Tribune* in 1997, he has served as the paper's Justice Department correspondent and White House correspondent. He played a central role in the paper's coverage of the Ken Starr impeachment investigation, the contested 2000 election, and the September 11 attacks. Before coming to the *Tribune*, Bendavid worked at several other papers, including the *Miami Herald* and *Legal Times*. Bendavid lives outside Washington, D.C., with his wife and two children.